Hitler Youth,
1922–1945

ALSO BY JEAN-DENIS G.G. LEPAGE
AND FROM McFARLAND

*Aircraft of the Luftwaffe, 1935–1945:
An Illustrated Guide* (2009)

The French Foreign Legion: An Illustrated History (2008)

*German Military Vehicles of World War II:
An Illustrated Guide to Cars, Trucks, Half-Tracks,
Motorcycles, Amphibious Vehicles and Others* (2007)

The Fortifications of Paris: An Illustrated History (2006)

*Medieval Armies and Weapons in Western Europe:
An Illustrated History* (2005)

*Castles and Fortified Cities of Medieval Europe:
An Illustrated History* (2002)

Hitler Youth, 1922–1945

An Illustrated History

Jean-Denis G.G. Lepage

McFarland & Company, Inc., Publishers
Jefferson, North Carolina, and London

LIBRARY OF CONGRESS CATALOGUING-IN-PUBLICATION DATA

Lepage, Jean-Denis.
[Hitler Jugend. English]
Hitler Youth, 1922–1945 : an illustrated history /
Jean-Denis Lepage.
p.   cm.
Includes bibliographical references and index.

ISBN 978-0-7864-3935-5
(softcover: 50# alkaline paper) ∞

1. Hitler—Jugend—History. 2. National socialism and youth.
3. Germany—Politics and government—1918–1933. 4. Germany—
Politics and government—1933–1945. I. Title.
DD253.5.L4613   2009
943.086083′5—dc22   2008048788

British Library cataloguing data are available

©2009 Jean-Denis G.G. Lepage. All rights reserved

*No part of this book may be reproduced or transmitted in any form
or by any means, electronic or mechanical, including photocopying
or recording, or by any information storage and retrieval system,
without permission in writing from the publisher.*

Cover image ©2008 Photos.com

Manufactured in the United States of America

*McFarland & Company, Inc., Publishers
Box 611, Jefferson, North Carolina 28640
www.mcfarlandpub.com*

Table of Contents

Preface 1
Introduction 3

1. Beginnings to 1923   9
2. The Road to Power 1924–1933   19
3. Prelude to War, 1933–1939   27
4. Hitler's Boy Soldiers, 1939–1945   123

Appendix 1: Chronology   163
Appendix 2: Song of the Hitler Jugend   166
Bibliography   168
Index   169

Preface

Few historical subjects are so emotional as the Nazi Third Reich, few have stimulated so much general interest, and few have been subjected to such close scrutiny. Adolf Hitler continues to fascinate and to horrify, and his barbaric regime still defies imagination. The Nazi regime is fortunately dead and buried, but the questions raised by its terrible history continue to demand explanations. Countless books have been written on the Nazi period, including many about the Hitler Youth, some of which have now become classics of their kind. In 1979, the historian James P. O'Donnell remarked that the British Library and the Library of Congress listed over 55,000 items on Hitler and World War II. Even the superficial student of that period of history is aware of why Hitler attached so much importance to the German youth, and the process of indoctrination leading to full-scale militarization is now well known. Conscious of sailing in the wake of many renowned historians and aware that my book would not make waves in the history of the now well-known *Hitler Jugend*, I've endeavored to approach this topic with a mind toward accessibility.

Everything relevant in the past has its message for the future, and to that extent the past is never quite dead. Vigorous selection has been required to keep the book within a reasonable length, but I hope that all major aspects are covered. Inevitably, my own attempt to present the Hitler Youth will reveal subjective preferences and areas of interest, and I have not shrunk from exercising value judgments where these seemed warranted. I am, of course, fully responsible for whatever errors of fact or interpretation appear here. This book is not a specialized full-length academic work, nor does it pretend to scholarship. Its aim is both simple and ambitious: to bring some light to one aspect of the Third Reich and to give a general overview of the Hitler Youth for the professional and amateur historian, teacher and student, and the intelligent general reader. I would like to thank Jeannette and Jan à Stuling, Véronique Janty, Anne Chauvel, Michèle Clermont, and Monique Brinks for their support, as well as Eltjo de Lang and Ben Marcato for their computer skills.

Jean-Denis G.G. Lepage • *Groningen*

Introduction

In the 1920s, after the horrors of World War I, many people believed that the twentieth century was realizing the idea of progress. These people were soon in for a great disappointment. After a period of illusory political stability and apparent economic recovery between 1924 and 1929, the Great Depression ushered in the nightmare of the early 1930s. People began to fear that progress was a phantom. Everywhere the demand was for security. Many nations tried to live in autarky, a state of economic self-sufficiency, by regulating, controlling, guiding, and rescuing their own economic systems. In countries where democratic institutions were strongly established, this trend advanced the principle of the welfare state and social democracy to protect individuals against unemployment and the price fluctuation in the unpredictable and uncontrolled world market. In nations where the democracy was not established, the same economic trend became one aspect of the totalitarianism which spread alarmingly in the 1930s. The cry was for a leader, a strong man who would act, assume responsibilities, make decisions and get results. This opened the way for dictators, unscrupulous and ambitious political adventurers whose purposes and final solution to all problems—economic, political and social—was war. By 1939 only ten of twenty-seven European states remained democratic. They were Great Britain, France, Holland, Belgium, Switzerland, Czechoslovakia, Finland, Denmark, Norway, and Sweden. Totalitarian regimes had been established in Italy, Germany, the Soviet Union, Poland, Spain, Hungary, Greece and Portugal.

Totalitarianism, as distinct from dictatorship, was an outgrowth of a long development in the past. The state was an institution that had continuously acquired new power ever since the Middle Ages. Step by step it had assumed jurisdiction over courts of law and men at arms, imposed taxes, regulated churches, guided economic policy, operated school systems and devised schemes of public welfare. The twentieth-century totalitarian states, more particularly Hitler's Germany, went even further. National Socialism was the most evil manifestation of megalomania in history. It claimed an absolute domination over every department of daily life and carried the development of state sovereignty and *raison d'état* to a new extreme. From cradle to grave, a German man or woman would be part of a Nazi-controlled organization.

Nazism was not merely anticlerical but explicitly anti–Christian, offering, or rather imposing, a total—if vague and contradictory—philosophy of life. Churches, both Catholic and Protestant, were "coordinated"; their clergy were forbidden to criticize the state, international ties were discountenanced, and efforts were made to keep children out of religious schools. The government encouraged anti–Christian pagan, Teutonic and Germanic movements.

The Nazi ideology drew heavily upon a historic nationalism which it greatly exaggerated. It derived in part from the organic theory of society, which held that the nation was a kind of living organism within which the individual person was but a single cell. The individual had no independent existence, but received life itself and all ideas from the culture of the nation into which he was born and by which he was nurtured. He was meaningless outside the collective body. Hitler claimed to represent the absolute sovereignty of the German people; he was presented as a kind of modern messiah and was the object of popular worship. The new order was thought of as being absolutely solid, like one huge monolith in which no particle had any separate structure. Given such a theory, it made no sense to speak of individual freedom, to allow individuals to have their own opinions or to count up individual opinions to obtain a merely numerical majority. In Nazi Germany, all political parties except the National Socialist were forbidden and destroyed. Valid ideas were those of the cultural and racial group as a whole, of the nation as a solid block. The Nazi Party was itself violently purged on the night of June 30, 1934, when many of the SA brown-shirt leaders—representing the more "social-revolutionary" wing of the movement—were accused of plotting against Hitler and were summarily shot.

Even science was the product of the society: there was thus a Nazi science which was bound to differ in its conclusions from democratic, bourgeois, western, capitalist, communist and "Jewish" science. Art—including music, painting, poetry, fiction, and architecture—was good insofar as it expressed the society in which it grew. The avowed philosophy of Nazism was basically subjective. Whether an idea was good or true depended on whose idea it was. Truth, beauty and right only corresponded to the inner nature, interest, or point of view of the Nazi Party. Law itself was defined as the "will of the German people," in fact solely operating in the interests of the Nazi state. Propaganda and repression were the principal branches of government. The Nazis demanded total faith in their view of life, they manipulated opinion, duped the country, rewrote history and forged "scientific" proofs. The very idea of truth evaporated. Barred from independent sources of information, having no means by which any official allegation could be tested, no one could escape the omnipresent state doctrine, the political expediency, the wishes and self-interests of the men in power. Endlessly repeated, the most extravagant statements came to be accepted, even contradictions, lies and rubbish were believed—at least overtly—by the German people. A secret political police, the Gestapo, and a system of permanent concentration camps in which thousands were detained without trial or sentence, suppressed all ideas at variance with the Führer. The severe repression thwarted the efforts of a few dedicated people to develop a broad resistance movement.

Racism was a further exaggeration or degradation of older ideas of nationalism and national solidarity. It defined Germany in a tribal sense as a biological entity, as a group of chosen people having the same ancestry, similar physical characteristics and a common blood. A latent hostility to Jews had always been present in the Christian world, but it arose nowhere more brutal than in Nazi Germany. Jews were considered un-German, and presented as unfair competitors in professions and business but also as decaying and parasitical elements putting the pure German race and culture in danger. The Nuremberg laws of 1935 deprived Jews of all citizenship rights and forbade intermarriage between Jews and "Aryans."

The term "Aryan"—closely related to Nazism—will be frequently used in this book, and therefore needs a bit of explanation. The term was coined by the German philologist and Sanskrit scholar Friedrich Max Müller (1823–1900) to replace the earlier term "Indo-European" that described people who had migrated from India to northwestern Europe around 1000 B.C. Müller's interest was principally linguistic; he denied any Aryan racial existence and warned against misuse of the term. By "Aryans" he simply meant those who spoke an Aryan/Indo-European language.

The accepted nature and extent of the "Aryan race" was difficult to assess, and it was impossible to scientifically prove. The French writer on racial theory, the charlatan Arthur Gobineau (1816–1882), developed the thesis that human races were unequal and that the Nordic Aryans were superior to all. His theories received widespread acceptance in Germany and were used to support the hazy Nazi ideology. Of course Gobineau believed the French to be Aryan. Hitler included the British and the northern Italians. By the end of the war, the ultra-racist SS, desperate for recruits, included Croatians under the leaking umbrella. The same theory with similar result was also developed by an Austrian writer named Guido von List. No easy boundaries could be ascribed to the Aryan world, but for the Nazis the heartland was clearly Nordic lands (e.g., Scandinavia and, of course, Germany). Without scientific proofs, historical facts and rational evidence, Hitler and the Nazi ideologists believed in German racial superiority, and asserted that the real Aryans were those taking up the struggle against Jews and Slavs in the "Aryan" kingdom of the Third Reich.

An entire nation was forced to accept the intuitions of a badly educated politician whose theories on racial matters belonged in a theater of the absurd. Jews were beaten, hounded, driven from public office, ruined in private business, fined, allowed to flee the country only after being stripped of all their possessions, and later, after 1942, systematically put to death in extermination camps. Anti-Semitism was inflamed by Nazi propagandists who wished people to feel their supposed racial purity more keenly and to forget the deeper problems of Germany, such as poverty, unemployment and social inequality. The Nazi ideology pretended that differences between rich and poor were of minor importance. It pointed alarmingly to the dark menace of Bolshevism (a radical doctrine based on Karl Marx's communism, defined by Lenin in 1903), and declared that all social classes stood shoulder to shoulder in slab-like solidarity behind the Führer. The Nazis blamed the grave troubles of the time on forces outside the country. They accused dissatisfied persons of conspiring with foreigners—with being the tools of western imperialism, of communist and international Jewry. They transformed the inner conflicts between rich and poor into a struggle between nations and gave the impression that war was the only solution for social ills.

Violence—its use, acceptance and glorification—was one of the most distinguishing characteristics of the totalitarian state. In Nazi ethics, war was noble, the love of peace a sign of decadence. As early as the late 1920s, the Nazis had private, uniformed gangs, the *Sturm Abteilung* (SA—storm troopers), who mistreated, abused and even killed other German citizens with impunity. For the first time in centuries, in one of the most "civilized" parts of Europe, torture was officially reintroduced. The mind decayed and the body-cult flourished. The ideal was to turn the German people into a race of splendid, disciplined animals. Contrarily, euthanasia was adopted for the insane and was even proposed for the aged. Camps were created for "asocials," political opponents and nonconformists. During World War II, when Germany ruled over a large part of Europe, the anti-Semitism of the fanatical SS descended to positive bestiality, the Nazis destroyed millions of human beings using infamous scientific and industrial methods.

The application of Nazi ideology depended on two types of force directed against individuals and social groups. The first was coercion and terror organized by the SS for security, political policing and elimination (and later genocide) of real and supposed enemies of the regime; this was organized on illegal bases by the Reichsführer SS, Heinrich Himmler. The other side of the coin was the control of the German people through indoctrination and propaganda; this was organized within the regular institutions of the Nazi state by the minister of propaganda, Josef Goebbels. Himmler and Goebbels—using different methods—aimed to implement Hitler's ideas and give structure to them.

No single target of nazification took higher priority than Germany's young people. In order for the Nazi regime to survive for a "thousand years," there had to be support fostered for in future generations. Hitler was well aware of this and made plans for it. The Nazi regime indoctrinated the rising generation in schools and universities. It instituted a youth movement, the *Hitler Jugend* (HJ—Hitler Youth). This appealed to a kind of juvenile idealism. Young men were taught to value their body but not their minds; young women were taught to breed large families and to look with awe upon their virile mates. In the view of Hitler, the nation's adults had been exposed to too many dangerous ideas over the years and had become accustomed to thinking and acting independently. German children were malleable, they could be separated from the old ideas and inculcated with the new Nazi precepts. "I begin with the young," Hitler said in a private talk with Hermann Rauschning. "We older ones are used up. We are rotten to the marrow. We are cowardly and sentimental. We are bearing the burden of a humiliating past, and have in our blood the dull recollection of serfdom and servility. But my magnificent youngsters! Are there any finer ones in the world? Look at these young men and boys! What material! With them, I can make a new world. This is the heroic stage of youth. Out of it will come the creative man, the man-god." The Führer went on: "When an opponent says to me, 'I will not come over to your side,' I reply calmly, 'Your child belongs to us already... What are you? You will pass on. Your descendants, however, now stand in the new camp. In a short time they will know nothing but this new community.'"

Before 1933, Germany's educational system, from kindergarten to the university, had been admired throughout the world for its comprehensiveness. After the Nazi takeover, the system underwent an immediate and chilling change. During the first few months of Hitler's rule, Jewish and politically unreliable teachers were dismissed, while female teachers were confined to domestic tasks. Not content with having persuasive control of the school system, the Nazis intruded even further into the lives of students, teachers and parents through the *Hitler Jugend* movement. A 1936 law confirmed the existence of an institution which had been in place since the creation of the Nazi Party and the establishment of the Third Reich. The *Hitler Jugend* was Hitler's tool to ensure that the younger generations would be totally loyal to the Nazi regime and willing to fight in the upcoming war. Hitler believed that the youth were the only ones that he could trust without reservation. The *Hitler Jugend* was an important vehicle for propaganda. The organization's boys were paramilitarily organized, deeply and fanatically indoctrinated in Nazi racist ideology. The Hitler Youth—and its female counterpart, the *Bund deutscher Mädel* (League of German Girls) (BdM)—carried widespread appeal, initially appearing as a challenge to more conservative forms of authority and giving youth a sense of collective power. But gradually the organization was used to enforce the Nazi ideology and it became merely a nursery for military mobilization. Appealing to passion more than to reason, the Nazi system could easily exploit the conformism, enthusiasm, commitment and sacrifice of the German youth. A whole generation of children were fooled by the state. The constant psychological indoctrination and the hard physical training to which German youth were submitted had declared aims: to brainwash the nation's youth to think German and act German, and to fill the ranks of the army, the SS and the regimented labor force. From cradle to grave, a German man or woman would be part of a Nazi-controlled organization. "They will never be free," Hitler said, "for the rest of their lives."

A note on the orthography maintained in this book: All German words and names are given in their exact German spelling with the sole exception that -ß- has been rendered -ss-.

1

Beginnings to 1923

The Nazi Party

The Nazi movement originated in Munich as the *Deutsche Arbeiterpartei* (DAP—German Worker's Party), one of a number of radical nationalist groups founded right after the First World War. The DAP was created by a toolmaker named Anton Drexler and a journalist, Dietrich Eckart. In September 1919, Adolf Hitler (1889–1945)—the son of a petty Austrian customs official, *Gefreiter* (corporal) of World War I, homeless laborer, failed artist, and Munich beerhouse activist—became a member of the DAP. In April 1920, the name of the party was changed to *Nationalsozialistische Deutsche Arbeiterpartei* (NSDAP—National Socialist German Worker Party). A convenient acronym, "Nazi," was formed from how the word "national" is pronounced in German (*na*-tsi-o-*nal*). In July 1921, Anton Drexler was kicked upstairs as honorary president and Hitler took command of the party. Drexler became a background figure in the Nazi Party and died, forgotten, in Munich in 1942. The new leader extended the NSDAP activities into the media with the acquisition of a newspaper, the *Völkischer Beobachter* (the Popular Observer) and into paramilitary activism with the formation of the *Sturm Abteilung* (SA).

Hitler's anticapitalist, anti-Semitic, extreme nationalist ideology was expressed in a 25-point program drawn up in February 1920 and reaffirmed after 1926. The main points were these:

- the rejection of the Versailles Treaty of 1919, and formation of a strong national army
- the union of all Germans in a greater Germany
- the demand for additional territories for food production and settlement of excess German population (*Lebensraum*—living space)
- the determination of citizenship by race (no Jew was allowed to be a German citizen; the crude Nazi race theory desperately sought scapegoats for post–World War I Germany's political, social and economic crisis)
- the demand that all citizens work for the general good
- the confiscation of all income not earned by work (an anticapitalist clause never applied)
- the nationalization of all large business

trusts had to be nationalized, and strengthening of small business
- a thorough reconstruction of the education system.

The Nazi program was constantly modified according to circumstances, and never offered the voter well-defined politics and economics. Vagueness was a deliberate basis of Hitler's ideology. Hitler achieved unprecedented personal power by systematically promising anything to anyone, while making secret deals with anyone who could be of some use to him, no matter how much difference there was between secret promises and public official oratory. What the Nazis proposed and promised was not particularly new. The ideology was simple, even simplistic, and often contradictory, with the emphasis on anti–Semitism, ultra-nationalism, the concept of Aryan racial supremacy, contempt for liberal democracy, and the principle of unique leadership. Greatly influenced by Mussolini's Fascism, the Nazi program was designed to appeal to everyone with a grievance of some kind. More than an intellectually constructed doctrine, it was a flexible movement aiming at aggressive action, a kind of religion leaning on blind faith, on irrationality, and on exploitation of subconscious fears and basic instincts. The ide-

NSDAP duty overcoat, **Bereichsleiter.** *The Nazi Party did not appeal to reason but to passion, and this was evident in its regalia and uniforms. Hitler was perfectly aware of the impact of regalia, and one is struck by the extraordinary and elaborate minutiae of Nazi uniforms, emblems, insignia, armbands, daggers, swords, flags, banners and the like. Hitler had a good sense for symbols and knew something of colors, having in his early days of scratching for a living in Vienna painted aquarelles and posters for shopkeepers. Hitler took such matters as the design of regalia and uniforms very seriously for he believed that the success of his nascent movement depended to a considerable extent on the use of strong symbols immediately comprehensible.*

ology was a jumble of vague generalizations, prejudiced ideas and a hodge-podge of various misappropriated philosophical principles lent from such theorists, writers, and artists as Charles Darwin, Johann Gottlieb Fichte, Jakob Grimm, E. M. Arndt, H. S. Chamberlain, Paul de Lagarde, Richard Wagner, Heinrich von Treitschke, Adolf Stöcker, Adam Muller, Rühle von Lilienstern, G. W. F. Hegel, Friedrich Nietzsche, and Hans F. K. Günther. In addition, historical falsifications were created and "scientific facts" were forged by Nazi "philosophers" (notably Walther Darré and Alfred Rosenberg), and used to excuse brutality, ruthlessness, megalomania, and a complete disregard for democracy and individual rights, the only goal being the absolute power of Hitler toward the absolute hegemony of Germany. A vital component of Nazism was the "Führer principle," the cult of the leader whose ideas were crucial in defining the nature of Nazi eclecticism. Indeed, from the start, the ambitious Hitler thought big and wanted to turn the tiny local Bavarian group into a national movement. The early conception of the NSDAP was revolutionary. Encouraged by the success of Mussolini's march on Rome in 1922, Hitler made a bid for power by force. On November 9, 1923, Hitler and a group of followers tried to seize power in Munich with the intention of sparking the takeover throughout Bavaria and Germany. The ill-prepared coup, known as *Marsch auf die Feldherrnhalle* or the Munich Beer Hall putsch, was bloodily repressed by the Munich police. Sixteen Nazi members were killed, the party was outlawed, and Hitler was arrested, tried for conspiracy, and sentenced to five years prison. Apparently his political career was broken and finished. While the leader was in prison, the Nazi Party fell into disarray.

Early German Youth Associations

A multitude of organizations

The Hitler Youth—*Hitler Jugend* (HJ, for short)—was officially formed at the second *Reichsparteitag* (Reich Party Day) on July 4, 1926. Although the *Hitler Jugend* (hereinafter not italicized) would become the only youth organization of Germany shortly after the NSDAP came to power in 1933, it was certainly not the first attempt to formally organize German youth along political, social, or religious lines. It was also not the only youth organization in existence at the time of its formation. German youth had been a major focus of numerous groups during the early 1900s including both left- and right-wing political parties, as well as groups generally benign in nature. German youth had always been highly organized, but the phenomenon of youth organizations in the beginning of the twentieth century was not limited to Germany—they were found in nearly all parts of the world. The Boy Scout movement, still active today, was founded in the United States in 1910, and offically chartered by Congress in 1916. In fascist Italy, paramilitary *Ballilas* (uniformed groups of children aged 8 to 12) were organized by Mussolini and very popular in the 1920s. In communist Soviet Union from 1922 to 1990, children aged 10–15 were indoctrinated in the so-called *Komsomol* or Communist Union of Youth.

In the years after 1919 and during the time of the Weimar Republic, the number of youth groups in Germany exploded. Some were political groups but many others were not political at all. Referred to as *Bünde* (leagues), those included the *Adler und Falken, Deutsche Falkenschaft, Geusen, Scharnhorst Jugend, Hindenburg Jugend, Bismarck Jugend, Jugendbund Graf von Wartenburg, Jungwolf, Jungdeutscher Orden, Freischar junger Nation, Freischar Schill, Deutsche Freischar,*

Jugend-Internationale, Jugendverbande, Tannenbergbund, Jungstrom Kolberg, Deutsche Kolberg, Deutsche Pfadfinderbund, and many more. To generalize about these groups is not possible, for they included a wide scale of attitudes and philosophies; some were comparatively large and open to all, others small and restricted to an "elite" membership. Many groups emerged spontaneously, not as the result of intellectual reflection. Some of them were basically apolitical forms of opposition to a society that had little to offer the young generation, a protest against the lack of vitality, warmth, emotions, and ideals. Some of these groups wanted to develop sincerity, decency, and open-mindedness, to free members from petty egoism and careerism, to oppose to artificial conventions, snobbery, and affectation, by hiking together, participating in common activities, and forming lasting friendships. Other groups were overtly patriotic, with the focus on nationalism, tradition, and occasionally chauvinism and racism. Others were against blind industrialization, materialist consumerism, and soulless society, and stressed the need to return to nature, to a simpler and healthier life. Some groups were individualistic, composed of young people who had no other motive than to live their own lives, and who had no clear aims, and no program; but other groups had defined goals, hierarchy, written manifestos and conventions, official ideology, political aims, and relations with political parties. Some had books and periodicals commenting on and announcing ideals and activities.

Germany had traditionally been a country marked by a quest for the unconditional and absolute, the unwillingness to accept reality, to compromise and live with imperfection, which has been at the root of most of its highest achievements and the cause of many of its greatest disasters. Against this romantic background youth organizations developed, which were always the movements of a minority. Accurate figures do not exist, but it seemed likely that the German *Bünde*, from 1890 till 1933, never exceeded 60,000. It was on the whole bourgeois in its social composition. Members of the youth movements were as a rule between 12 and 19 years of age.

The history of youth movements from the end of the nineteenth and the begining of the twentieth centuries until 1933 is very complex, and even the limited scope of those that existed exclusively in Germany is nearly impossible to fully document. But as complex as the subject may be, no study would be complete without a mention of some of them, as they were direct or indirect forerunners to the Hitler Youth.

Wandervogel

The *Wandervogel* (roughly, bird of passage or migratory bird) was a small movement created by a certain Karl Fischer (1881–1941) in 1896, in Steglitz, a suburb of Berlin. Its focus was youth-led nature hikes and excursions. The concept of youth-oriented nature hikes was by no means unique, but what was new was that they were now being led by other youth and not adults. The *Wandervogel* was in its truest form a movement against the values of the time (the Wilhelmine period) and an attempt to reevaluate the social situation with the idea of creating a better human condition. This was a noble and lofty goal indeed, but one in direct response to the conditions experienced by many lower- and middle-class youth. The *Wandervogel* movement was at first a romantic and rather innocent protest against a society in which young people were superfluous. It was also a very limited and completely unofficial affair. It consisted of teenagers meeting to discuss ways to break free of the seemingly repressive system of values dominant in Germany at the time. It is often said that the countercultural hippie movement of the 1960s finds its historical predecent in the early idealistic German *Wandervogel*. Anyway, the "migratory birds" were annoyed by the fact that many Germans had emigrated from the countryside to the big cities, and they decided to reverse the process. They organized treks to explore the vast German countryside in attempts to both free themselves of parental control and to gain a better sense of values through the experience of friendship, hardship and raw nature. They were disgusted with the materialism and—protesting against the burgeoning industrial life—they communed with nature in mountains and the woods. Their goal was to revive romantic Teutonic idealism, and there was a focus on traditional German folk stories, folk songs, and national heroes. In the early days the movement was neutral on political, religious and racial matters, but gradually anti-establishment nationalism and anti–Semitism were emphasized. After 1913 the *Wandervogel* accepted no longer Slavs and Jews in its ranks. As a result, the Zionist Jewish youth created its own movement, called *Blau Weiss* (Blue-White).

In November 1901 the *Wandervogel* formally became an association, even though it had informally existed for nearly five years. It was officially called *Wandervogel, Ausschuss für Schülerfahrten* (Committee for Schoolboys' Rambles). The name "*Wandervogel*" was proposed at the November 1901 meeting by a young man named Wolf Meyen. The term seems to have first appeared in a poem by Joseph Freiherr Von Eichendorff published in 1837, and was first used with a wider meaning, referring to human beings, in a poem by Otto Roquette in the 1850s. The writer Heinrich Sohnrey (1859–1948) was elected president of the association, and together with leader Karl Fischer drew up a constitution to give the committee a proper legal façade. The *Wandervogel* movement, not unlike many other youth movements that would soon follow, adopted a specific style of dress, a ranking system, and even a system of addressing fellow members. All the youth groups were selective, with standards and criteria that varied greatly from group to group and at different places and times, but nobody became a full member at once. Newcomers to the group started with the rank of *Scholar*, and gradually—after more or less elaborate tests and complicated achievements—became *Bursche* (student) and later *Bachant* (fellow). The authority of the leader *Oberbachant* (senior fellow) was unquestionable, but there was an *Eufrat* (Parents and Friends Advisory Council) which helped to "rule" the movement. Their greeting was "*Heil!*"—later adopted by the Nazis. The movement was divided into units: a *Gruppe* or *Horde* totaled between eight and twenty members. Each group had a *Heim* (nest or home), a meeting room decorated with the emblem of the movement, possibly a small library and other collective property including flags and banners, trumpets, pipes and drums, as the soldier gradually supplanted the strolling scholar as the ideal type. Several groups were united in an *Ortsgruppe* (local branch), and all local branches in a given province had a central organization called a *Gau*.

In the early days everybody turned up in different garb—often wearing short pants and flamboyant hats with feathers. In the 1920s the wearing of a uniform became obligatory: this included short trousers; blue, white, brown, green or gray shirts; heavy marching shoes; and neckties, as well as badges as marks of identification and pins for distinction and achievements. The swastika was frequently used by both the *Wandervogel* and the extreme anti–Semite Right after 1918.

At first the movement consisted exclusively of boys, but after 1907 girls were allowed. Questions of sexual morality and homosexuality preoccupied the youth movement for years. As the leadership thought females would be a distracting and disruptive element, girls were only tolerated, and the sexes were never integrated. In fact the organization chose to ignore sexual problems. Half-baked ideas prevailed on the subject. It was argued that in mixed groups boys would become effeminate, and the girls would tend to become wild. The meeting of the sexes was generally delayed beyond the age of seventeen. Before that girls were tolerated at some of the boys' meetings and festivals, though never on their trips and hikes. In accordance with the strict moral code of the day, the official line was to create separate exclusive boys' and girls' groups, who had to sublimate their juvenile libidos until marriage. This attempt was, of course, doomed to failure and, in individual cases, could cause or aggravate sexual maladjustments later on. Before World War I some leaders and members advocated a much freer relationship between sexes, to the scandal of Wilhelmian society.

Homosexuality had already been outlawed in Germany under the Penal Code of 1871, but in the liberal climate of Weimar Germany after 1918, and especially in Berlin with its café life, bars, cabarets and night clubs, there had been proposals for repeal. Earlier in January 1914, a speaker of the Catholic Center Party had denounced the *Wandervogel* as a "club of homosexuals" and a den of free love. The movement spread rapidly and became more conformist. About 25,000 members met in October 1913 at the Hohe Meissner mountain south of Cassel. The historical meeting saw the first crack in the movement and a crisis dividing the leadership into "conservative" Right and "progressive" Left. At the beginning of the First World War (1914–1918), an immense wave of patriotic and national enthusiasm rose within certain circles of the youth organization. But gradually as the conflict dragged on, it caused disappointment and even rejection. The war gravely affected the fortunes of the movement. Many of its

Member of the **Wandervogel** *movement*

leaders and members—some of whom did not regard military training as part of their ideology—were mobilized, while activities were narrowly circumscribed and greatly disrupted. Things had turned out very differently from what the enthusiasts had expected. The war destroyed an entire generation of German youth, and many *Wandervogel* were killed. About 14,000 members saw military service, most in front-line duty; of these, one in four never returned from the trenches.

Youth leagues

BÜNDE

In the late 1920s and early 1930s, some of the *Wandervogel*—those who were happy just to have survived four years of World War I butchery—remained politically neutral and uninterested after the postwar crisis had passed, but for others, the youth movement had taken on a political coloration. The *Wandervogel* had been a movement of reform and protest, but the society it hoped to reform and against which it protested—that of Prussian Wilhelmian Germany—had been swept away by World War I. Romanticism, songs and hikes—the very spirit of the early days—were totally out of place in 1919 Germany, so some thought. The *Wandervogel* had been critical of society, but it had never assumed that its mission was to change the world. The immediate postwar years caused a radicalization both on the Left and on the Right, and the *Wandervogel* could not maintain its unity. The most active and determined members were divided by political questions about how to change the world. The individualistic civilian period, during which youth was led by youth, drew to a close. Elements of the former *Wandervogel* continued after the First World War, in numerous more or less disciplined and organized *Bünde* (leagues), with new political ideas, new collective and paramilitary activities, and—most notably—led by adults. The word "*Führer*" (leader; hereinafter not italicized) began to appear with its connotation of domination and blind obedience. To children whose fathers had been killed in World War I, the leaders of these groups became surrogates; to teenagers disturbed by a fragmented society, they offered solidity; to students who knew that nothing awaited them upon graduation from college, they offered immersion in the group; to alienated youth drifting into dreary, unfriendly cities, they offered companionship; to those thirsting for absolute meanings, they provided absolute answers. The word "*Bund*," with its mysterious undertone of conspiracy, was linked with adventure and excitement as though it hid a deep secret. At the same time, the *Bund* often offered a convenient, dreamy haven of refuge from the pressing problems of the day. The lyric romanticism of the early *Wandervogel* tended to be replaced by duty, service, obedience, the servile subordination of the mind under the yoke of an ideology, and sacrifice for a cause. A small but vocal and influential minority joined the communists and socialists. A considerably larger group joined right-wing extremist groups. The story of these small rightist leagues—between 1919 and 1933—is an uninterrupted chain of unions, quarrels, splits, exclusions, rivalry, mutual recriminations and reunions. The great number of numerically small organizations—some short-lived—and the number of leaders involved makes it impossible to trace in detail all of their complex developments. In such groups there generally was much sympathy for Hitler, but no or little inclination to join the Hitler Jugend, whose rowdyism, narrow-mindedness, and low cultural level were frequently deplored; moreover they refused—on the whole—to identify themselves with any particular political party.

The earlier movement divided into several different streams. Many former *Wandervogel* found their way directly from the German Army into the *Freikorps* (unofficial armed militias) a part of which would later become Hitler's *Sturm Abteilung*. Youngsters such as the league of *Knappenschaft* (Young Novitiates) and *Freischar* (free groups) took part in street brawls to fight out the political issues of the day. The *Schilljugend* was an Austrian youth nationalist movement created in Salzburg in spring 1924, headed by the former Freikorpsführer Oberleutnant Gerhard Rossbach. The *Schilljugend* had many similarities with various Nazi *Jugendbünde* and held close contacts with Hitler's NSDAP.

The *Jungstahlhelm* (Young Steel Helmet) was the youth organization of the *Stahlhelm*. The *Stahlhelm* (Steel Helmet) was an organization formed in December 1918 by nationalist ex-servicemen. It played a prominent role in politics in the 1920s and early 1930s. In the presidential elections of March 1932, the association supported Hitler. Once in political power, the Nazis wanted no opposition of any kind, and the veterans association was closely controlled and renamed National-Socialist League of Ex-Servicemen. In July 1933, the youth movement *Jungstahlhelm* was incorporated into the Hitler Jugend. In 1951 the veterans' organization *Stahlhelm* was revived in more modest and apolitical form, with headquarters at Cologne.

The *Jungdeutscher Orden* (also known as *Jungdo*) was founded by ex–*Wandervogel* lieutenant Arthur Mahraun in 1919. It was an extreme-right antirevolutionary youth group with somewhat confusing ideology. They wanted a strictly disciplined nation but rejected dictatorship; they were strongly nationalist but advocated a rapprochement with France; they rejected racial supremacy but nevertheless excluded Jews from their ranks. Mahraun spent the twelve-year Hitler era breeding sheep in central Germany and died in 1950, a man forgotten by all but the small community of the faithful.

Some *Bünde* also changed course—the *Oberland Bund*, for example. *Oberland* was a small Munich paramilitary group originating from a right-wing *Freikorps*; its leader—Friedrich Weber, a local veterinarian and another former *Wandervogel*—was ideologically close to the Nazis, and marched with them in the failed Munich Beer Hall putsch of November 1923. Later, however, radical socialist demands were put forward, and a part of Oberland moved for a while toward Bolshevism and some of its leaders became communists.

The *Jungnationale Bund* (known as *Junabu*, League of Young Nationalists) had been created by a certain Heinz Dähnhardt. Staunchly nationalist, the *Junabu* was one of the most effective leagues and remarkably free from the cultural narrow-mindedness that was prevalent in German right-wing circles. Its leadership had strong reservations about National Socialism, sarcastically criticizing Hitler's evasions of clear stands on socio-economic questions. Toward the end of the 1920s, however, with the aggravation of the political crisis, the *Junabu*'s moderation failed to attract or hold the younger generation; several former leaders of the *Junabu* were brought to trial in Essen in 1937 and sentenced to penal servitude.

Artaman League

The *Bund der Artamenen* (Artaman League) was another youth group that influenced the future HJ. The name came from the ancient Indo-German word "Artam" that was supposed to mean "revival through forces of the origin." The *Bund der Artamenen* was a tiny organization of young ultranationalists created in the early 1920s by a young man by the name of August Georg Kenstler. Participants were devoted to the concept of soil and to the idea of German race. The idealist members of the back-to-the-land league wished to escape decadent and corrupt urban life through farming. They preferred to work on farms in lieu of military service. The Artamans were strongly chauvinist, anti–Slav and urged that Polish farmers living in Germany be returned to their own country. Sympathizing with the Nazis, they had a flag displaying a swastika and a motto: "We want to march to the East!" Their device was "Blood, Soil and the Sword"—a slogan which was to become a basic principle of the SS. Many Artamans journeyed to farms in eastern Germany to defend the fatherland against the Slavs. The movement intended to mobilize hundreds of thousands of young Germans, but never succeeded in enlisting more than 2,000. It was not a success because the leaders quarreled, and also the idealism of these young people from the cities appeared insufficient to pass the severe test of agricultural labor. It was easier to rhapsodize about blood and soil than to buckle down to a working day of ten hours. The Artamans were also preoccupied with occultism and mysticism; they held that by communing with the ghostly spirits present in nature, mysterious veils of the past would be lifted. Their rituals tried to recreate that primordial kinship with nature which they supposed ancient Germans to have had. They abhorred science and reason as enemies of the life of the soul. Many of them became vegetarians and teetotalers, a few observed abstinence from sex, as they believed that the purification of the physical body would help the soul to see "reality." They threw over orthodox medicine for spiritual and herbal healing, which were somehow felt to be closer to the primal source. They were thus open to the theory of the Nazi "philosopher" Richard Walther Darré (1895–1953), who preached selective breeding, the agrarian philosophy of *Blut und Bodem* (blood and soil) and the protection of the peasantry as the "life source of the Nordic race." More and more the movement took on the character of an anti–Semitic society seeing the Jews as the exemplar of the bourgeoisie, and the urban bourgeoisie as the source of all misery. As the situation deteriorated in the late 1920s, some of the Artamans were drawn deeper into politics, and engaged in a holy war against their enemies: liberals, democrats, Free-Masons and Jews. Eventually many members of the Artaman League turned to National Socialism. Among the Artaman leaders in 1924 were two men destined to infamy in the Third Reich: Heinrich Himmler, who would later become Reichsführer SS, and Rudolf Hoess, later the commander of extermination camp Auschwitz. The small league was dismantled and incorporated into the Hitler Jugend in October 1934 as the Nazi youth movement gained strength.

Eberhard "Tusk" Köbel

Among the leaders of the pre–1933 German youth movements there was one who became a legend in his own lifetime. Eberhard Köbel—better known as "Tusk"—was born in Stuttgart in 1907, the son of a senior government official. Köbel joined a *Wandervogel* group as a boy, then became a member of the *Freischar* and leader of the Wurttemberg region of that group in 1928. In 1929, Tusk founded his own movement known as *DJ 1–11* (*Deutsche Jungenschaft*—German Youth Movement of November 1). He revolutionized the youth press, radically changing newspapers' layout, making them simpler, livelier and more attractive by using catchy illustrations and photographs. He introduced a new form of tent (the *kohte* from Lapland) which became very popular throughout the youth movement. The eccentric Tusk also introduced the banjo and balalaika; new songs and dancing styles were imported from Northern Europe. There was fanaticism and even ecstasy apparent in his speech and behavior. He was a visionary who thought in terms of a community for life, with all-embracing demands upon the individuals. Finding even the Prussian tradition too mild, Tusk introduced extreme militaristic practices and held up the ideal of the ancient Japanese warrior caste known as *samurai*. His dream was to forge German youth into one great army of followers who were to become models of intrepidity, an elite of radiant physique and character, free from all bonds. Tusk's *Jungenschaft* was a school of character. It became popular—other groups envied his boys' verve and élan, and often imitated their innovations, including attire and songs. He also met with jealousy and derision, and many rival leaders ridiculed his artificial pathos and tendency to swank. Tusk was a German nationalist but not an extreme one. As all right-wing leaders, he denounced the iniquities of the Treaty of Versailles, and attacked democrats, Marxists and Jews, but he never gave intelligible purpose to his feverish activities. His attitude in 1933 was more and more inconsistent. For a while he joined the Communist Party, and displayed much interest in Zen Buddhism. He advised members of his *Deutsche Jungenschaft 1–11* to join Hitler's youth and try to gain positions of command in order to subvert the Hitler Jugend from within. It seemed that Tusk nursed illusions of being appointed head of the Hitler Jugend. This was unthinkable and in January 1934 he was arrested by the Gestapo. Released in June 1934, he left Germany for Sweden and England where he stayed until the end of World War II, making a living as photographer and studying Far Eastern languages. In August 1944, Tusk, trying to make up for his own past political mistakes, expressed the hope that his former followers would fight as partisans against Hitler in the final phase of the war. The charismatic, legendary and eccentric Eberhard "Tusk" Köbel—regarded as both a genius and a charlatan—died in East Berlin in 1955, a sick, lonely and forgotten man.

As illustrated by the few examples above, it is impossible to generalize about the *Bünde*. Some pursued defined purposes of a political, social, or religious character. Others aspired to be free of any tie to the world of adults. Others considered their league to be an end in itself. Some wanted, like Jean-Jacques Rousseau, to return to nature.

As Nazism grew, many former *Wandervogel* and *Bünde* turned to National Socialism, and many leagues were merged into Hitler's youth movement. *Wandervogel* and *Bünde* provided fertile ground in which early Nazi ideas might grow. The Hitler Jugend would take on the notion of "youth led by youth" and incorporate it into its core of ideals, while the unique style of dress pioneered in the *Wandervogel* would continue on in many forms among the new organization.

Hitler's National Socialism came to power as the party of youth; its cult of youth was pronounced and Hitler never lost opportunities to declare that his movement was a revolt of the coming generations against all that was old, senile and rotten with decay. From the beginning, the Nazi movement was anxious to win control over the extreme-right-wing leagues originating from the *Wandervogel* and *Bünde*, a goal in which it was highly successful.

2

The Road to Power, 1924–1933

The *Kampfzeit* (Time of Struggle)

Paradoxically, Hitler's failed coup of November 1923 turned into a triumph since it helped him build up a national reputation. Hitler only served a year of a prison sentence (from 11 November 1923 to 20 December 1924), enjoying an easy and comfortable detention. When he started anew in February 1925, Hitler had learned a few things and henceforth decided to observe "legal" principles for political success: unity under his unique leadership, vigorous opportunistic propaganda, gaining the army's support, and making maximum use of the democratic means that were available. After leaving prison, however, Hitler was forbidden to speak in public, and the road to power was long and difficult.

The years between 1925 and 1933 were called by the Nazis the *Kampfzeit*, the "heroic" time of struggle, a period of intense effort and sacrifice against overwhelming odds. It was part of the carefully created Nazi mythology, and the idea of the highly idealized *Kampfzeit* was taught, after 1933, as part of the school curriculum.

During the period 1925–29, the Weimar Republic was stabilized, the economy was partly restored, and social agitation was controlled. The insignificant NSDAP was threatened by disunion. Hitler succeeded in winning over the deviating northern contingents of the NSDAP led by Gregor Strasser. With difficulty the stubborn Hitler eliminated all opposition and finally obtained unlimited power within the party. He established his authority through a series of loyal party officials known as *Gauleiters* (district leaders). By the end of the 1920s, it seemed like Hitler's party had no political future, but the international crisis of 1929 worked as a detonator. Beginning in the United States, the economic crisis was followed by a huge depression which rapidly affected the whole world, and particularly the fragile German economy, with currency collapse, bankruptcies and large-scale unemployment.

After 1930 the Nazi Party, cunningly using the framework of the democratic constitution, made tremendous progress combining the vote of disillusioned workers and ruined middle classes, and working backstairs intrigues with financial and industrial magnates fearing the triumph of the communist opposition. Encouraged by the apparent

success of his strategy, Hitler played a double game. Below the surface, the SA militia terrorized and victimized its opponents. Officially, however, Hitler sought power through election to Germany's highest office. After complicated and tortuous political moves in 1931 and 1932, Hitler did not seize power. He was jobbed into office by intrigues and political bargain. The growth and the triumph of the Nazi Party were not fortuitous. Despite the large support he had won, Hitler came to power not as the result of any irresistible revolutionary movement or a popular victory at the poll, but as part of a shoddy political deal, due to the bad judgment of his temporary supporters and because of the division of his political opponents. January 30, 1933, was a landmark for Germany and the world when President Hindenburg appointed Hitler chancellor (corresponding to prime minister). Hitler never abandoned the cloak of legitimacy, instead he turned the law inside out and made illegality legal. Within a few months, after having arbitrarily crushed all opposition, the cunning Hitler established a dictate. He was proclaimed Führer of Germany, which became a one-party state by the act of 14 July 1933. The Nazi Party had some 27,000 dues-paying members in 1925; 49,000 in 1926; 108,000 in 1928; and 178,000 by the end of 1929. The NSDAP had 210,000 members in March 1930 and 850,000 in January 1933. By September 1939 this had increased to more than 4 million, with 150,000 officials. By January 1943 the NSDAP numbered 6.5 million, and they party peaked with 8.5 million in 1945.

One of the six million German unemployed in 1932. The sign reads: "I am looking for a job, no matter what!"

Creation of the Hitler Youth

Jugendbund der NSDAP

The first NSDAP-related organization of German youth was the *Jugendbund der NSDAP* (League of the Youth of the National-Socialist Party), which was formed by a fanatical young Nazi supporter named Gustav Lenk. It seemed that Gustav Adolf Lenk (born in October 1903 in Munich, thus aged only 17) could not join the party. Instead of waiting, he decided to create a Nazi youth branch and started recruiting members in late 1921. The Nazi youth organization headed by Lenk was announced in March 1922 in the *Völkischer Beobachter*. An article was published inviting "all national-socialist-minded youth, aged between 14 and 18, regardless of their social class, whose heart suffered under the pitiful conditions of Germany, who wanted to fight the Jewish enemy, shame and suffering, and who wished to serve the cause of the Fatherlands" to join the Nazi Youth League. On Sunday, 13 May 1922, Lenk's Nazi youth group was officially created during a meeting at the Bürgerbräukeller beer hall in Munich. The youth organization was divided into the *Jungmannschaften* (boys 14–16) and the *Jungsturm Adolf Hitler* (16–18 years old). As the youth league needed some sort of backing, it was decided to organize and place it under the command of the *Sturm Abteilung* (SA storm troopers) headed by Lieutenant Johann Ulrich Klintzsch, and the 300 youth members wore uniforms similar to those of the SA. The SA, as already mentioned, were the early private militia of the Nazi Party. It was intended originally to protect the party mass meetings and oppose rival political parties by force. The SA men were young roughnecks brought in largely from the *Freikorps* (Free Corps), the post–World War I nationalistic freebooters.

The first public appearance of the *Jugendbund* was in the "Battle of Coburg" on 14–15 October 1922, when elements of it took part along with some 800 SA members. In early 1923 the *Jugendbund* held its first national congress, having expanded beyond the boundaries of Bavaria. Owing to Lenk's energy, small Nazi youth groups were created in Nuremberg, Dresden, Hanau and Dortmund, and contacts were made with Nazi-minded and extreme-right groups in Austria and Sudetenland. In spite of local successes, the development of the Nazi youth movement was limited. Lenk tried to launch his own newspaper, *Nationale Jungsturm*, but as there were too few subscribers, the paper flopped. Another attempt to launch a Nazi youth newspaper, this time called *Nationalsozialistische Jugend*, also failed. Temporarily the Nazi youth movement would have to be content with a published enclosure in the existing Nazi Party paper *Völkischer Beobachter*. This was indeed a formidable challenge, because in the early 1920s, the Nazi Party, its SA and youth movement were small groups of penniless activists without significant influence, deprived of important means and facing rival ultra-right, nationalist and anti–Semitic political formations.

After the failed Munich putsch of November 1923, Hitler was sentenced to five-year imprisonment and the NSDAP, the SA and the Nazi Party youth movement were declared illegal. None of these disappeared, however, but continued to exist under cover. During the time the NSDAP was outlawed, Lenk was briefly imprisoned. When he was released he made two attempts to resurrect the *Jugendbund*, first as the *Vaterländische Jugendverband Grossdeutschlands* (Patriotic Youth League of Greater Germany) and later as the *Grossdeutsche Jugendbewegung* (GDJB; Youth Movement of Greater Germany), but both attempts ended with his arrest. Another young Nazi, Kurt Gruber, who had been leader of the *Jugendbund* in Saxony, also made an attempt to resurrect it; he too used the name *Grossdeutsche Jugendbewegung* (GDJB). His attempt was more successful, both because the authorities in Saxony did not ban his GDJB and he because he cooperated with other organizations of the far right. Gruber's GDJB was renamed *Frontjugend* (Front Youth) when it became the youth branch of the *Frontbann* (Front squad, a cover name used by the SA), but later changed its name back to GDJB. Another large Nazi youth organization during this time was the *Schilljugend*, formed by Gerhard Rossbach in Austria and led in Germany by SA Gruppenführer Edmund Heines.

Kurt Gruber

When Hitler started anew in February 1925, he relaunched party and the SA. Simultaneously the youth organization was also reorganized. Hitler did not immediately decide on who should lead the new official youth movement of the NSDAP. Gustav Adolf Lenk had shown little talent to lead the youth movement, had expressed deviating ideas, and was charged with embezzlement. Accused of being a traitor, he was forced to resign and soon faded out of the picture. Following the refusal of Rossbach to accept Hitler as the leader, the task was handed in May 1925 to Kurt Gruber (born in October 1904). An interregnum followed, in which the *Schilljugend*, a right-wing extremist *Bund*, became for a time the official youth movement of the Nazi party NSDAP. Gruber soon showed great organizational talent. He succeeded in uniting the various pro–Hitler youth groups, and in April 1926 the very descriptive name Hitler Jugend appeared for the first time, revealing the personality cult devoted to Adolf Hitler. The named Hitler Jugend is said to have been coined by Julius Streicher, the editor of the Nazi newspaper *Der Stürmer*. From the start, the name Hitler Jugend had two meanings: the first applied to the entire German youth movement, including the organizations for girls; the second designated the group of male members aged fourteen to eighteen.

On 3–4 July 1926, at the *Reichsparteitag* (Reich Party day) held in Weimar, the Hitler Youth was formally established by Hitler, and Kurt Gruber was appointed *Reichsführer der Hitler Jugend* (leader of the Hitler Youth). Gruber did not move his headquarters to Munich, but chose to keep it at Plauen. By that time there was no question of independence for the youth movement; apparently Hitler did not feel confident of independent success in this field; the HJ remained a part of the SA. The first national HJ rally was held in August 1927 with 600 boys present, and a year later 2,500 boys took part in the party rally in Nuremberg.

Gruber did good organizational work. He divided the Nazi youth movement into the same units as the Nazi Party. He introduced the concept of "youth led by youth," and issued a youth uniform based on that of the SA, composed of a brown shirt, black shorts, and red armband with swastika. He introduced strong symbolic flags, insignia and emblems such as the S-Rune. He also defined the main activities of the movement—including culture, education and propaganda, and encouraged the practice of sport, camping, marching and music. Gruber created the *Jungvolk*, the junior branch for boys aged 10 to 14, and founded two newspapers, *Die Junge Front* and *Hitlerjugend Zeitung*. The achievements of Gruber were far from neglible but—despite close contacts between Gruber and other rightwing *Bünde*—the Nazi youth organization did not make much headway. Moreover, there was rivalry and jealousy at the top of the Nazi leadership. Gruber, in spite of his talent, was heavily criticized. Prominent members of the Nazi Party were critical of the human material collected by the HJ. Repeated complaints were made of indiscipline, and even drinking orgies among the Hitler Youth. The first leader of the Artaman League, H. Holfelder, wrote a letter to

Hitler in 1925, urging that local Nazi leaders should be instructed to refuse membership to former members of the Artaman who were wanted by the police for robbery, or living on the earnings of prostitutes. This throws a revealing light not only upon Hitler's party but also on the more elitist Artamans. In 1929 a certain Baldur von Schirach, a successful leader of Nazi students, who was something of a poet in his spare time, reported to the Führer that the Hitler Jugend was "badly led and its discipline indifferent." Moreover, the HJ had not significantly increased its membership. This, of course, did not please Hitler. In 1926 the organization counted 700 members; a number that rose to 13,000 in 1929. In spite of Gruber's effort, the Hitler Youth remained a negligible force. In 1931, Hitler ordered the HJ headquarters to be moved to Munich, and Kurt Gruber was soon forced to leave his post. Like Gustav Lenk before him, he soon disappeared from the leadership and sank into oblivion.

Baldur von Schirach

The new post of *Reichsjugendführer* was created to head the youth movements of the NSDAP, including the HJ, the *National-Sozialistische Schülerbund* (NSS—Nazi school league), and the *Nationalsozialistischen Deutschen Studentenbund* (NSDStB—National Socialist German Students' League). A young man named Baldur von Schirach was appointed to the position in October 1931. Von Schirach was also head of the NSDStB and Adrian von Renteln was made head of the HJ and NSS.

Early SA man with Nazi flag (c. 1921)

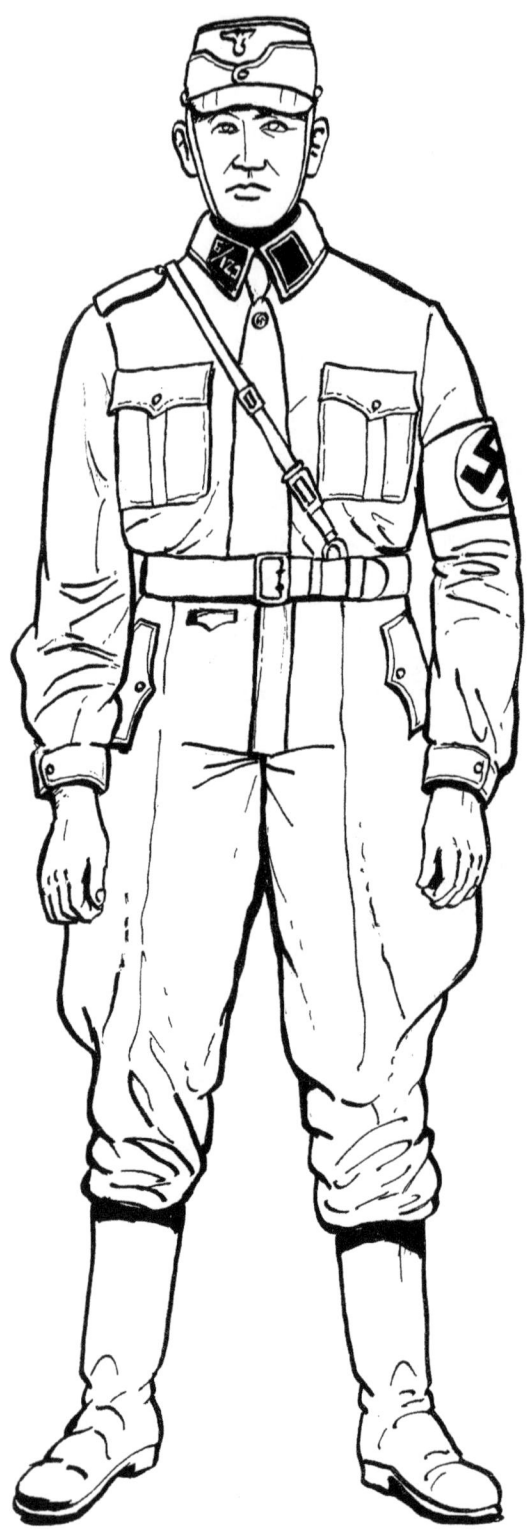

SA man 1933.

Baldur Benedikt von Schirach was born in Berlin on 9 May 1907 to a wealthy family. His father was an officer and later a theater director. His mother was American, and his grandfather had lost a leg at the battle of Bull Run in 1861. Baldur grew up in a milieu of music and literature, and showed talent for poetry. A romantic and sentimental child, he longed for adventure and action. He joined the Young German League at the age of ten. As a student he became anti–Semitic, anti–Christian, full of contempt for Germany's ruling class, and was regarded as a renegade by his peers. During 1924–27 he studied history and Germanic folklore in Munich where he got acquainted with the Nazi movement. In March 1925, at age 18, he joined the NSDAP as member number 17,251 and became a member of the SA. He attracted Hitler's attention with his lyrical, flattering poetry and became one of his henchmen. Von Schirach had published a book of lyric poetry in Munich in 1929 untitled *Die Feier der neuen Front* (The Feast of the New Front). In 1929 von Schirach was appointed head of the National Socialist German Students' League (NSDStB), with the task of promoting Nazism in the universities. In October 1931, Hitler made him Reich Youth Leader of the NSDAP, a post in which he proved himself to be a master organizer in the prewar period. Von Schirach was also promoted to the rank of *SA Gruppenführer* (General) and rapidly moved into Hitler's inner circle. On 31 March 1932, his link with the Führer was reinforced when he married Henriette Hoffmann, the daughter of Hitler's private photographer Heinrich Hoffmann. Hitler and SA chief Ernst Röhm were his groomsmen at the wedding. In the meantime, Adrian von Renteln resigned in 1932, having done much to rid the HJ of many incompetent or otherwise unsuitable leaders, most of their replacements coming from the middle- and upper-class-dominated NSS and NSDStB. Von Schirach took over his posts and the NSS was soon merged with the HJ.

The Hitler Jugend and Kampfzeit

By the beginning of the 1930s, the HJ was one youth organization among many and by no means the biggest. Von Schirach had to be patient in his battle against the other youth organizations, and confined the HJ to a propaganda role. The Hitler Jugend and SA participated in the *Kampfzeit* resulting in the seizure of power by the Nazis in January 1933. They propagated the ideology by passing out leaflets, spreading pamphlets and placards, chanting slogans, marching in impressive rallies and mass parades, and holding prestigious meetings. The essential purpose of such manifestations was to display strength and physical force, to create a sense of power and a feeling of unity, and to show to all that the success of the Nazis was irresistible. On 17–18 October 1931, a token mobilization of Nazi forces took place in the town of Brunswick with a large number of uniformed participants. This impressive display of strength alarmed the Weimar authorities. In December 1931 a national ban was imposed on all political uniformed militia, including the communist fighting squads, but also the Nazi SA, SS and Hitler Jugend. This proscription remained in force until June 1932 but proved to have little practical effect, as street violence, disrupting of rival meetings and political hooliganism did not diminish. Illegality also seemed to have acted as a stimulus and the Nazis gained new sympathizers and adherents. The HJ was made independent from the SA on 13 May 1932, not least to prevent it from being banned along with the SA by the Weimar authorities, however it was banned along with its parent organization from 13 April to 17 June 1932.

SA Gruppenführer *1933.*

There were indeed many fights and skirmishes against parties and youth groups opposed to Nazism. Between 1931 and 1933, twenty-one boys and one girl of the Hitler Youth were killed in violent action. Semi-qualified doctors, dentists, physicians and pharmacists (students of the HJ in their final years) could be helpful within the Sanitäts-SA, the medical corps of the stormtroops. With violence frequently accompanying SA activism and hooliganism since the beginning of the *Kampfzeit*, it was essential to have medically qualified personnel at hand.

In 1931, after calculated hooliganism in theaters, the Nazis forced the government to ban the further showing of Lewis Milestone's film *All Quiet on the Western Front*. The film had been adapted from the German novel by Erich Maria Remarque. Made in 1930, the film was bold, interesting, and strongly anti-militaristic. It was the story of a youth brought up to believe in the value of patriotism, militarism and glorious death, who came to find that war colored things differently. The youth returned on leave to his school where the master—who had taught him the values that he now despised—greeted him ecstatically. As a fighter he was treated with great respect, and the eager young children waited to be stirred by thrilling tales. He had none. There was no heroism, no glory. The atrocious reality was different from the official myth. The film was totally committed to showing the pointlessness and evil of war. It gave war its true face, a face of degradation and bestiality that applied not only to World War I which was portrayed, but to *all* war. This was obviously in total opposition to Nazi ideology. Propaganda master Josef Goebbels distributed to members of the SA and Hitler Youth a number of tickets for the theaters where the film was playing in Berlin. The Nazis (in civilian dress) crowded into the places and during the shows released mice, set off stink-bombs, and created other agitation. The police were called, but could trace no obvious culprits as all present merely stated that they wanted to see the film in the following days, the press was full of the story of the so-called "spontaneous" eruption of popular anger and the government banned the film as likely to be the cause of more disturbing the public order. The Nazis were jubilant to know that terror on the streets could dictate the government's actions.

From the start, von Schirach sought to reeducate the German youth in the spirit of National Socialism. As youth leader, von Schirach's efforts were concentrated on building up the Hitler Youth as quickly as possible. However, all through the twenties, the Nazi youth movement remained a negligible force. The following figures give the approximative prewar membership:

1923—1,200
1924—2,400
1925—5,000
1926—6,000
1927—8,000
1928—10,000
1929—13,000
1930—26,000
1931—63,700
1932—99,586

3

Prelude to War, 1933–1939

Growth of the Hitler Youth

Gleichschaltung

In January 1933 the Nazis seized power, and in the eventful spring that followed a truncated and terrorized *Reichstag* voted to give Hitler unlimited power. Then broke out the time of *Gleichschaltung* began, the complete coordination of all activities by the regime, the fusion of every element of German life into a functioning Nazi political and social machine. Through a series of laws, the government system was changed. Trade unions were forbidden and replaced by a single body known as the German Labor Front (DAF). The first concentration camps were established for opponents, and the first steps taken which would lead later toward the systematic extermination of Jews. Goebbels was made minister of propaganda and all political parties except Hitler's NSDAP were forbidden and dissolved. The state was remodeled upon a totalitarian plan, a state in which there could be room for only one youth organization. Baldur von Schirach was—in Hitler's own words—the ideal man for the leadership of the Nazi youth. Schirach, who had already distinguished himself among his fellow students, undoubtedly deserved credit for having founded a solid organization. Under his dynamic leadership, the growth of the Hitler Jugend rocketed. Following the seizure of power, by the end of 1933 there were 812,038 of the 7.5 million German boys and girls in the fourteen-to-eighteen age group belonging to the HJ. By the end of 1934 the figure was 1.25 million. The reasons for this rapid growth in membership were various. In 1933, the Hitler Youth seemed to be the great wave of the future. Many young people joined because of their enthusiasm for the Führer, and in the hope that their free time would be purposefully and rewardingly occupied; these people had been in general sympathy with Nazism for some time, and for them joining the movement was simply the logical thing to do. Others, whose approval had been more reserved, were swept into the movement by the huge tidal wave of nationalist emotion. Others joined as a result of pressure exerted both by the HJ organization and the Nazi Party upon their parents, teachers or employers, or because of anxieties about their future careers or places in higher education. Parents also argued that their own jobs would be more secure through their children's contribution within the Hitler Jugend. Among these opportunists or reluctant converts, the motives varied, as did their subsequent behavior. It must be remembered that the early 1930s was a period of disarray and desperation. The middle classes were hardly less seriously hit by unemployment than the working class. Everything seemed undermined by the general economic decline, and the specter of poverty was becoming a grim reality. Choosing Hitler was often not a conscious political decision, nor the affirmation of a known program or ideology. For many who were hopeless it was simply a desperate acceptance in the absence of an alternative, an omission rather than a commission, or an act of faith. Some were willing to surrender their own critical judgment, with varying degrees of reluctance, to abdicate all responsibility, to abandon democracy and freedom, and to trust Hitler, who they thought would know best what to do. In 1933 who knew where it was all leading? Only a few people in Germany or elsewhere understood and foresaw that Nazism was heading inevitably toward barbarism, a new world war and genocide.

In addition, during *Gleichschaltung*, many youth organizations were dissolved and merged with the HJ, increasing the number of involuntary members. Baldur von Schirach succeeded in bringing all youth movements under his control, even including the religious organizations.

Absorption of non–Nazi youth associations

In 1933 there were about four hundred youth organizations, leagues and associations in Germany which had nothing to do with the Nazi Party. The first casualties of the rise of the Nazis to power were the youth organizations of the left-wing German political parties. Soon membership in other youth organizations was officially discouraged and these disintegrated under pressure.

Following the seizure of power, parties and working-class youth organizations were forbidden and suppressed, including the powerful, highly popular and rival Communist Youth Association (KJVD), the Social-Democrat Socialist Youth (SAJ) and the German Socialist Youth Association (SAP).

The HJ soon endeavored to coordinate youth organizations of the bourgeois and right-wing parties as well, which were seen as ambiguous competitors. Indeed—as already said—many of these *Bünde* also submitted to a vehement nationalism and anti-Semitism, worshipped war and violence, condemned democracy, and called for a new Greater German Reich under the leadership of a powerful and authoritarian Führer. But many of these "elite," well-mannered middle-class groups looked upon the Hitler Youth as a collection of uncouth upstarts. Their leadership did not want to take sides, and in the end their perplexed, temporizing attitudes were no protection against the Nazi storm. Hitler himself had no use for such movements; he had contempt for them. For him, "*Wandervogel*" was a term of derision. The Hitler Jugend wished to realize its totalitarian aspirations even with regard to youth associations whose political temper approximated their own. One could only be a National Socialist and not a National-Socialist and something else besides. One could be a National-Socialist youth exclusively within the Hitler Jugend. The youth organizations of the right-wing parties (such as the *Jungstahlhelm*, *Scharnhorst Jugend*, and many others) were submitted to hard pressures. The order of the day was this: join or dissolve. They were denounced by spokesmen of the HJ as "nationalist philistines," attacked as "unteachable sentimentalists indulging in moonlight romanticism," "aristocrats who would never soil their hands to support the proletariat in its struggle," "indifferent to the suffering of the working class," and so forth. Such anticapitalist, quasi-revolutionary language played a great part in HJ propaganda. This was found necessary during the early 1930s, a period of acute economic crisis, when the HJ tried to attract the working-class youth. The nationalist groups and associations were on the defensive, and many leaders who had been in close contact with Hitler's party for many years could not bear to accept von Schirach's authority. Those who attempted to resist the rising flood were easy prey for the fanatical, savage and one-sided Nazis. Some groups were attacked by the Hitler Youth in their camps, on excursions, or in their town centers. They were soon swept away, and if some of the former periodicals published by the right-wing youth movements were permitted to exist, it was a concession for which they had to pay a high price in conformity. *Gleichschaltung* triumphed and the youth organizations of the right-wing parties more or less voluntarily dissolved themselves and merged with the HJ. Many of their leaders endeavored, with almost indecent haste, to secure seats on the bandwagon. Most of them capitulated ignominiously to get positions, responsibilities and ranks in the HJ. By the end of 1933 all such groups were made part of the HJ, which took over some of their nebulous ideas—for instance, the concept of youth led by youth, the rejection of the bourgeois society, and the exaltation of comradeship, but there was serious resistance too. Vice Admiral Adolf Trotha and conservative youth groups (e.g., the *Freischar* and *Geusen*) made a last-minute effort to save the *Bünde* from extinction and incorporation. In March 1933 they set up an alternative youth group to the HJ, called the *Grossdeutsche Jugendbund* (Greater German Youth League). Although marching under the banner of the swastika, the Greater German Youth League wanted to enter the new emerging Nazi Reich in accordance with their own *bündisch* traditions. This of course could not be tolerated, and the Hitler Jugend attacked them as "Communist." After several acts of violence, the leaders of the *Grossdeutsche Jugendbund* began to despair of their chance of survival as a separate entity. On Whit Monday 1933, police, SA and HJ detachments surrounded a camp where the *Jugendbund* held a rally, and its 15,000 participants were sent home. The league was forced to disband and merged with the HJ on 17 June 1933. Three year later von Trotha was compensated with the award of a ceremonial post: commander-in-chief of the Marine HJ, an honorary rank he received from von Schirach as an assurance that the ban had been directed against the *Jugendbund*, not against him personally. He then became one of von Schirach's most faithful collaborators.

The extreme, "elitist," *völkisch* and anti–Semitic Artaman League was also submitted to a combination of threats and blandishments. Friendly declarations produced among them a mistaken impression; their "beautiful romanticism" was to be replaced by a new "creative romanticism of steel." The League had done a good job in the 1920s, but it was time now to recognize that a savior had arisen in the person of Adolf Hitler. Soon the leadership, under increasing pressure, announced their intention of joining the HJ. The *Bund der Artamenen* merged with the Nazi Youth and became *Landjahr der HJ* in 1934.

The process of absorption affected also the youth groups independent of political parties, which, in the tradition of the *Wandervogel* and the Boy Scouts, took their members on hikes in order to experience nature and comradeship. The Nazis tried to justify the ban by saying that "more and more individuals hostile to the National Socialist State and their youth movements have become in effect a haven for opponents who dispute the Hitler Jugend's monopoly as the guiding force of young Germany."

The process of *Gleichschaltung* inexorably continued. Soon the Hitler Youth took over the running of the network of *Jugendherbergen* (German Youth Hostels), enabling them to determine who could or could not spend the night in one.

In 1934, it was decreed that every teenager who wanted to join a sporting association or to win sports certificates had to be a member of the HJ. In this way Baldur von Schirach usurped the leadership of these organizations and young athletes and sporting associations were effectively incorporated into the Hitler Jugend. By that time most surviving youth associations had been incorporated into the Hitler Jugend by deals, coercion and voluntary joining.

Absorption of religious youth movements

Von Schirach had almost achieved his goal. All that remained outside his authority were Roman Catholic and Protestant youth organizations. The Protestant youth groups were strongly influenced by the *Wandervogel* and the 1920s *Bünde*, and were frequently indistinguishable from them, except for the stress they put on religious motives and their cultural activities. Numerically they were strong. With the rise of Nazism whole groups of Protestant youth went over to Hitler. This was not altogether surprising, because the German Protestant Church had never felt at ease in the democratic Weimar Republic; it still wanted an all–German empire in which throne and altar were one. It put a strong emphasis on Teutonic traditions, opposed the disruptive ideas of the 1789 French Revolution, and inveighed against an "international Jewish-capitalist-atheist conspiracy" aiming to destroy the "true" Germany. Ludwig Müller (1883–1946) was a former armed forces chaplain and an outspokenly nationalist anti–Semite; with Nazi support he had been elected Reich Bishop of the German Protestant Church in early 1933. There was, however, a strong resistance movement in the German Protestant Church declaring that Christianity was not compatible with Nazism; the *Pfarrer Notbund* (Emergency League of Pastors) had been founded by Protestant bishops and other outspoken men like pastor Martin Niemöller (1892–1984) to defend the traditional Lutheran Church. But in spite of protest and the opposition of the Emergency League, an agreement between von Schirach and Reich Bishop Müller on the organization of Protestant Youth brought 800,000 young people into the HJ in December 1933. However, there were limits to von Schirach's expansion plan, at least temporarily.

The struggle with Roman Catholic Church youth organizations was more protracted, because their existence had been formally guaranteed by a concordat with the Vatican. Hitler's concordat, signed in July 1933 with Pope Pius XI (Achille Ratti, born in 1857, pope from 1922 until his death in 1939) prevented him from getting the Catholic youth organizations within his grasp. In the agreement, Hitler assured that German citizens could profess and practice religion, guaranteed the right of the Church to administer itself and maintain a role in education, and agreed to tolerate Catholic organizations. In return the Church declared that German Catholics should take no part in politics and nor be expected to put themselves without reservation at the service of the new National-Socialist regime. However, regardless of the binding character of the concordat, the status quo was not respected, and the activities of the Catholic Church youth were gradually circumscribed. In 1935, a decree forbade the Catholic youth associations to wear uniforms or insignia, to parade, hike or encamp in large groups, to fly banners, flags and pennants, or to practice or receive instruction in sports. Harassment and threats followed, and the precarious balance was lost in February 1936 after the violent occupation of the central headquarters of the Roman Catholic youth organizations in Düsseldorf. The premises were closed and fifty-seven leaders and priests were arrested. In April 1936, the German Catholic episcopate effectively ordered the dissolution of the Catholic youth organizations, associations and leagues. In March 1937, Pope Pius XI issued the extraordinary encyclical *Mit brennender Sorge* (In Deep Concern) in which he expressed the Vatican's dissatisfaction with the Nazi application of the terms of the 1933 concordat. The pope reminded Hitler that humans possess rights that must be preserved and which cannot be denied, suppressed or hindered; the same week he condemned atheistic communism in a letter titled *Divini Redemptoris*. The Holy See's concerns were totally ignored by the Nazis, and Catholic resistance was doomed to be crushed. It should be noted, however, that some of the official Catholic historians writing since 1945 have exaggerated the extent of Catholic resistance. Some Catholics went very far in their efforts to accommodate Catholicism and National Socialism.

By 1936, Baldur von Schirach had reached his goal and claimed to have—and apparently did have total control over the education and indoctrination of German youth. An entire generation of young Germans was forced to follow the route mapped out by Hitler.

An independent branch of the NSDAP

In the early phase of the dictatorship, in 1933, von Schirach repeatedly underlined the socialist revolutionary mission of the organization. He stayed, however, at a careful distance from the SA, although the Hitler Jugend had been since the start officially a sub-branch of the SA, and despite the fact that he was himself an *SA Obergruppenführer* (general), immediately subordinate to *SA Stabschef* Ernst Röhm. The *Sturm Abteilung* were since 1921 the paramilitary militia of Hitler's party, composed of patriots and nationalists, but also street bullies, hooligans and gangsters who played an important role in Hitler's rise to political power. Once power had been gained, there was little left for them to do. The cumbersome SA battalions were an embarrassment for Hitler and his party and endangered the Führer's position. A bitter struggle was engaged in between Hitler and Röhm, resulting in the physical elimination of the SA leadership on 30 June 1934 (the so-called Night of Long Knives). Von Schirach, who prudently had chosen Hitler's camp, survived the assassination of the SA.

After the purge, the Hitler Youth became fully independent of the SA and good contacts were made with Himmler's SS. Baldur von Schirach's position was further strengthened by that time, but it was entirely based on Hitler's goodwill. By 1936, Baldur von Schirach was a very popular and honored personality of the Third Reich. Ranking near the top of the hierarchy, he was presented by propaganda as a sort of demigod who embodied all that was fine and noble in German youth. His pictures were second only to Hitler's throughout Germany. However von Schirach was not popular within the Nazi top circle. Because of his early commitment to Nazi activism, he had not been able to graduate from school, and he felt rejected by the academics. At the same time he was not a "tough guy"—the type cherished by the Hitler Youth. His naïve sentimentality, lyrical poetry, effeminate behavior, baby face and plump appearance were ridiculed. Jealous rivals did not want to take him seriously; his enemies spread the rumor that he was homosexual and that his pretty wife Henriette had been at one time Hitler's mistress. Von Schirach was never quite able to live up to his own ideal type of the hard, rough, quick Hitler youth.

Von Schirach's ambition was fueled by two basic ideas: young people had to be led by young leaders and the HJ should be autonomous. Moreover he demanded—under his direction—the unity of education, a fusion of the school system and Hitler Jugend, encompassing all spheres of life for young Germans. He attempted to create an independent copy of the Nazi state within the Hitler Jugend, answerable to Hitler alone. This meant in part warding off or channeling the influence of the NSDAP and the state, while at the same time usurping greater and greater areas of education. Cooperation with the party, army, SS, SA, ministry of education and other Nazi organizations was regulated by contracts, which were always designed to guarantee the sovereignty of the Hitler Jugend. Cooperation with any one organization immediately brought the other competitors into a fray, since they feared losing influence and new recruits. The alternating attempts of the Wehrmacht and the SA, and later the SS, too, to take in hand the pre-military training of the HJ and von Schirach's efforts to extricate himself are all impressive testimony to this. After the seizure of power, von Schirach was responsible first to the minister of the interior, Wilhelm Frick, and then to the education minister, Wilhelm Bernhard Rust.

In spite of all his efforts, von Schirach did not achieve his aim, the Hitler Jugend did not become the autonomous state youth organization he was dreaming of, but remained a *Gliederung* (a limb or a branch) of the NSDAP. After 1933, when the HJ became part of the Nazi state apparatus, it began to lose whatever spontaneity and independence it may ever have had.

From voluntary to compulsory membership

In the beginning, membership in the HJ was supposedly voluntary, but the student who demurred encountered a combination of blandishments and pressure that only the hardiest could resist. Hitler knew what he was doing when he got the HJ together. If he were able to capture the minds of young children and persuade them to become dedicated to his cause, to accept his theories on what was right and what was wrong, he would then be able to hold the whole country captive and he would gain complete control. At first the Nazis offered different incentives to the children, things that would fascinate and attract them to their cause, such as uniforms, knives, drums and bugles. The next step was the peer pressure on those who still had not joined. Remarks like "your friends are members, why aren't you?" indicated that if they did not join they might lose their friends. And a friend would rather join friends with reservations than lose those people they hold close to their heart. Such a remark as "you should belong to our group and have fun like we do, be a member!" also pointed toward friends and enjoyment. As all people want to enjoy themselves, and as children hate to be isolated, this kind of pressure would really get to the children, and it got many children to join in to help Hitler's rule.

The development of the Hitler Youth organization did not keep pace with the rapid increase in membership. Leaders, premises and money were in short supply. Compulsory membership was decided by law in 1939. That year was a milestone in the history of the Hitler Youth. In March the female *Bund deutscher Mädel* (BdM) and the male HJ membership became compulsory by law for all youth between 10 and 18 years old. The Hitler Youth was declared a form of honorary service to the German nation. Parents who objected were submitted to various pressures and even heavy fines. The large-scale nazification of the German youth was achieved and the preparation for war was well underway. In 1933 the HJ counted 2,292,041 members. In 1934 the number grew to 3,577,565. In subsequent years the membership grew to 3,942,303 (1935), 5,437,602 (1936), 5,879,955 (1937), 7,031,226 (1938) and 7,287,470 (1939).

The Nazi hold on youth

The Hitler Jugend accepted youngsters from the age of 10 to 18. At 18, the young man was graduated from the youth organization. Then he was called for six months into the *Reichsarbeitdienst* (RAD—the state labor service) in which he was subjected to manual labor and strict discipline. After this, he went into the *Wehrmacht*, the national armed forces, for two years of military service. In this way the Nazi state never relinquished its hold on German youth from age 10 to 21. During the twelve years of Hitler's regime from 1933 to 1945, three separate groups passed through adolescence, the years between the fourteenth and eighteenth birthdays. Each group had its own experience of Nazism. The first group, those whose teen years fell in the period 1933–36, had its formative experience before the National Socialists came to power. They had experienced the crisis of the early 1930s and were on the whole receptive to the benefits offered by the new regime, such as reduction of unemployment in the rearmament program of 1935–36. The promises of the restoration of national greatness might also have had a certain appeal. The second group, the young people of the years 1936–39 had no such memories. They all had gone to schools that bore the stamp of Hitler's regime. For them the Hitler Youth was taken for granted. There was no alternative, and group comradeship, uniforms and exciting leisure activities had a considerable impact, even though occasional irritations in the form of brutality, intolerance, drills and demagogy could have discouraged some of them. The third group were those teenagers whose adolescence occurred during the war in the period 1939–45; their experience was characterized by coercion, drill and active participation to the war. To this "war generation," the grip of Nazism was at its most far-reaching and increasingly repellent.

Organization

No one in the HJ was paid, apart from the seniors officers; but there was a professional service responsible for the finance, administration and training of the Hitler Jugend, called *Reichsjugendamt* (Reich Youth Office). At the top of the organization was the *Reichsjugendführer* (Leader of the Reich Youth), Baldur von Schirach—and later Arthur Axmann. Schirach's close collaborators were a team of young men including Hartmann Lauterbacher, Karl Nabersberg, Werner Altendorf, Erich Jahn, Günther Blum, Horst Krutchinna, Alfred Loose, and Georg Usadel. The average age of the leadership was between 24 and 30. The youth organization was financed by the NSDAP, the Nazi Party, through a complicated and bureaucratic channel of treasurers. The Ministry of Interior financed the local structures such as the construction and maintenance of homes, meeting halls, clubs, youth hostels and sport installations.

The Hitler Youth Office was a large national organization. At the top it administered various services, including these:

- Service L: physical education and sport
- Service KE: shooting, aviation, navigation, and driving
- Service HBA: installations, buildings and materials
- Service O: general organization
- Service S: social affairs
- Service G: health and hygiene
- Service Pr: press, radio and propaganda
- Service WS: political formation and education
- Service K: culture
- Service A: relations with German youth living abroad
- Service GV: foreign politics
- Service JHF: travels, hiking and youth hostels
- Service V: administration
- Service P: personnel

In April 1933, the Hitler Youth was

officially reorganized into two main groups. For boys there was the Hitler Jugend for teenagers aged 14 to 18. The HJ had a sub-branch for boys aged 10 to 14: the *Deutsches Jungvolk in der Hitler Jugend* (DJ—German Young People in the Hitler Youth). For girls there was the *Bund deutscher Mädel in der Hitler Jugend* (BdM—German Girls League in the Hitler Youth), for girls aged 14 to 18. The BdM had a sub-branch for young girls aged 10 to 14: the *Jungmädel im Bund deutscher Mädel in der Hitler Jugend* (JM—League of Young Girls). Units of the four organizations of the HJ had a military structure and ranks were copied from those of the SA.

Deutsches Jungvolk

The sub-branch of the HJ for boys aged 10 to 14 was created in December 1928 by Kurt Gruber. Originally called *Jungmannschaften* (youth teams), then *Deutsche Knabenschaft* (German young boys), the sub-organization was formally established and renamed *Deutsches Jungvolk in der Hitler Jugend* (DJ—German Young People in the Hitler Youth) on 27 March 1931.

After 1936, the education of German youth was carefully regulated. At first came the preliminary steps. By March 15 of the year in which he would celebrate his tenth birthday, every German boy had to register with the Reich youth headquarters. After a thorough investigation of the boy's record and that of his family, with special attention to his "racial purity," he was admitted into the *Deutsches Jungvolk*. An initiation ceremony was held on Hitler's birthday (April 20) in the presence of NSDAP and HJ functionaries. The failure of any children to join the HJ was regarded as a violation of civic responsibility.

From 10 to 14, *Jungvolk* boys were called *Pimpfen* (cubs, or little ones). Ten boys formed a group called *Jugenschaft*, headed by leaders (the equivalent of NCOs who were a few years older than the boys themselves) called *Hordenführer*, *Oberhordenführer*, *Jungschaftführer* and *Oberjungschaftführer*. Four *Jugendschaften* (about 40 *Pimpfen*) formed a squad called *Jungzug*, headed by leading members titled *Jungzugführer* and *Oberjungzugführer*. Four *Jungzüge* formed a *Fähnlein* (a squadron of 160 *Pimpfen*), headed by officers called *Fähnleinführer*, *Oberfähnleinführer* and *Hauptfähnleinführer*. Three or five *Fähnlein* formed a *Stamm* (company) commanded by young adult officers called *Jungstammführer* and *Oberjungstammführer*; each company was divided into four groups: group 4, boys aged 10; group 3, boys aged 11; group 2, boys aged 12; and group 1, boys aged 13. Four or six *Stämme* formed a *Jungbann* (battalion), commanded by young adult leaders carrying the titles of *Jungbannführer*, *Oberjungbannführer* and *Hauptjungbannführer*.

Sew-on patch worn by members of the DJ. The emblem—also used by the SS—displayed the Sieg rune, symbolic of victory.

Kern Hitler Jugend

From 14 to 18 years old, members were *Hitlerjunge* (Hitler's boys) belonging to the

Kern Hitler Jugend (Hitler Youth proper). Prior to the establishment of a paramilitary rank system, the Hitler Youth maintained a simple hierarchical system with only three ranks: *Reichsjugendführer* (National Youth Leader), *Hitlerjugendführer* (Hitler Youth Leader), and *Hitlerjunge* (Hitler Youth member). When the HJ organization grew in number, more elaborate units and ranks were developed, based on the SA model.

Ten to fifteen HJ boys formed the smallest unit, a group called *Kameradschaft* (literally "comradeship") commanded by leaders called *Kameradschaftführer* (Comrade Unit Leader) and *Oberkameradschaftführer* (Senior Comrade Unit Leader). Three or four *Kameradschaften* formed a squad of fifty to sixty HJ boys called a *Schar*, headed by a staff of *Scharführer* (Squad Leader) and *Oberscharführer* (Senior Squad Leader). Three or four *Scharen* formed a *Gefolgschaft*, commanded by *Gefolgschaftführer* (Cadre Unit Leader), *Obergefolgschaftführer* (Senior Cadre Unit Leader) and *Hauptgefolgschaftführer* (Head Cadre Unit Leader). Each *Gefolgschaft*, roughly the size of a military company totaling 150–190, had its own flag and was the primary unit with which each Hitler Youth boy identified himself. Each company was divided into four groups: group 4, boys aged 14; group 3, boys aged 15; group 2, boys aged 16; and group 1, boys aged 17. Three or five *Gefolgschaften*, totaling 600–800; formed an *Unterbann* (a kind of battalion), headed by *Stammführer* (Battalion Leader or Major) and *Oberstammführer* (Senior Battalion Leader). Four or six *Unterbanne* formed a *Bann* (a regiment), totaling about 3,000, commanded by a *Bannführer* (a kind of Colonel). An *Oberbann* (division) consisted of five *Banne* totaling 15,000, commanded by officers called *Oberbannführer* (Division Leader) and *Hauptbannführer* (Senior Division Leader, equivalent to a general). Twenty *Deutsches Jungvolk Jungbanne* and twenty *Hitler Jugend Banne* formed a *Gebiet* (district) headed by a *Gebietsführer* (District Leader), with each *Gebiet* totaling about 75,000. There were 42 *Gebiete* which constituted six *Obergebiete* (regions), with each *Obergebiet* totaling about 375,000 boys.

At the national level, there were *HJ-Gruppen* (groups). In 1931, these included:

1. HJ-Gruppe Ostland: East-Prussia and Danzig
2. HJ-Gruppe Ost: Brandenburg, Ostmarkt and Mecklenburg
3. HJ-Gau Berlin
4. HJ-Gruppe Nord: Hannover (south and east), Schleswig-Holstein, Hamburg and Weser-Ems
5. HJ-Gruppe Nordwest: Westphalia (north and south), Düsseldorf, Essen, Cologne and Achen
6. HJ-Gruppe West: Hessen-Nassau (north and south), Hessen-Darmstadt and Cologne-Trier

Identification badge worn on left upper sleeve. Left: South Baden (in existence before 1933, this district was distinguished by a yellow braided bar). Right: West Cologne–Achen. The cloth triangles were black with their lettering and edging machine-woven in white thread.

Member of the Hitler Jugend with flag.

7. HJ-Gruppe Südwest: Württemberg, Baden, Palatinate and Saar
8. HJ-Gruppe Süd: Bavaria (Upper and Lower), Swabia, Upper-Palatinate and Franconia
9. HJ-Gau Munich
10. HJ-Gruppe Mitte: Saxony, Thüringen, Halle-Merseburg and Magdeburg
11. HJ-Gruppe Silesia
12. HJ-Gruppe Austria

Female organizations

Girls were also accepted in the Hitler Jugend. They could join the HJ in two sub-organizations created in December 1928 by the leader Karl Gruber: the *Jungmädelbund* (JMB—League of Young Girls, aged 10 to 14) and the *Bund deutscher Mädel* (BdM—German Girls League, aged 14 to 18). Originally called *Schwesternschaften der Hitler Jugend* (Nurse teams), the sub-organization was later renamed *Bund deutscher Mädel* in July 1930. Another organization for girls, the *National-Sozialistische Schülerinnenbund* (NSS—Nazi League for Schoolgirls) also existed but it was merged with the BdM in July 1932. Altogether the BdM had 125,000 leaders, who were trained in thirty-five provincial schools, most of them on a part-time basis. But, like the whole of the Hitler Youth, the BdM always suffered from shortage of suitable leaders. Both BdM and JMB sub-groups aimed at providing an outdoor life that would keep young girls healthy, at the same time as it developed their understanding of National Socialism and made then them feel part of the German *völkisch* community. The essential purpose of the BdM and JM movement was defined by Jutta Rüdiger, one of the BdM's national leaders; the organization would bring out in the girls "character, and the ability to perform, not useless knowledge, but an all-round education, and an exemplary bearing." The female organizations were intended to give girls and young women a sense of pride and self-worth, and produce political and racial conformity in the young so that they would go on as adults to have unquestionable loyalty and faith to the Führer, Adolf Hitler. For this purpose the girls' sub-branches were organized along the strict military HJ lines.

The *Mädelschaft* (squad) was the smallest BdM unit, with 10 to 15 *Mädel* and *Jungmädel* (girls) under command of a *Mädelschaftsführerin*. The *Mädelschar* (platoon) consisted of three or four *Mädelschaften* totaling 50 to 60, under command of a *Mädelscharführerin*. The *Mädelgruppe* (company) headed by a *Mädelgruppenführerin* consisted of three or four *Mädelscharen*, totaling 150–190. The *Mädelring* (battalion), commanded by *Mädelringführerin*, had four to six *Mädelgruppen*, totaling 600–800. The *Untergau* (regiment), under command of a *Untergauführerin*, was composed of five or six *Mädelringe* totaling 3,000. The *Gau* (district), headed by a *Hauptmädelführerin*, comprised five *Untergaue* totaling 15,000. The *Obergau* (region), under command of an *Obergauführerin*, consisted of five *Gaue* totaling 75,000, and the *Gauerband* brought five *Obergaue* together, totaling 375,000.

The *Deutsche Jungmädel* ranks (girls age 10 to 14), from the lowest to highest, were *Scharführerin*, *Gruppenführerin*, *Ringführerin*, and *Untergauführerin*. The BdM top leaders, Jutta Rüdiger and Melitta Maschmann, had the title of *Reichsreferentin*. The top leadership of the HJ women was formed at three institutes situated at Potsdam, Godesberg and Boydent. The middle ranks were formed in 44 schools, and the lowest ranks by weekly training at local clubs and homes, but at all levels of the HJ there were a lack of good leaders.

BdM girls enthusiastically participated in the firm establishment of Nazi rule in Germany, even though they were assigned to duties in keeping with the Nazi viewpoint on the role of females. Hitler thought that men were superior to women. The primary role of the female, he believed, was to give birth to healthy, racially pure "Aryan" baby boys. All girls' and women's organizations were thus regarded as auxiliaries below their male counterparts. All girls of the BdM and JM were constantly reminded that the great task of their lives was motherhood.

The girls' sections of the Hitler Youth were organized along different lines. Although the ranks and units of the JM and BdM girls were similar to those of the boys, the physical requirements were scaled down. A ten-year-old girl had to sprint 60 meters in 14 seconds, long jump two meters, throw a softball 12 meters, jump in cold water from a height of three meters and also perform two somersaults forward and two backward. She had then passed the Jungmädel test and was entitled to wear the neckerchief and special neckerchief ring. While a greater emphasis was placed on the mastery of domestic tasks, in keeping with the Nazi doctrine on the subordinate, home-making role of the woman, girls received physical training and ideological indoctrination that ranged from tumbling to memorizing names of Nazi martyrs. BdM girls were taught the three "Ks" ruling their future life: *Kinder, Kirche, Küche* (children, church, kitchen). BdM girls also worked in nurseries and hospitals, and on farms. To a certain extent, the BdM association proved to be a modernizing force in many practical day-to-day respects and could provide emancipatory openings. The organization allowed girls to travel beyond the narrow confines of home, bringing them in contact with youth from other regions. Girls could pursue activities which were otherwise reserved for boys. Those working as functionaries for the organization could escape from the female role model centered around family and children, and they might even approach the classic "masculine" type of the political organizer who was never at home. Such opportunities remained very limited, however, and were withdrawn increasingly, owing to the Nazis' general discrimination against women. The man in the street had nicknames for the function of the girls' organization, lacking reverence but clear and relevant. *Bald deutsche Mütter* (German mothers-to-be), *Bund deutscher Milchkühe* (League of German Milk-cows), *Bedarfsartikel deutscher Männer* (Requisites for German Males), and *Brauch deutsches Mädchen* (Make Use of German Girls) were some of many mocking interpretations of the initials "BdM."

Women in the Third Reich

Faith and Beauty (Glaube und Schönheit)

BdM service ended at 18 but 21 was the proscribed age for admission to the official *NS Frauenschaft* (NSF), the National Socialist Women's Association. In January 1938,

BdM badge worn on the left breast of tunic

the transitory organization *Glaube und Schönheit* (Faith and Beauty) was created to fill the gap. The new organization's pompous name was typical of the Nazi regime. The organization housed girls between 18 and 21 in what could be compared to homes for ascetic beguines or dwellings of Roman vestal virgins and the wise women of Germanic antiquity, where they were offered means to personal development. The whole "Faith and Beauty" venture was intended to further an ideal of the perfect Nazi woman, known as *"Hohe Frau"* (Exalted Woman). The flower of young "Aryan" womanhood was cultivated with an eye toward perfection. The organization was open to a select circle of blonde and blue-eyed females who, apart from their staunch devotion to the Nazi ideology, were blessed with "superior intellectual gifts and grace of mind and body." After a probation period of three months they could become full members and were grouped in small communities of 10 to 15 young women, strictly overseen by the Youth National Department. The "Exalted Women" wore the same uniform as the younger BdM girls and had to submit to the same rules and engaged in the same activities, including sport, collective gymnastics, folk dance, music and singing, manual and domestic work, and political indoctrination. In addition the women's curriculum included riding, swimming, car driving, and pistol shooting. The organization *Glaube und Schönheit* had a high membership cost which had to be paid by parents. It was intended to teach domestic handiness and foster homespun feminine charm. It also aimed at developing the social, spiritual and physical graces by dancing, riding, tennis playing, and sunbathing. The girls were encouraged to be creative and free to specialize in their own spheres of interest within limits: sports/training of the body; gymnastics/natural movement; hygiene/knowledge of the human body; and baby care. Nazi indoctrination was, of course, continued, and girls also received advanced training in fashion design, domestic science, cookery, housekeeping and preparation for marriage. Groups of dancers were formed which performed at special functions like Nazi Party rallies. Some especially pretty girls became prize exhibits for the National Socialist conception of the ideal woman. Their job was to meet the demand for wives among the praetorian guard of the National Socialist regime. They were expected to choose a racially worthy spouse from the leadership corps of the NSDAP and the SS.

During the war, the purpose of the organization shifted and adapted to the grim situation. Dancing, singing, and frivolity were discarded and replaced by domestic activities, administrative duties and nursing in overcrowded hospitals full of wounded soldiers.

Women Association

There were two other ways of maintaining party tutelage over young women who had outgrown the BdM and the organization Faith and Beauty: the *Reichsarbeitsdienst der weibliche Jugend* (RAD/wJ—Reich Labor Service for Young Women) which will be described later, and the *Nationalsozialistische-Frauenschaft* (NSF—National Socialist Women's Association).

Women formed a distinct social group, forced into compliance with Hitler's regime. Nazism was very much a male movement in tone and character; it emphasized physical struggle, toughness, and military-style camaraderie, leaving very little place, if any, for feminine values. From the start, women's position in society was inferior and the NSDAP had barred females from membership. According to the anti-feminist ideology, women could not think logically or reason objectively, since they were ruled only by emotion. One of the few women officially involved in Nazi activities was the self-assured Leni Riefenstahl, who directed mountaineering and skiing movies as well as important heroic propaganda films such as *Victory of Faith*, *Triumph of the Will* and *Olympics 1936*. The other woman to have some status in Nazi Germany was Anna Reitsch (1912–1979), a champion glider and a test pilot who was awarded the Iron Cross. The *Luftwaffe* was the only German arm massively employing females in uniform (*Helferinnen*, about 100,000 in 1944), serving as auxiliaries in air warning, telephone and teletype departments. On the whole women were repressed and had little official influence. From 1933 to 1937, women were expelled from work, had their rights of inheritance curtailed, were refused entrance to higher education, and were barred from senior professional posts. The removal of women from many sectors of employment caused resentment. However, during 1938–1945, the Nazi regime launched a wide-scale rearmament program, and during the war the majority of males were drafted into the armed forces. This created a large labor shortage and Nazi officials found themselves in the contradictory position of having to encourage, even demand that women work. Increasingly, women opted for better-paying jobs in heavy industry and weapons plants in the larger towns, leaving behind housework and nursing, servant's work and the hard life on the farm.

Nazism had a certain appeal among women, resulting from a series of legislative measures that sought to encourage marriage and raise the birthrate in the Third Reich. The creation of new roles within party and public organizations—such as the NSF—made possible the active involvement of many women in the Third Reich. The NSF was a *Gliederung* (segment) of the NSDAP. It was created in October 1931 and led by Elsbeth Zander. The *NS Frauenschaft* was reorganized after the Nazi seizure of power in 1933. It was the overall body coordinating all existing women's groups and associations; these included the *Frauenwerk* (Federal Organization of Women), the Women's League of the Red Cross, the Women's League of the *Deutsche Arbeitsfront* (the German Labor Front), and the Women's Labor Service. The purpose was to keep German women firmly under the control of the exclusively male NSDAP party.

The NSF was placed under the leadership of Gertrud Bäumer and then under Gertrud Scholtz-Klink. A blonde, blue-eyed, slender little woman with classic features and fresh complexion, Gertrud Scholtz-Klink was married to a postal clerk and bore him six children. Active in various Nazi organizations, she was promoted to *Reichs-*

Emblem of the **Nationalsozialistische-Frauenschaft** *(Nazi Women League). The emblem bore the initials of the German words for Faith, Hope and Charity.*

frauenführerin (leader) of the NSF and other women's organizations in 1934. Despite the imposing title she possessed, her leadership was more token than actual, and her views on a woman's role closely mirrored those of the male-dominated Nazi Party and state. She was the prototype of the militant Nazi woman, expected to tread softly, avoid difficult issues and teach all German women how to organize their households according to the policies of the party, consistently praising the "sacred character" of Nazi conquest and struggle. Although it tolerated a small but vocal faction of women, the NSF firmly encouraged them to pay deference to male supremacy, to embrace their secondary role, to emphasize the joys of labor and childbearing, to raise their children as patriots, to support the ideas and beliefs of Nazism, and to see that all commands of the party were unconditionally carried out in daily life. NSF members gave aid and comfort to fatigued mothers, they instructed adolescent girls, they dealt with cases involving children, they offered enlightenment on such subjects as cooking leftovers, dressmaking with good German cloth, and raising babies. The NSF brought further opportunities to be involved in political activism, especially to women who had few formal qualifications. Not all of the NSF's activities were benevolent, though. The leadership of the organization, mirroring Hitler's view, regarded any kind of feminism or women's liberation as anathema. Some of its members became guards in concentration and work camps for Jewish and "deviating" women. During the last year of World War II, women of the *NS Frauenschaft* provided rear-echelon support to the *Volkssturm* (Home Guard). After March 1945 some of them were issued firearms and *Panzerfaust* (portable anti-tank weapons).

By 1935 about eleven million out of the country's thirty-five million females belonged to the *NS Frauenschaft*. Their official uniform consisted of a dark blue-black suit,

NS Frauenschaft *female work leader in dress uniform*

including a jacket, a skirt and a fedora. On the upper left sleeve of the jacket was sewn a silver-gray national emblem (with eagle and swastika). The wearer's district affiliation was indicated by a silver-gray cuffband, often worn on the lower left sleeve. An enamel organization badge was usually worn on the lapel of the jacket.

Nursing and motherhood

The Weimar Republic had granted the vote to women in 1919. As a comparison, French women were not given that right until 1945. Of course, the Nazis—beginning with Hitler himself—were well aware of the benefit they could get from controlling this bloc of voters. On the whole, the changes brought about by Nazism were far from liberating for women. In fact, demands on them increased, as women were forced to combine the roles of mother, housewife, Nazi propagandist and industrial worker subjected to military discipline. Wrapped up in mock-heroic verbiage, the NSF was only a loose framework designed to contain outbursts of excessive zeal, and its functions were mostly restricted to trivial welfare work and propaganda.

Confined to their role as breeding machines and beasts of burden, German women contributed their fair share to the war effort, and certainly suffered alongside their menfolk. The Allied air war brought the horrors of the front line to every German town, and women suffered appallingly when they fell into the hands of the vengeful Russians in 1945.

Hitler was always very firm in his contention that women were to perform their most important task by administering their homes, taking care of their husbands, and producing future leaders and soldiers.

The idea that a "woman's place was in the home" was not new, but Hitler's regime put it into practice. All Germany was familiar with the following slogans which were

Staff member, NS Frauenschaft

taken seriously, without a trace of irony: "Women are the eternal mothers of the nation"; "Women are the eternal companion of men in work and battle"; "The triumphant task of women is to bear and tend babies"; "Men are willing to fight, but when they are wounded, women must be there to nurse them."

Hitler simply did not accept women as equals. He wanted them to embrace motherhood as an ideal and regarded any kind of feminism or women's liberation movement as a "Jewish idea" deliberately designed to weaken society. Rather than attend to their rights, women had to concern themselves with "the duties that Nature had laid upon them in the interests of communal survival." Gertrud Scholtz-Klink and the NSF had little impact on Nazi policymakers, who excluded her from meetings at which issues affecting women were discussed. When appearing in public before a female audience, Hitler never forgot to extol the outstanding importance of women but he also constantly reminded them that the highest aim for the German girls and women was—and must remain—home, health and marriage. Marriage of course was not an end in itself but had to serve the multiplication and preservation of the "Aryan race." Families were encouraged to have at least four children.

The family and sexual relations were no longer altogether a private matter, but a supreme duty to the German community. Their ultimate aim was the maximum propagation of the species. Elitist, mystic fanatics like Heinrich Himmler and Walther Darré wanted quality, but a brutal realist like Hitler was only concerned with quantity of human material, as a rising birthrate gave promise of more future troops which could be hurled into the international fray. What the Führer needed was a disciplined human mass dedicated to Nazi faith, blind obedience and service.

Social measures included allowances and benefits encouraging maternity, including prizes and financial privileges for large families, and gifts to newborn infants. Should the husband of a barren wife form an extramarital liaison which produced a child, he was not to be legally charged with adultery but merely obliged to pay maintenance. *Kindertagesstätte* (nursery schools) were created for children of preschool age. Marriage loans were provided to help married couples in setting up housekeeping. Between 1933 and 1936, the Nazi regime financed 694,367 marriages. Similar measures included a heavier tax on bachelors and childless couples who were considered as "deserters on the home battlefield." Added to the financial inducements was a strong propaganda campaign based on emotion. Bearing children was celebrated to the point of adulation. "*Kindersegen*" (blessed with children) was an emotional term constantly used by Nazi leaders to promote the birthrate. During the first three years of World War II, because of this social policy, there was no drastic mobilization of German women for war work. In late 1943 and early 1944, however, the crisis became so acute that women had to take the place of the men called to the colors.

The term "family" was limited to households with four children or more. There were special honors for mothers who contributed children to the regime. A medal was instituted in December 1938. The *Ehrenzeichen der deutschen Mutter* (Cross of Honor of the German Mother), also known as the *Mutterkreuz* (Mother Cross), was an elegant blue and white enamel cross worn on a narrow blue and white ribbon. It was awarded to the mothers of large families, in three classes: bronze for four or five children, silver for six or seven children, gold for eight or more children. The crosses were awarded to the prolific mothers on Mothering Sunday (the second Sunday of May) or on 12 August (the birthday of Hitler's mother) at a public ceremony. The Mother Cross was regarded as a prestigious distinction of the highest order. Its wearer would be saluted by sentries, enjoy unrestricted access to Hitler (in theory), and occupy a supreme place of honor in the German state.

Hitler's gamble on women's emotionality, capacity for devotion and desire for domination was a huge success. A common feature in many Nazi homes was a "Hitler Corner" composed of a portrait of the Führer and flowers. These altars were regarded as good-luck charms. During the war it was claimed that walls adorned with a portrait of Hitler would withstand a bomb blast. As for the bachelor and childless Führer himself—"the saviour of the Nation"—he could not be considered a "deserter on the home battlefield." Goebbels' propaganda had created the sacred image of an asexual man who had renounced marriage and children, whose bride was the German people to whom he devoted his entire life and sacrificed himself in the service of the community. Practically nobody in Germany knew that Hitler had a girlfriend named Eva Braun.

The Nazis had no sense of humor at all. Making jokes about the Führer was severely repressed. A woman who entertained colleagues with the following lampoon was sentenced to two years' imprisonment in 1943:

> He who rules in the Russian manner
> And imitates Napoleon
> Was born in Austria
> Trims his moustache English-fashion
> Salutes like an Italian
> Asks our wives for lots of children
> But can't produce any himself.
> He is the leader of Germany.

The ideal German woman

Beauty was whatever pleased the Führer, his paladins and cultural administrators. Owing to the female youth organizations, the Nazi regime was rather successful at altering the appearance and habits of women. The NSDAP regarded such things as fash-

Ehrenzeichen der deutschen Mutter *(Cross of Honor of the German Mother)*

ionable clothing, makeup, and pants on women as evidence of "Weimar and Jewish decadence." Maintaining a slim figure, drinking alcohol and smoking were branded as detrimental to health and fertility, and thus un–German. The Führer's aversion to meat, liquor and tobacco was firm and categorical. His dream was to convert the German people to a vegetarian diet. The fanatical abstainer sometimes said that meat-eating paved the way for drinking and smoking. Hitler's attitude, being well known, was grist for the mill of crusading health faddists and hidebound fanatics of decorum alike. Alcohol was regarded as a source of mental debility and criminality, sexual impairment and hereditary degeneration. Germany had the world's strongest anti-smoking movement in the 1930s and 1940s, supported by Nazi medical leaders worried that tobacco might prove a hazard to the race. German epidemiology was the most advanced. Doctors Franz Muller, Eberhard Schairer and Erich Schoniger were the first to research and document lung cancer, coronary disease, heart attack, and other serious illnesses caused by the use of tobacco. In the press, nicotine was denounced as a cause of premature senility, a nerve and gland poison. Popular educators went so far as to assert that smokers became frigid, impotent and ultimately infertile. Women smokers were threatened with particularly dire consequences: atrophy of the ovaries, poisoning of the breast-fed infant, and loss of personal freshness, beauty and youthfulness. Therefore the Nazis launched a campaign against drinking and smoking by women. In many restaurants and public places hung conspicuous signs reading *Die deutsche Frau raucht nicht* (the German woman does not smoke), and owners of cafés were barred from selling tobacco to female customers. The success of such campaigns was probably minimal, but they did result in some harassment of women who dared to smoke in public. Smoking was banned in many workplaces, government and public buildings, public transport (train, bus, tramway), air raid shelters, hospitals and rest homes. One of Hitler's plans was to mark cigarette packages with warnings in big red letters, such as "Tobacco kills" and "Smoking will damage your health." This order was never implemented but it has been adopted in the European Community today. In spite of the anti-tobacco campaign, which culminated between 1939 and 1941, smoking rates rose dramatically in the years of Nazi rule: German per capita tobacco use between 1932 and 1939 rose from 570 to 900 cigarettes a year. This rise has sometimes been explained as representing a form of cultural resistance.

In addition, German women were encouraged not to "paint their faces" and not to "wear fashionable fripperies." Although Hitler favored women with elegant and slim figures, the official image of the ideal woman was of a plump, broad-hipped and full figure suggestive of fertility. The regime promoted a rustic looking, fresh-faced, primly gowned, unadorned peasant girl with simple folk dresses, blond hair pulled into a bun or coiled braid: a female cliché suggesting fertility more than sensuality. Those who deliberately defied this stereotype were harassed, might be disciplined by the NSF and publicly denounced as "trouser-wenches with Indian warpaint," and in the worst cases were fired from their jobs.

In art, Hitler condemned modern painting but approved of female nudes, so long as they exhibited what he considered as ideal Nordic racial traits and a virginal wholesomeness. The result was technically accomplished painting and sculptures, but since there were executed according to the stereotypes of Aryan manliness and female virtue, Nazi art was ultimately dull, cold and predictable.

Sexuality

Given that the German nation aimed to combat the declining birthrate, it is not surprising that contraception and abortion were forbidden and severely repressed. Homosexuality also merited no mercy, more for a simple piece of arithmetic than morality. In terms of population policy, homosexuals were seen as zeros who failed in their duty of racial preservation by producing no children: in a Third Reich obsessed with the birthrate, this was an unpardonable crime. Homosexuality had been outlawed in Germany since 1871, but in the liberal climate of Weimar Germany, and especially Berlin with its café life, bars, cabarets and night clubs, there had been proposals for repeal. Persecution of homosexuals varied in intensity throughout the period of Hitler's Third

Reich. After the Reichstag fire of February 1933, decrees were issued against public indecency, homosexual bars were closed, and gay magazines were banned. While many members of the performing arts and political leaders (notably the SA leadership) enjoyed an unofficial immunity, police supervision, castration, imprisonment in concentration camps, and even the death penalty were included in the range of punishment applied to others. Lesbianism, too, was forbidden, but it presented no practical reproductive problems; a lesbian could, after all, bear children.

Rules governing sex education were strict. The problem of adolescent sexuality had to be solved by self-restraint; by showing self-control one showed one's sense of duty to the community. According to the Nazis, the neglect of physical education and an excessive emphasis upon intellectual development led to unhealthy sexual imaginings and libertine tendencies. The giving in to such pleasures was seen as being especially dangerous because this could lead young men to consort with prostitutes, and hence to run the risk of contracting venereal diseases. It was thought essential that through sport and gymnastics boys should be "hardened like iron" to prevent them from succumbing to the urges of their libidos. Self-discipline, however, was not to be confused with the "pettifogging morality of yore," with the religious appeals for self-denial made by bourgeois Christian society. Besides, one of the Nazis' major preoccupations was the question of how to produce more male children to make up for those who were going to be killed in the war. Departing from Lutheran Puritanism and Catholic prudishness, the Nazis urged that the mating of vigorous young males with healthy females was so important to the future of the white Aryan race that procreation was no longer a private matter, but a duty to the state. As a budding soldier, the young HJ male should joyfully acknowledge his sound instincts and practice self-control from "a sense of duty to the German community," rather than from ethical, religious or moral considerations.

The official call for asceticism was thus not taken too literally, and somewhat more liberal standards were applied to the young people. Hitler himself admitted that sex and war went together well. A rigorous upbringing, one that alone could produce the type of warrior he needed, was impracticable unless it had the safety-valve known as "wholesome delight in existence." Sound instincts make sound humans. Baldur von Schirach applied this educational formula regarding sex to the Hitler Jugend. His policy was to establish "harmless contacts" between boys and girls, and given the official Nazi birthrate policy, this was more of an invitation than a limitation. Before yielding to homosexual blandishments, the adolescent boy would do better to practice a little sexual indiscipline in female company. Irresponsible youths were encouraged to produce children out of wedlock, and unwed mothers were elevated to hitherto undreamed-of heights. Children—even "illegitimate" children—were always welcome, provided they were healthy and "Aryan."

Von Schirach felt that he had cured the Hitler Youth of the homosexual and pedophile symptoms so often attributed to it. How efficient his methods were and how well founded was his confidence is difficult to estimate, as many cases of suspected or proven homosexual and pedophilic relations were secretly reported and these cases were probably only the tip of an iceberg. Pedophilia and homosexuality among Hitler Youth were officially blamed on the old youth-group past of many members and leaders, when a homoerotic ideal had been fostered. It is indicative that both von Schirach for the HJ and Himmler for the SS attached such importance to the dangers of homosexual liaisons that inevitably arose in all-male communities.

Lebensborn

The obsession with increasing the birthrate in Germany resulted in the creation of sinister, official Nazi eugenic institutions. For the purpose of transforming the German nation into a "super race" through selective breeding, Himmler organized a program called *Lebensborn eingetragener Verein* (Fountain of Life Society) and took a personal interest in all minutiae, from conditions for admission to nutrition. Created in December 1935, the *Lebensborn* society was directed by the *SS Standartenführer* (Colonel) Dr. Gregor Ebner who was placed directly under Himmler's personal headquarter, headed by Karl Wolff. The organizational part was in the hands of the *Rasse-und Siedlungshauptamt* (RuSHA—the SS Race and Settlement Main Office). The society's object was the mating of vigorous males with healthy females, with the aim of maximal propagation of high quality "Aryan" children. The *Lebensborn* stressed the duty of German women to bear racially sound children, and took care of wives and girlfriends of police and SS members. Special nonprofit maternity homes were established in order to encourage a higher birthrate even for unmarried women. Homes were established at Steinhöringen, Polzin, Klosterheide, Hohehörst, and Vienna. Later more hospitals, children' homes and sanatoriums were added from former Jewish properties. During the war, new establishments were created at Bromberg, and in Holland and Belgium. Fantastic rumors surrounded the secret *Lebensborn* homes, supposed to be a cross between SS brothels, maternities, and stud farms. The truth was far simpler and less lurid. In fact *Lebensborn* was a rather bourgeois institution and the homes, far from being brothels, were obstetrical clinics founded in conformity with a conservative sexual code, serving to keep up an appearance of middle-class respectability, and carefully managed in accordance with an almost monastic set of regulations, looking after unwed mothers and their babies. Most unmarried girls using the homes belonged to the *Bund deutscher Mädel*. The selected girls (only forty out of a hundred applications were considered) were taught that their duty was to make children for the Third Reich, and encouraged to be pregnant by racially sound SS men who, married or not, were relieved of any responsibility for the children. Every SS officer supported the program with his dues, 5 to 8 percent of his salary, and encouraged to be a member or a "conception assistant." Himmler encouraged them to overcome their bourgeois qualms about fathering children out of wedlock, as, in his own words, "*Lebensborn* was the basis for a new advance of the Germanic race." Genetically valuable mothers were compelled to swear an oath of secrecy. After careful investigations of their "Aryan racial purity," they were supervised by selected matrons, received wholesome meals and an allowance of 400 marks, and could attend maternity courses. Single women acquired a certificate of racial suitability and later could legally marry SS men. The homes had their own facilities for registering births in a way which satisfied legal requirements but precluded public scrutiny. The system was however strongly eugenic and racist. Only healthy and sound children were kept alive. Children born with a physical or mental handicap were killed in a "euthanasia" program. Himmler must have been disappointed with the total output of new beings from *Lebensborn*. In 1938, two years after the program officially started, the homes accepted only 653 mothers, 40 percent of the applicants who had applied. In 1945, after nine operational years, the official figure for *Lebensborn* births was recorded as 12,000, of which half were "illegitimate," some raised by their own mothers, others adopted by selected "racially sound" foster parents.

During World War II, the *Lebensborn*/RuSHA program also included a guarantee for the health and survival of German mothers and babies living abroad. Of course, the most stringent measures were taken against abortion. Abortion among foreign women was encouraged unless they were pregnant by a German male. In occupied Europe, the *Lebensborn* society and the RuSHA took an even more sinister aspect: the wholesale kidnapping and importation of Aryan-looking foreign children. The sole purpose of this inhumane and predatory scheme was to add to the breeding stock of the Third Reich. The selected children were given German names, placed by the society with reliable, racially trustworthy and suitable German families, and they were raised in special Nazi schools. The project never became fully operational and the number of children involved in this particularly heinous part of the Lebensborn program has never been clearly established. Estimations are difficult to make, as the traces were obliterated after the abduction and renaming of the victims. Probably some 340,000 children were kidnapped from Russia, Poland, Yugoslavia, France, Norway, Denmark, Holland and other occupied European lands.

The SS *Lebensborn* program was only a beginning. Hitler, Himmler, Reinhard Heydrich and Martin Bormann had many plans for the future when the war would be over and won. In 1943 they had prepared a project for a fundamental reform of the marriage laws, including the legalization of bigamy—not universally though, but as a mark of distinction, rewarding war heroes. These privileged members of the "master race" would be given farms in the conquered eastern territories, exempted from taxation, and allowed two wives in order to produce more children.

Nazi People's Welfare Organization

There was rival organization, placed under the auspice of the Nazi Party: the NSV. The *Nationalsozialistische Volkswohlfahrt* (NSV—the Nazi People's Welfare Organization). Like the DAF (the German Labor Front directed by Robert Ley), the NSV was the "social arm" of the Nazi party. The NSV was devoted to the welfare of party members and their families, especially mothers and juveniles. The NSV was founded in September 1931 by a Nazi municipal councilor, Erich Hilgenfeldt, in the district of Wilmersdorf in Berlin. Originally its function was modest. The NSV was designed as an emergency aid group providing relief for party members during the depression of 1929–1932. Soon its activities encompassed the whole city of Berlin, with the support of Josef Goebbels and the patronage of Hitler. After the seizure of power in January 1933, the NSV grew in influence and stature, as Erich Hilgenfeldt received Hitler's mandate for all matters of charity and the people's welfare in May 1933. Hilgenfeldt soon usurped the place of both private and public welfare agencies, effectively subordinating organizations like the German Red Cross. The NSV became the second largest party organization, with some sixteen million members in 1942. The structure of the NSV was copied after the organ-

Emblem **NSV Nationalsozialistische Volkswohlfahrt** *(Nazi People's Welfare Organization)*

ization of the Nazi Party itself, and was divided into *Block* (a various number of homes), *Zelle* (an urban neighborhood or a village), *Ortsgruppe* (a town or several villages forming a district), *Kreis* (region) and *Gau* (province). The NSV had several sub-agencies, including the WHW (Winter Relief), Tuberculosis Relief, Dental Relief, Mother and Child Relief, and several others. The Nazi welfare organization constituted a large empire within Germany, disposing of millions of Reichsmarks raised by millions of "voluntary" dues-paying members, state funds, collections and donations. "Voluntary" contributions were docked from salaries and wages, while failure to give spontaneously and generously was reported to higher authorities and police. Like the DAF, the NSV was corrupted but it enjoyed a relatively high reputation among the German population. There were rumors of large-scale corruption, with the claim "There goes the Winter Relief!" accompanying the passage of Nazi Party cars in the streets. During the war, the NSV's official task was to, feed, house and comfort German civilians who were injured or who had lost everything because of Allied mass air raids. But there was more. Apparently an innocuous organization, the NSV—as with other branches of the Nazi Party—had an inhumane vocation: the implementation of Hitler's racial policy. In fact the NSV was not solely or primarily a welfare and charitable organization. It was designed to strengthen the collective, biologically and politically—not to feed the hungry, give water to the thirsty or clothe the naked. Instead of merely pursuing social policies and assisting needy individuals, the NSV participated in political indoctrination, the "purification" and strengthening of the body of the nation in accordance with strict racial lines. The items of clothing and money collected under the aegis of Winter Relief were not made universally available to the needy. From the start, Jews, Gypsies, "asocial" persons, the "hereditary ill" and other "enemies of the regime" were excluded and disqualified from the benefits of the organization. Racial objectives were also pur-

NSV auxiliary. The volunteer of the Nazi Women's Organization wears a dark blue suit with jacket and skirt. On the upper left sleeve of the jacket is displayed a silver-gray national emblem, and on the lower left sleeve a dark-blue cuff band with silver-gray lettering indicating the wearer's district affiliation. On the lapel of the jacket is worn an enamel organization badge of triangular shape.

sued by the NSV's Mother and Child Relief. Only the "biologically valuable parts of the German nation" received support. Women who were allegedly "hereditarily ill and inferior" or of an "asocial disposition" were disbarred from postnatal care. Women, babies and young children were categorized according to whether they were worthy of help, hereditarily healthy, or of lesser value. From 1935, the NSV became involved in the field of adoption with racial-political objectives, and by 1937 a new sub-agency was created, the NSV Reich Adoption Service, providing for only "healthy and racially pure" children. During the war, the NSV's attempts to appropriate the field of adoption led to conflicts with the SS's *Lebensborn* agency. Questions of respective competence, in fact the institutionalizing of barbarism, were settled in a spirit of compromise. In the occupied Netherlands, for example, the NSV was responsible for the care of children born to German soldiers by Dutch mothers. In occupied Norway, the SS *Lebensborn* agency secured a monopoly on germanizing mothers and children in their care. Both the NSV and the *Lebensborn* were involved in kidnapping of "Aryan" children in occupied Europe. Orphans of "German blood" were taken from homes or from their foster-parents, or were simply abducted from kindergarten, schools, or off the streets. They were placed in NSV homes, given new names and educated along Nazi lines in the Hitler Jugend in military and racial fashion.

HJ Uniforms and Regalia

Regalia, in its strictest sense, means the insignia of royalty—crown, orb, scepter and other appurtenances of a sovereign. But like many another word it has come to be used where it fits conveniently. It has been borrowed by church, civic, military, political and masonic groups to describe the uniforms and ornaments that make them recognizable to outsiders and, within their own fraternities, to display their degrees of authority and achievement. Regalia and uniforms, the heraldy of war, have always been an inducement to men to take up arms. They make a distinction between civilian and military, confer glamour on their wearers, demonstrate national unity, and give a sense of identity with country, common cause, and comrades. They provide a link between the purely functional need for immediate identification and the need of humans to dress themselves for the occasion of war. Flamboyant, colorful uniforms typical of the eighteenth and nineteenth centuries were adapted to the demands of twentieth-century modern warfare. During World War I, uniforms became drab and functional. For concealment and camouflage, they were khaki, green or brown in order to merge as much as possible into smoky, bracken and wooden backgrounds.

The Hitler Youth adopted many of the outward trappings of the German youth movements which had been absorbed, notably their uniform and organizational structure. The HJ was a kind of juvenile brotherhood with sectarian rules and rituals. The children had insignia, flags, banners, badges and a device: *Blut und Ehre!* (Blood and Honor). The primary concern was not the education of individual character, but training future members of the Nazi Party, the army and the SS. Therefore the compulsory uniform was stylized evidence of a National Socialist uniformity of outlook transcending all class barriers, and exemplified the totalitarian trend toward complete regimentation of all citizens—children and adolescents included. Although it aroused a measure of indulgent ridicule and anxiety abroad, the pageantry of Nazi Germany was a decisive element in pulling Germans together behind Hitler in the early and mid–1930s.

Nazi uniforms and regalia were designed, manufactured, controlled and sold by the *Reichszeugmeisterei* (RZM—central ordnance office of the NSDAP). The *Reichszeugmeisterei*, literally the National Material Control Office, can be thought of as a government procurement office. The *Reichszeugmeisterei* was established at almost the moment that Hitler took over the government of Germany. By July 1934, the RZM was in place with a director, staff and offices in Munich at Tegernseer Landstrasse 210. Officially, it had the solitary purpose of selecting suppliers and sellers of certain NSDAP uniform-related products. The RZM made certain that standardized merchandise in sufficient quantities could be received from a variety of suppliers at stipulated prices. It had exclusive legal authority to design and control quality and costs of uniforms, badges, medals and other regalia. Since its mission was on behalf of the Nazi Party (the RZM was a branch of the Treasury Department) its jurisdiction included material for use by both the *Gliederungen der NSDAP* (Nazi party organizations) and *Angeschlossende Verbände* (associated units). Secondarily, the RZM was charged with making sure that the production of all that they ordered was carried out in "Aryan" manufacturing plants, with materials of German origin whenever possible. Producers authorized by the RZM were not allowed to employ "non-Aryan" workers, and had to give preference to Nazi Party members when promoting workers and dealers. The basic products under RZM control were wearing apparel (shirts, trousers, tunics, overcoats, and caps), and other accessories, such as belts, buckles, belt straps, flags, crash helmets, daggers, knives, standards, buttons, insignia, arm bands, car pennants, neckties, drum eagles and meeting badges. Each firm authorized to produce or sell RZM material was issued an RZM registration number and it was required that the number appear on all finished products they made or sold. The RGBI I-1269 law promulgated on 20 December 1934 punished by imprisonment or forced labor the illegal manufacture, wearing of Nazi uniforms and bearing of regalia. The official RZM shops for retailing Nazi Party badges and equipment were shown by a white metal sign with the inevitable swastika/eagle emblem and the words, "*Zum Verkauf parteiamtlicher Gegenstände zugelassen NSDAP Reichszeugmeisterei*" (sale of official party items authorized by the National Quartermaster Department of the German National-Socialist Workers' Party). The RGBI I-844 law from 26 June 1935 punished by imprisonment any person who insulted, despised, or mocked Nazi regalia, uniforms and flags.

The RZM system applied to Nazi Party equipment and insignia only. The control did not extend to non-party organizations, like the *Heer* (army), *Kriegsmarine* (navy) and *Luftwaffe* (air force).

Boys' uniforms

The wearing of a uniform was intended to erase social differences. It was also intended to give a strong and united image of youth. Far from being evidence of a new social order, however, the uniform merely exemplified the totalitarian trend toward complete regimentation of all German citizens, children and adolescents included. Uniforms of all branches of the HJ were rather expensive and often a financial burden for large families. Parents of slender means had no choice but to obey the official call for uniforms "transcending all class barriers."

The early HJ uniform was civilian dress, including ski caps, leather shorts and various shirts and tunics—in the countryside, sometimes in traditional folkloric fashion. The brown SA shirt (worn with black shorts) was authorized for the young Nazis as early as 1926, which caused some members to be killed because they were mistaken for SA activists. This prompted the design of a unique, practical and durable HJ uniform. In 1933, several standardized HJ uniforms were offered for sale through strictly licensed Nazi RZM "brown shops."

Hitler Jugend's early dress   *Hitler Jugend* **Scharführer**

HJ Rottenführer *(left)* and HJ Stammführer *(right)*

HJ Gebietsführer *in winter-duty overcoat* *Hitler Jugend* **Stabsführer**

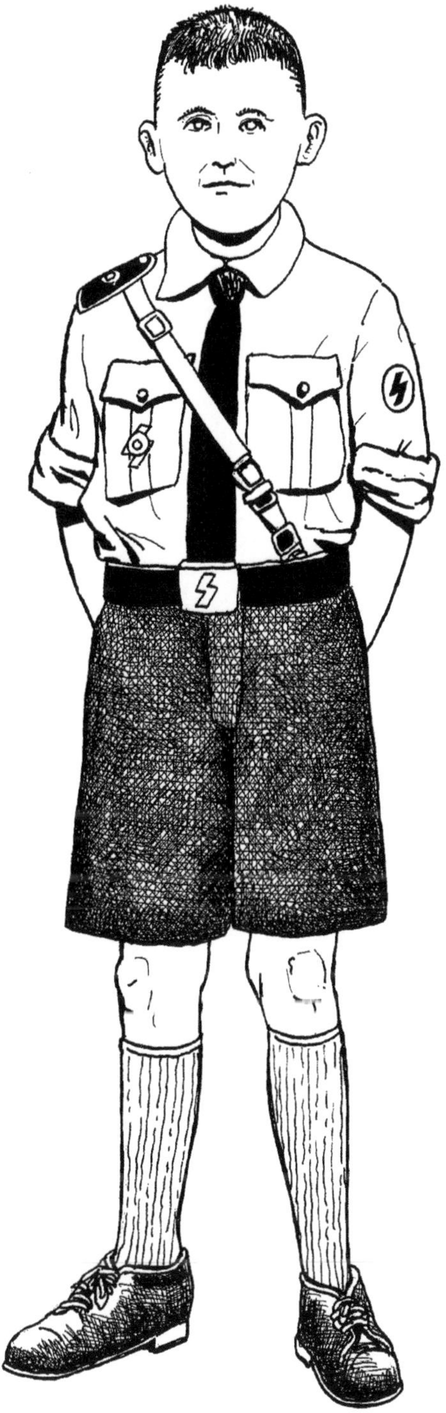

Pimpf, Deutsches Jungvolk *(junior Hitler Jugend)*

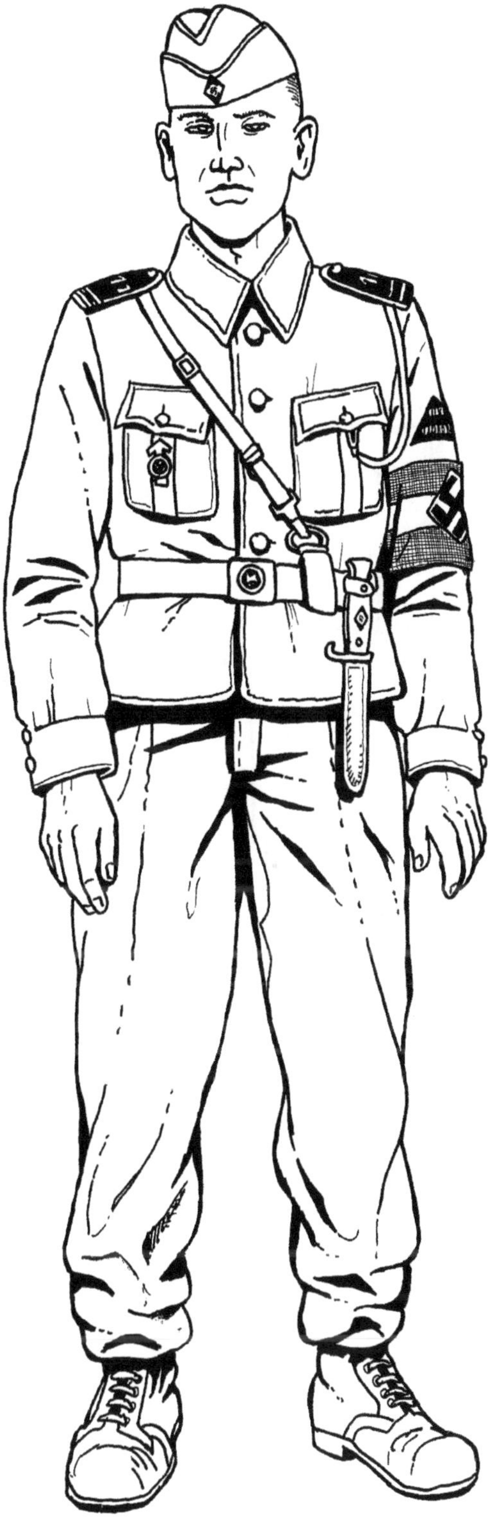

HJ dark-blue winter uniform

HJ winter blouse

HJ belt buckle

Junior HJ members wore a uniform composed of a khaki forage cap, a khaki shirt, a black neckerchief (held in place by a brown leather toggle), a four-pocketed tunic, an armband with swastika, black corduroy shorts, a waist belt, a shoulder belt, white or gray stockings and *Bundschuhe* (heavy marching shoes). In 1934, a dark-blue ski suit was introduced as a winter uniform. This included a black ski cap with the HJ diamond badge at the front and a dark-blue, two-pocketed, pullover blouse. The latter had shoulder straps piped red for the general HJ branch, with *Bann* (regiment) number. On the left upper sleeve there was a black triangular badge indicating the *Obergebiet* (corps district) and the *Gebiet* (divisional district). Under the badge on the left sleeve there was the HJ red-and-white armband with black swastika. The short, dark-blue winter jacket existed also in a double-breasted variant with large collar and two front pockets. There was a black leather waist belt with buckle, and an HJ knife in a sheath. Long trousers were tucked into white socks, and heavy marching shoes were worn. Hair was always short in a military cut.

Adult leaders wore a single-breasted, four-pocket khaki tunic with black trousers and a peaked cap with the political eagle above the HJ diamond-shaped swastika insignia. They also wore the black "region" triangle on their left sleeves, and black shoulder straps indicated the rank. The waist belt worn by leaders and troops was decorated by a buckle displaying an eagle holding in its claws the triangular HJ swastika and the motto *Blut und Ehre!*

Girls' uniforms

Members of the League of German Girls were at first issued a simple brown costume. Hitler—who wished the girls to look pretty and attractive—found the uniforms "old sacks" and ordered them to be redesigned. In 1936 a group of Berlin designers created a stylish new costume. In summer, the girls of the BdM wore a white (often short-sleeved) blouse, a black scarf or a black neckerchief with an interwoven leather slipknot, and a light-brown short-waisted jacket, or a white poplin blouse with long sleeves,

HJ forage cap

HJ cap

BdM uniform (and four-pocketed warm tunic)

3. Prelude to War, 1933–1939

BdM-HJ variant dark-blue winter blouse

- *Untergauführerin*: double-narrow edging
- *Gauführerin:* one thick and one narrow edging
- *Obergauführerin*: double-narrow gold edging
- *Reichsführerin*: gold oak-leaf border.

Insignia

Sleeve triangles were worn by all members of the Hitler Youth on the upper left arm. HJ and DJ members had black cloth triangles with lettering and edging machine-woven in bright yellow or white-silver thread. Girls of the BdM wore black cloth triangles with their lettering and edging machine woven in white thread. The lettering was usually in two lines. The upper line showed the wearer's *Obergebiet* (region) and the lower line showed the individual *Gebiet* (district). HJ or BdM units that had been in existence before 1933, known as "Tradition Units," had a gold braided bar (HJ) or silver bar (BdM) sewn along the bottom of the triangle.

four-button-front fastening, and two breast pockets. A general feature was a navy-blue or black pleated skirt with belt loops around the waist, and two internal front pockets. Black or white ankle socks, and various footwear including marching and civilian shoes were worn. In addition, for cold weather, there was a warm four-pocket, single-breasted climbing jacket; this had five front buttons, and was made in light-brown imitation-suede material. The Hitler Youth patch was worn on the upper left sleeve. Below this patch was worn the red-white diamond-shaped Hitler Youth insignia with swastika in the center.

The uniform for the permanent senior BdM leaders included a dark-blue, single-breasted tunic with pockets, a matching dark-blue skirt, a white blouse and high-heeled shoes. A shield-shaped cloth patch with embroidered eagle, swastika and unit number was worn on the left breast. Rank was indicated by silver and gold-colored cord edging and badges embroidered in matching wire, as follows:

- *Gruppenführerin*: no patch edging
- *Ringführerin*: narrow, silver-cord edging

The racial doctrine of the Nazis held that *Auslandsdeutsche* (Germans in foreign lands) retained their affiliation with the homeland. There were also foreign Nazi parties such as the German-American Bund founded in the United States in 1935 by Fritz Kuhm. There were several special agencies of the Nazi Party responsible for spreading Nazism abroad and to make contact with and supervise Germans in foreign lands. Children of *Auslandsdeutsche* and foreign German Nazis were encouraged to belong to the Hitler Youth and—where permitted—wore their uniforms to official functions or on their return to Germany. They were distinguished by foreign triangular badges bearing the name of their land of origin (e.g., the United States, Kap-Stadt, and China).

Members of the HJ and BdM who voluntarily served a year working on the land wore a green triangle. The lower left sleeve

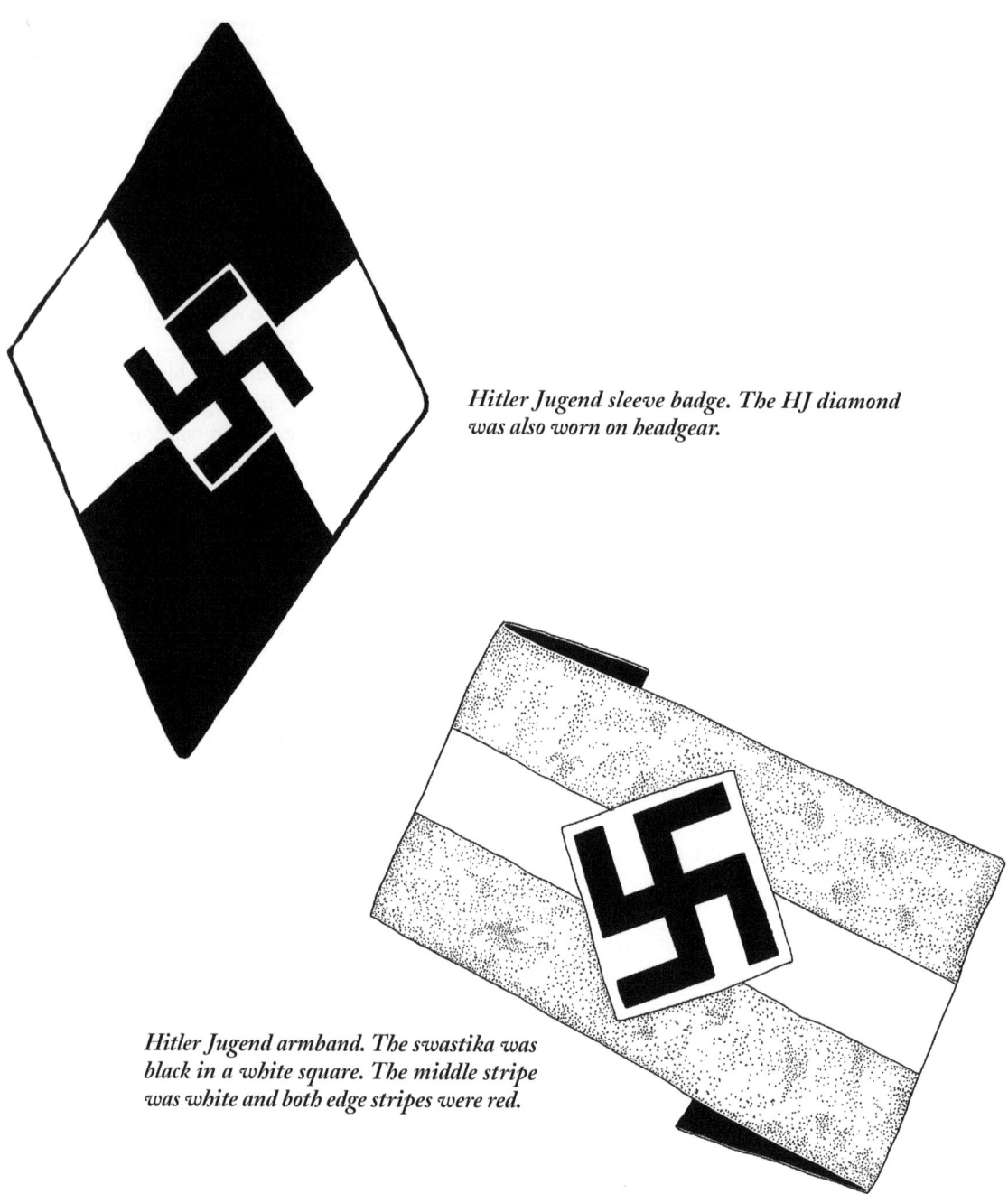

Hitler Jugend sleeve badge. The HJ diamond was also worn on headgear.

Hitler Jugend armband. The swastika was black in a white square. The middle stripe was white and both edge stripes were red.

Opposite: *Kern-HJ shoulder straps. The ranks, from the lowest to highest: 1.* Hitlerjunge, *2.* Rottenführer, *3.* Oberrottenführer, *4.* Kameradschaftsführer, *5.* Oberkameradschaftsführer, *6.* Scharführer, *7.* Oberscharführer, *8.* Gefolgschaftsführer, *9.* Obergefolgschaftsführer, *10.* Hauptgefolgschaftsführer, *11.* Stammführer, *12.* Oberstammführer, *13.* Bannführer, *14.* Oberbannführer, *15.* Hauptbannführer, *16.* Gebietsführer, *17.* Obergebietsführer, *18.* Stabführer. *From 1 to 15 stripes, stars and oak leaves were silver. From 16 to 18, they were gilded.*

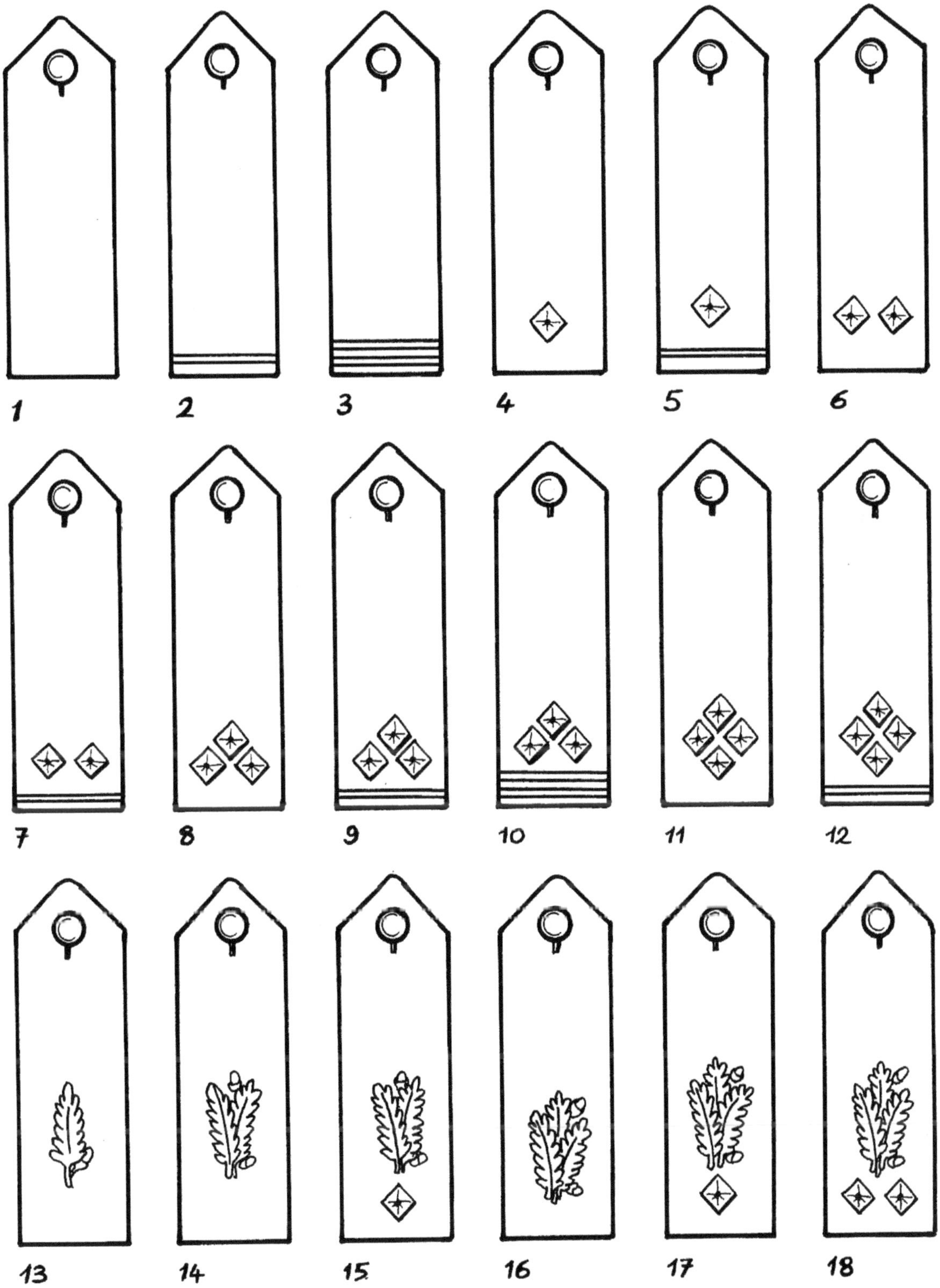
1
2
3
4
5
6
7
8
9
10
11
12
13
14
15
16
17
18

could also carry badges indicating skills that the young wearer might have acquired. The *Armelbinde* (armband) was worn by all HJ boys and leaders on the upper left arm. It consisted of a black swastika in a white square; the middle stripe was white and the edges were red. A sew-on patch was worn by members of the DJ instead of the arm band. The color denoted the *Oberbann* (region) to which the wearer belonged. Members of DJ wore a single shoulder strap on their right shoulder, without piping. Their unit number was shown lengthwise as opposed to HJ's across. Members of the BdM did not wear shoulder straps as part of their uniform. *Schulterklappen* (shoulder straps) were very complicated before 1938. The system was simplified from 1938 to 1945. All HJ shoulder straps were black (navy-blue for Marine-HJ). The colored piping represented the *Oberbann* and the number indicated the wearer's *Gefolgschaft* (unit). Rank was indicated on the shoulder strap by means of a series of pips, stripes, squares and oak leaves.

The girls did not wear armbands. Instead they wore a Hitler Youth diamond patch sewn to their left sleeve under the triangle badge. BdM sew-on badges indicating rank were worn on the left breast of the tunic. Cuff titles were not worn by the HJ. There were, however, three exceptions. The *Landdienst der Hitler Jugend* (agriculture service) insignia was worn by members who volunteered to work on the land for a year. The cuff title *HJ Streifendienst* was worn by members of the Hitler Youth Patrol Service. A cuffband with the inscription *Kinderlandverschickung* (KLV) was worn by girls involved in the wartime evacuation of children.

Flags and banners

All units of the Hitler Youth had flags, banners and pennants. Nazi flags played an important role. At the same time dramatic and menacing, waving in the wind, proudly paraded by standard bearers in the streets, draped about buildings, they added a touch of color to the austere parades and rallies, and their numbers were often impressive. They were regarded as holy. It was on their unit's flag that HJ boys and girls swore an oath of allegiance. When left unattended, flags and banners had to be stood erect, and on no account was the cloth to touch the ground, as this was symbol of defeat. It was also forbidden to lean them against a tree, a building or the like, as this was a sign of neglect.

The flag of the Hitler Youth Organization proper (*Hitler Jugend Organisationsfahne*) was a red-white-red striped flag (the white stripe being slightly narrower). In the center there was a white square standing on its point, with a black swastika. The width-length ratio was 29:50.

The flag of a company-size unit of the (main) Hitler Youth (*Gefolgschaftsfahne*) was the same design, with a white square in the upper left, with the numerals of the company and battalion. The Hitler Youth regimental flag (*Bannfahne*) was a red-white-red striped flag (as described above). In the center there was a black Prussian-type regimental eagle (the type of eagle used on Prussian regimental flags since the eighteenth century) with a white

HJ sleeve badge of the Obergau South Swabia

Hitler Jugend Organisationsfahne *(Hitler Youth Organization flag)*

sword and hammer in its claws. Above the head there was a white scroll with the regimental letter. The width-length ratio was 29:50. The "Trumpet" flag of the Hitler Youth (*Fanfarentuch*) was the same design but the white stripe was placed vertically.

The *Deutsche Jungvolk*, the organization for boys between 10 and 14, had its own flags. The flag of the German Youth Organization (*Deutsche Jungvolk Organisationsfahne*) was a black flag with a white sieg rune (the runic letter S). Its width-length ratio was 4:5 or 10:11. It was in use until 1934. The "Trumpet" flag of the German Youth (*Fanfarentuch der deutsche Jungvolk*) was the same flag but square. The flag of a company-size unit of the German Youth (*Deutsche Jugend Fahnleinfahne*) was the same, with a white square placed in the upper left side indicating the number of company. The German Youth Regimental Flag (*Deutsche Jungvolk Jungbannfahne*) was different in design. Instead of a rune sign the flag featured a white eagle decorated with a black swastika, holding a white hammer and a sword in its claws on a black field. Its width-length ratio was 8:11. It was in use from 1934 onward.

The flags of the *Bund deutscher Mädel* included the following. The pennant for a district of the German Girls League (*Bund deutscher Mädel Untergauwimpel*) was a red-white-red striped pennant with a black spread-wing eagle (a little like the one on old Prussian flags) with white swastika on its breast. Above the head in black was the unit number. The width-length ratio was 2:3. The pennant for a group of League of German Girls (*Bund deutscher Mädel Gruppenwimpel*) had a black swastika in a black square and indication of the company number in the upper left.

The *Jungmädel*, the organization for girls between 10 and 14, had several flags, too. The pennant for a district of the Young Girls (*Jungmädel-Untergauwimpel*) was a black triangle with an eagle carrying a swastika, surmounted by the number of the district. The flag of a group of young girls

Hitler Jugend Bannfahne *(regimental flag)*

Bannfahne des deutschen Jungvolks *(DJ regimental flag)*

Flag of a group of 160 HJ boys between ages 10 and 14
*(*Deutsche Jungvolk in der Hitler Jugend*)*

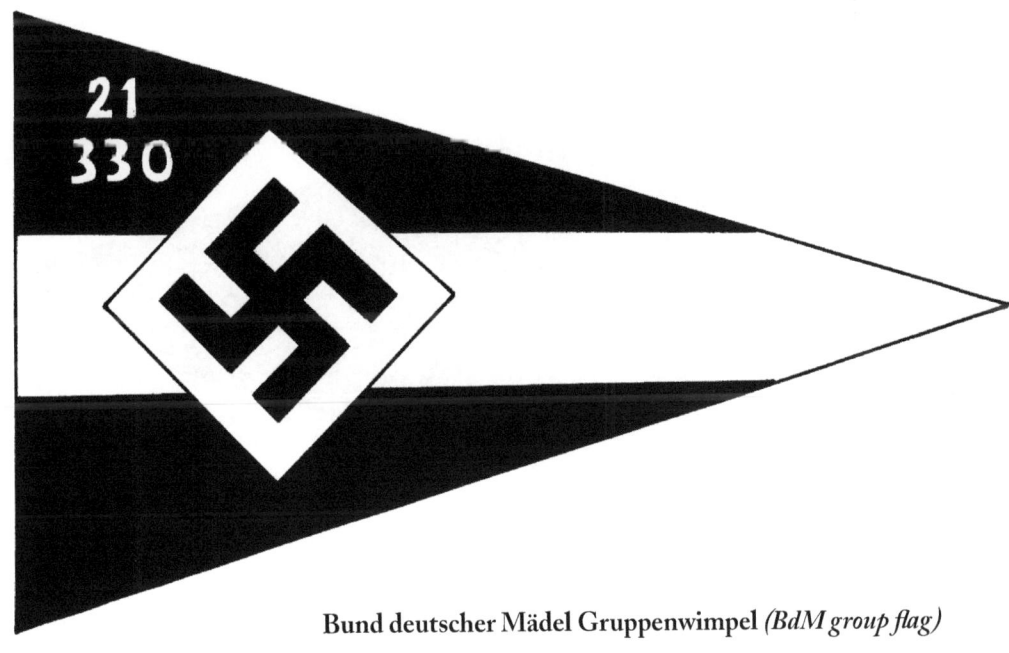

Bund deutscher Mädel Gruppenwimpel *(BdM group flag)*

Jungmädel-Untergauwimpel *(JM district flag)*

Jungmädel-Gruppenwimpel *(JM group flag)*

BdM girl with **Gruppenwimpel** *(squad flag)*

(*Jungmadel-Gruppenwimpel*) included a swastika and two diamonds and group number indicated by digits placed on the upper left of the flag.

Medals

Special medals were created for the Hitler Jugend. Some were intended to commemorate rallies, party meetings, holiday trips and other Nazi events; they were sold to those who participated. These commemorative medals were an obligatory purchase which made a source of income for the Nazi treasury, and had the effect of making the event seem important and bonding the participants into a united front. Other medals were personally awarded for years of membership, special individual achievements and great deeds in sport, training, or skill specialization, as well as tests of knowledge of Nazi arcana, such as the *Hitler Jugend Ehrenabzeichen* (Hitler Youth Badge of Honor) or the Proficiency Award. There were also badges for riding and handling horses and horse-drawn vehicles, for both adults and young people. The HJ also instituted shooting awards like the *Schiessauszeichnung* (HJ shooting medal) which came in the three classes: marksman, sharpshooter and expert sniper. Girls of the JM and BdM had discreet honor badges and brooches. For the party faithful there were even clips, rings, and necklaces, with black, white, and red

Junior Hitler Youth proficiency award for boys age 10 to 14

Hitler Jugend proficiency award (age 15–18) "Für Leistung in der Hitler Jugend" (for achievement in the Hitler Youth)

the usual colors and swastikas the dominant theme. Medals and awards for both boys and girls were worn with pride, sewn on breast pockets.

Knives

Knives, daggers and cleavers were an important part of the Nazi regalia. Introduced in December 1933, a sixteenth-century, "Holbein," Swiss-styled *Dolch* (dagger) was suspended by a chain to the waist belts of high NSDAP functionaries, and SA and SS senior officers. Other Nazi agencies and organizations were quick to follow, and before long uniform-conscious civil servants were clamoring for daggers of their own. Hitler, keenly interested in regalia and eager to support the world-renowned German blade makers' cartel in Solingen, approved many of the designs himself. The designs were created by students and masters at state trade schools. Once a pattern had been selected, it was submitted to the *Reichszeugmeisterei* (RZM) for final approval. Only then could organization members purchase and display their new sidearms. There was a profusion of gleaming blades. The late-medieval-styled SS dagger had a black wooden grip, bearing various decorations, such as SS runes, standard eagle and swastika, and motto ("My honor is loyalty") etched into the blade. The Reich Labor Service's sidearm was a hewing knife carrying the slogan "*Arbeit Adelt*" ("work ennobles"). That of the Hitler Jugend was a *Fahrtenmesser*

Hitler Jugend knife with leather scabbard. The blade carries the words "Blood and Honor!"

Dagger HJ leadership

(traveling knife) with the device of the organization carved into the blade: *Blut und Ehre!* (Blood and Honor). The HJ knife was carried in a metal sheath worn from the waist belt.

Hitler Jugend knives were awarded to qualified members who had participated in war games, sport, or a day-and-a-half-long march, who had achieved a set of minimum standards on the playing field, and passed tests of knowledge of Nazi arcana, including the words of the anthem, the "Horst Wessel Song." The Hitler Youth knife was an important part of the uniform and being allowed to carry it was a serious and prestigious matter in a boy's life in the Third Reich. The sidearm was purchased but not considered personal property, so when a holder was expelled or had to leave for any reason, the knife had to be handed back. Of all the edged weapons produced during the Nazi regime, the HJ knife was the most prolific. Between 1934 and 1945, over 20,000,000 were manufactured and well after the end of the war the makers continued production with the Boy Scout trefoil substituted for the Nazi decoration.

For daily use, the HJ also issued pocket knives (with hinged blades) decorated with the inevitable eagle/swastika design and a portrait of Adolf Hitler.

The German salute

All members of the HJ—as all members of the other NSDAP organizations—were taught to revere the Führer and greeted each other with the *Deutscher Gruss* (German salute). This was an adaptation of the ancient Roman salute and similar to Mussolini's Fascist salute. One stood at attention, left hand on the belt buckle, then the right arm was raised a little higher than the shoulder and one said enthusiastically, with clear and loud voice, "*Heil Hitler!*" with clicking heels. The salute expressed both a respectful and virile greeting, and wishing health and long life to Hitler. But, with the rigidly upraised arm it was more an aggressive gesture than a peaceful one. For the happy few who might meet Hitler personally, the salute was the same, but one said "*Heil, mein Führer!*" (Hail, my leader!). It is said that the salute was first used in December 1924 when Hitler was released from prison. It became common practice after 1925. After the Nazis came to power in 1933, the Hitler greeting was intended to replace the common and friendly "*Gutentag*" (good day) and the more religious "*Gruss Gott*" (God bless you). It was compulsory in all parades, meetings, and official and public events, and strongly advised in daily life, including at schools, offices, and so on. Everyone was expected to use the Hitler greeting throughout the day. It was an obligation for all citizens on every possible occasion, and Germany became a vast camp of Hitler saluters. Boys and girls of the HJ were encouraged to denounce everyone—even their own parents—for failure to use it or for reducing the salute to an infinitesimal movement of the arm accompanied by an inarticulate mumble.

Members of the Nazi Party addressed each other as *Kamerad* (comrade). The phrase "*Sieg Heil!*" (To Victory!) became not only the greeting and farewell of the Nazi Party followers but a chant to be reiterated endlessly on all public occasions. These melodramatic trappings helped to make and secure the lifeline that held Hitler to his public.

Training and Activities

The Hitler Jugend built upon many practices of the youth organizations of the Weimar and pre–World War I periods. It offered a wide range of leisure activities and, at lower levels (which in the everyday running of things were the most important) was

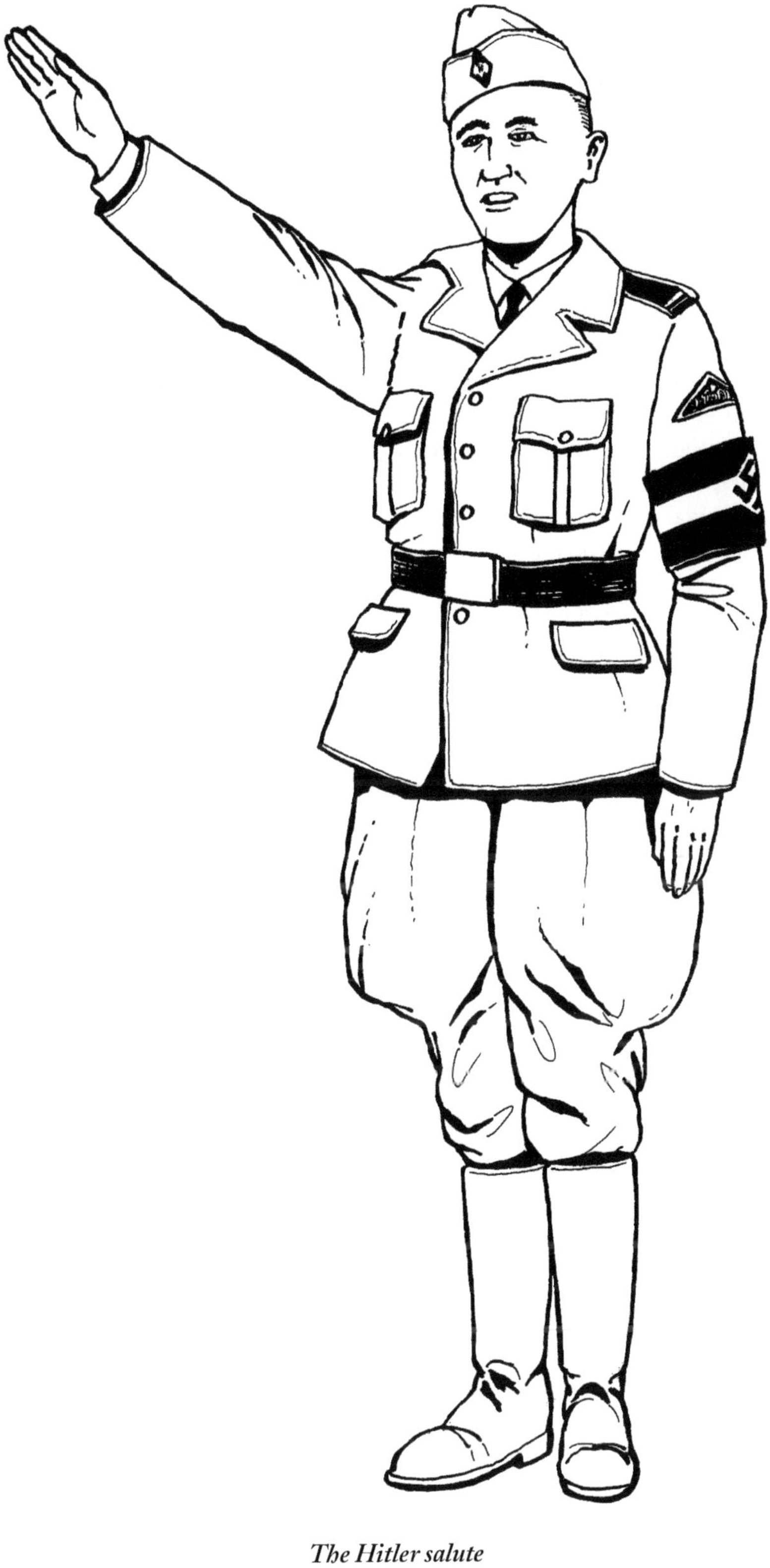

The Hitler salute

led not infrequently by people who had talent and previous experience in other, older, defunct youth organizations. In the German provinces, the arrival of the Hitler Youth after 1933 often meant the first access to leisure activities, the impetus to build a youth club, a swimming pool, a sport field, or the opportunity to go on weekend or holiday trips away from one's narrow home environment. For many young people, the HJ made life meaningful and exciting, developed comradeship and self-consciousness, and gave the illusion of equality, the feeling of belonging to the racially pure *Volksgemeinschaft*, the great, elite, classless German community. The organization had something for everyone: arts, crafts, sports, model planes, journalism, singing, music, traveling, and more. The romantic façade of tents and open-air cooking, field sports and campfires, snappy uniforms, impressive parades, and solemn vows of loyalty to the Führer were heady stuff for young people. All politics aside, for a large part of the German population the image of Nazism was characterized not by terror, mass murder, racist persecution and war but by reduction of unemployment, economic boom, guaranteed pay, attractive leisure activities organized by the KdF (Nazi free-time organization), tranquility and order. The period from 1933 to 1939 was for many Germans a good time. Every year a new theme was developed at the national level for the Hitler Youth. And so 1934 was the "Year of Training," 1935 the "Year of Apprenticeship," 1936 the "Year of the Junior HJ," 1937 the "Year of National Restoration," 1938 the "Year of National Reconciliation," 1939 the "Year of Hygienic Duty," 1940 the "Year of Ordeal of Capacity," 1941 "Living for the Führer," 1942 the "Year of Colonization and Rural Service," 1943 the "Year of War and Involvement of the Youth," and 1944 the "Year of the Volunteers." In all HJ activities lay also a strong competitive element intended to activate rivalry, instill a "winning spirit," and develop strength and courage. The principles of leadership and the emphasis on physical force in many cases helped to establish the domination not necessarily of the best but that of the strongest.

Sport

Sport reflected the Nazi value of fitness, health, and domination of the strongest. Sport and training were intended to create a race of splendid, disciplined, strong animals. The ideal was to eradicate the traditional German *Bierbauch* (beer belly), pipe smoking, the eating of greasy sausages and drinking beer without moderation. The emphasis was thus on virile outdoor activities, sports, competition and physical training. HJ candidates had to satisfy certain minimum requirements in the sphere of athletics, including running 60 meters in 12 seconds, long jumping 2.75 meters, swimming 300 meters in less than 10 minutes, throwing the softball 25 meters, and taking part in a 36-hour hike. HJ members practiced gymnastics, collective sports, sailing, diving, and swimming, but also such dangerous *Mutprobe* (tests of courage) as diving into a river from a bridge or leaping over a bonfire. Boxing was also introduced and practiced in order to develop aggression and overcome the fear of being hurt. In Hitler's own words, boxing was a sport which developed the "spirit of aggression," required "lightning decisions," and trained the body in "steely dexterity." Boxing became the favorite sport of the Third Reich. When Max Schmeling defeated Joe Louis in New York in 1936, he was greeted by Hitler himself. He became a national hero overnight, and became a central figure in racialist Nazi propaganda claiming the superiority of the white Nordic race over black athletes. In the return bout in 1938 for the heavyweight championship, Joe Louis's determination to win was clear. Schmeling went down in the first round and he was counted out two minute and four seconds after the start of the fight. In Germany his defeat was felt as a national disaster and a personal snub for Hitler. During World War II Schmeling enlisted in the German paratrooper corps and fought on the island of Crete.

Skiing instruction and mountain climbing were also very popular and part of the training given by various organizations, notably the *SA Gebirgsjäger* (Storm-trooper mountain units) drawn from professional German and Austrian alpinists, hunters, foresters and skiers. The Nazis were quick to realize that diving, flying and gliding, driving, skiing and other exciting activities were skills of the future, and they sponsored and promoted them both to enhance the image of a modern nation and to attract youth. Sports events were organized everywhere in Germany, and these were more manifestations of strength, power and collective consciousness than skilled performances.

The Olympic Games of 1936 were held in Berlin in August. Staged according to Goebbels' propaganda, the harsh persecution against the Catholic Church and the Jewish community was temporarily silenced, and the Games gave a large number of foreign athletes, reporters and visitors the façade of a modern, peaceful and dynamic German nation.

One amazing feature of Nazi Germany was how far short of athletic "Aryan" perfection most of its leaders fell. The men who claimed a providential destiny as saviors of the Aryan race, and who caused the horrible deaths of millions of innocent victims for their "racial inferiority" did not all have the appearance of the ideal, heroic, fair-haired, blue-eyed, athletic, tall Germanic *Übermensch*. Hitler's own ancestry was quite unclear. His presumed grandfather seemed to have been a wanderer, and his name was possibly of Czech origin. His stature was relatively short, his hair was dark, and his physical appearance was more Slavic than Germanic. He never practiced sports or even

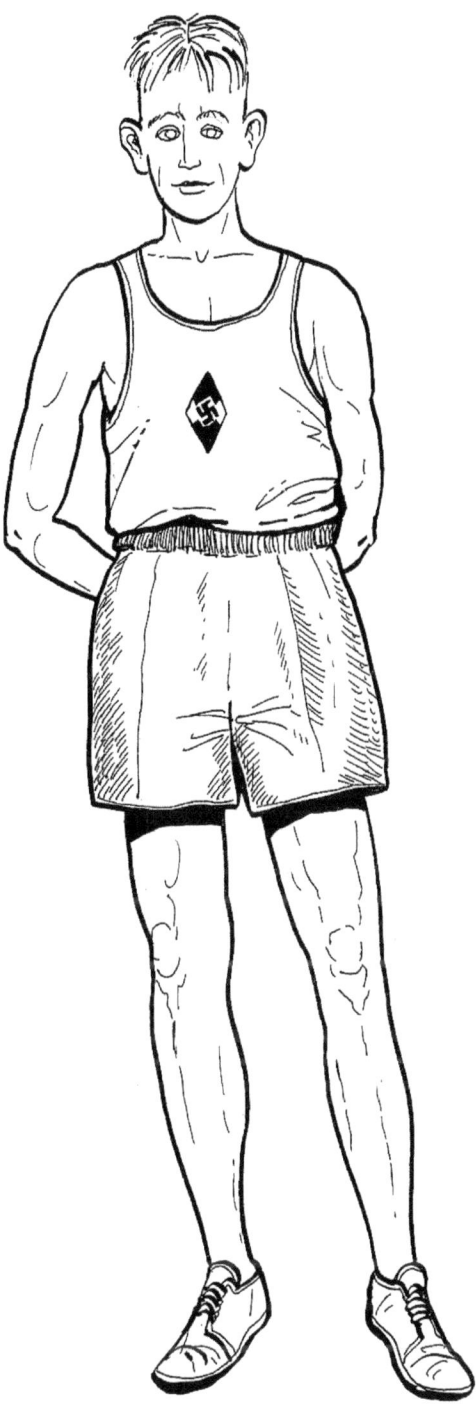

Hitler Jugend sport kit. The HJ sport kit was the same for boys and girls. It consisted of a white singlet bearing the HJ emblem, brown or black shorts, and black light-weight shoes, usually worn without socks.

physical exercise; he was lazy and moody, shy and awkward, distrustful and contemptuous, and there was something essentially ridiculous about him, as Charlie Chaplin brilliantly captured in his film, *The Great Dictator* in 1940. Hermann Göring, number two in the Nazi hierarchy after Hitler, had been a handsome man and a glamorous pilot in World War I, but later became a fat man addicted to drugs and luxury. Reichsführer SS Heinrich Himmler was a dull, short-sighted bureaucrat with a bullet head and poor health. Propaganda Minister Josef Goebbels was short, thin, dark-haired and physically disabled, with a club foot which left him with a pronounced limp and an inferiority complex. SA Chief Ernst Röhm was an ugly, short, fat homosexual. Hitler's deputy, Martin Bormann, was a short fat man with limited intelligence. The chief of the Labor Front, Robert Ley, was a fat drunkard with a psychologically labile and socially insecure personality. The extravagant Rudolf Hess (Hitler's deputy before his mysterious flight to England) was so mad that even his fellow Nazi leaders noticed. The ruthless Gauleiter Julius Streicher (publisher of the Nazi newspaper *Der Sturmer*) was mentally deranged and a pornographer, but apparently that was not a handicap in the Nazi movement. Had the times not been so unstable in Germany, these men would have remained a bunch of emotionally crippled misfits, impotently acting out their delusions on the fringe of politics.

Hiking

Sports and physical training reflected the Nazi emphasis on fitness. German youths also had to be capable of marching long distances. Hiking was intended to harden the youths, it was a preparation for a war in which infantry legwork would be decisive. Hiking in the HJ was not an afternoon of pleasure in loose groups of friends strolling about and having fun, it was marching in disciplined, military-like columns in close ranks. And hiking was more than physical training. It was intended to create a feeling of togetherness and to enhance the image of a new nation marching as one toward its glorious future. It was regarded as a national duty, as a mystical exercise to discover and love Germany, and as a mental preparation to defend her and—if need be—to die for the nation. It was rhythmic, with songs, fifes and drums, and flag waving ahead in the wind. In all weather, throughout the years, large columns of HJ/DJ boys and JM/BdM girls roamed everywhere in the land. Marching was not aimless though. The young people went on excursions, camping and hiking trips, and to "holiday" camps which were actually *Wehrertüchtigungslagern* (military training camps). These camps were designed, built and administered by the youths themselves. Always located amid pleasant countryside scenery, they could accommodate hundreds of youths. They invariably included a gatehouse with sentries, offices, rows of tents (or wooden dormitory huts), and barracks for the leaders, all placed in an orderly fashion along alleys leading to a central meeting square, site of the inevitable national and HJ flags. In addition each camp included athletic fields, training and marching grounds, and sometimes even a swimming pool. Of course these included collective facilities: kitchen, supply stores, refectory, showers and toilets. All this was maintained, tidied, and cleaned by the members themselves. Martial music was played from loudspeakers. Flowers, nicely mowed lawns, bushes and trees were planted inside the camp to make the environment a little easier on the eyes. The whole design radiated a sense of order, cleanliness and military strictness, which was intended to impress the youth. With everyone eating the same food, doing the same activities, and enduring the same disciplined hardship, life at the camps was also intended to reduce the sense of social class, and to develop equality, comradeship and team spirit. The activities at the camp were dedicated not to fun, relaxation and leisure, however, but to instruction, indoctrination and training. One did not idle away one's time. A typical day in the camp looked like this:

- 6:45 a.m.—Reveille
- 7:00 a.m.—Hoisting the colors
- 7:00–8:30 a.m.—Ideological and political instruction
- 8:30–9:00 a.m.—Breakfast
- 9:00–9:30 a.m.—Sports
- 9:30–10:30 a.m.—Medical and hygiene training
- 10:30–11:45 a.m.—Camp administration (cleaning, tidying up, etc.)
- Noon–2:00 p.m.—Lunch, followed by a rest period
- 2:00–3:30 p.m.—Assembly activities
- 3:30–5:30 p.m.—Field work, marching or hiking
- 5:30–6:30 p.m.—Free time
- 6:30 p.m.—Evening parade and lowering the colors
- 7:00 p.m.—Supper
- 7:30–9:00 p.m.—Campfire with songs
- 9:30 p.m.—Lights out

Under close supervision, the youth were shown the great achievements of the Aryan culture and those of the Nazi regime. They were taken to what the state considered historical places. Members of the HJ visited weapons factories, for example, and were taken on to a "pilgrimage" to such Nazi holy places as the village where Hitler was born (Braunau, Austria) on 20 April 1889 and the prison at Landsberg where he was imprisoned after the failed putsch of November 1923. Another Nazi shrine was the *Feldherrnhalle* (Hall of Heroes), the building in Munich in front of which the bloody confrontation between the Nazis and Bavarian police took place on 9 November 1923. After the Nazis came to power, the *Feldherrnhalle* embodied a shrine to the sixteen fallen Nazi martyrs who were killed during the failed putsch.

After 1935, Hitler Jugend members were submitted to the so-called *Adolf-Hitler-Marsch*: during a week, all HJ units had to march in disciplined and uniformed ranks to Nuremberg to participate in the *Reichsparteitag* (Reich Party Day) held in September.

To shelter hikers and marchers a network of *Jugendherbergen* (youth hostels) was developed in 1933. Youth hostels had long existed in Germany, but they were now officially taken over by the Nazi state. At rest camps and youth hostels hiking members of the HJ could rest in exchange for a modest payment. By 1934 some five million youngsters had taken advantage of the *Jugendherbergen*.

Hiking and outdoor activities, love of the German countryside, and a distaste for the ugliness of industrialization, inherited from the *Wandervogel*, built a strong "green" feeling in the Hitler Jugend.

Rallies and celebrations

The members of the Hitler Jugend attended public demonstrations in uniform, they organized and participated in Nazi Party meetings, mass rallies, torchlight marches, presentations, festivals, parades, reviews, games, exhibitions, commemorations, pagan rites (such as the consecration of flags), speeches and celebrations, all with a theatrical and festive air. These spectacular ceremonies—using every art, subterfuge and contrivance for mass persuasion—adapted the techniques of soap opera, drama and cinema. Their purpose was to keep the faithful in close and constant touch with the activities of the regime and to normalize the vicious message of National Socialism. They were displays of ruthless intimidation, of threatening force, and one of the more evil manifestations of megalomania known to history. They necessitated a huge organization and strict discipline for the marshaling, equipping, feeding and then dispersal—in the case of the annual Nuremberg rallies—of hundreds of thousands of men, women and children. They were astounding spectacles intended to impress both participants and spectators and to sanctify the new regime. They were expected to serve as substitutes for traditional religious high holy days.

January 24, the day commemorating the murder of the HJ "hero" Herbert Norkus, included a slow torchlight parade with solemn songs.

January 30 was the anniversary of the *Machtergreifung* (seizure of power) when Hitler had assumed the chancellorship in 1933. On that day each year the German nation was presented with a lengthy account of what Hitler had taken over and what he had done with the power entrusted to him. The day ended with a public ceremony, broadcast by radio from every street corner in the land, and torchlight processions. Eighteen-year-old members of the HJ who had proved their qualities were sworn in as full members of the Nazi Party.

February 24 was the "annunciation day" on which the National Socialist Party had been founded and its twenty-five-point program published in 1920. Year after year until 1943, Hitler liked to look back on the beginning of his career. The Führer presented himself as the "truest executor of the NSDAP's sacred heritage," recalled the movement's modest start and the great opposition it had overcome, and emphasized its achievements and successes which guaranteed Germany's victorious future.

March 16 was the National Day of Mourning, or Heroes' Remembrance Day, for the victims of World War I and Nazi martyrs. This was celebrated in the Kroll Opera House with a performance of the second movement of Beethoven's Third Symphony, a solemn "cultural" occasion attended by all foreign diplomats before World War II.

April 20 was Hitler's birthday (1889), celebrated with extravagant rituals. On that day delegations from all over the country brought presents, including pieces of art; these were passed on to the museum of Linz which Hitler hoped to turn into the greatest art gallery in Europe after the war. Representatives of the youth organizations solemnly pledged their allegiance to the Führer. April 20 was a significant day for boys aged 14 as they officially entered the HJ proper. The day culminated in a parade of the *Wehrmacht* (armed forces) through the Brandenburger Tor at Berlin before Hitler in his capacity of army supreme commander.

May 1 was National Labor Day—taken over from the socialist tradition—with popular feasts emphasizing the Nazi Party's solidarity with the workers (its "socialist" component) and Hitler's role in the creation of the welfare state.

The second Sunday in May was Mothering Day (originally invented by the flower trade to boost its turnover), during which prolific mothers were rewarded with medals, and young girls reminded of their duty toward the regime: to make children.

Strenuous efforts were made to introduce a romantic pagan feast on June 21 (summer solstice) dedicated to NSDAP martyrs and war heroes, with stirring speeches, night parades, public demonstrations and blazing bonfires.

The pièce de résistance of the annual Nazi cycle was the first week of September: the grandiose Party rally was held in Nuremberg from 1927 to 1938 in a climate of mystical ecstasy, sacred delirium, and nationalist exultation. For a full week the regime displayed its immense talent in jubilant colors, lights, music and festivities for its own self-glorification in the presence of thousands of participants. Homilies, slogans and speeches were addressed to pilgrims and faithful, providing displays of Hitler's rhetoric. Mass performances and mass demonstrations were held, including parades of soldiers with fixed bayonets in rows of twelve, SS and SA men with colorful spread-eagle standards, and *Luftwaffe* flying shows. Old Nazi fighters, representing the glorious past of the movement, marched ahead of the young generations: RAD (Labor Service) uniformed battalions presenting gleaming shovels, disciplined boys and girls of the Hitler Jugend, and dancing young women from the "Faith and Beauty" association. Women, veterans, farmers and workers, representing organizations overtly related to the Nazi Party as well as state agencies and services, paraded in an expression of the ideal of the national "racially pure" community and the self-dramatization of Hitler's messianic mission. Each year had a different theme. In 1933 it was the "Rally of Victory," in 1934 "Rally for Unity and Strength," 1935 was the "Rally of Freedom," 1936 the "Rally for Honor and Freedom," 1937 the "Rally in Honor of Work," and 1938 the "Rally of Greater Germany." The Party Week of September 1939 would have been devoted to peace, but it was canceled, and the hundreds of trains prepared for it were used for the mobilization of the army for World War II.

In autumn, the Harvest Thanksgiving Day on 1 October was a tribute to the German farmers, emphasizing the racist myth of *Blubo* (blood and soil), with an impressive celebrations, romantic ceremonies and parades in ancient folk costumes.

November 4 was the *Totengedenktag*, the Day of Homage to the Dead.

On 9 November somber pageantry lent mythical status to the "blood baptism," the commemoration of the anniversary of the abortive 1923 Beer-Hall Putsch in Munich. The march to the Feldherrnhalle was repeated in the precise order of 1923, along a route flanked by pylons of burning torches, with funeral music, tolling bells, and the slow recital of the names of the sixteen martyrs of the party who were honored for their self-sacrifice for the Nazi cause. This had a symbolic significance too: commemoration of the past with an eye on the future. The solemn, kitschy commemoration was broadcast over the whole country.

December 21 (*Yule*, winter solstice) was a celebration designed to replace the Christian festivals. In spite of the Nazis' efforts, it did not, however, supplant the traditional Christmas (with fir tree and offering of presents) and Sylvester Eve (New Year). As Christian holidays were too deeply ingrained, summer and winter solstices were treated with little reverence.

The Nazis also revived the *Althing*, an old Germanic institution, as a support for their ideology. The Viking *Althing* was originally a tribal assembly of free men, both a kind of parliament and a court of justice. Under the Nazis the custom was replaced by a powerful mixture of pagan romanticism, militarism and naïve patriotism to build up recruits for Hitler's war machine. The *Althing* became merely a theatrical show held in rudimentary natural theaters, incorporating hilly slopes and ancient ruins. The shows included music and songs, martyrs' commemoration, military tattoos, pagan oratorios, exhibitions of sport and horsemanship, circus acts and reconstructed battle scenes. Even the Germanic-oriented SS treated these ridiculous and showy occasions with irreverence.

Music

Music had always been (and still is) very vivid in Germany, and her contribution in the past had won the admiration of the whole world. However music in Germany underwent almost a total eclipse when the Third Reich was established. Hitler, the failed Austrian painter and architect manqué, was finally able to dictate German culture. The Nazis applied their policy of *Gleichschaltung* (coordination) to music and the official Nazi line was expressed through the medium of the Reich Chamber of Music. The glittering, flourishing and experimental music of the Weimar period was replaced by music inspired by tradition and folklore. American jazz (scornfully regarded as "Negro music"), experimental, modern and atonal music were banned, and German composers of Jewish origin—considered "degenerate" (such as Gustav Mahler)—were forbidden. In an effort to create a distinguished National Socialist style for the youth, a German Song Week was instituted in May 1934 and a Music School was created in Berlin in 1936. This was followed by another school founded at Weimar in 1937 and another at Graz in 1939. Music pupils studied not only German classical and traditional music by officially "Aryan" composers, but also popular theater, singing, mime, instrumental music, and conducting. Of course these studies were augmented by sports, political education and National Socialist ideology. In 1937, the music schools had turned out some 60,000 musicians. Graduates became musicians and bandmasters in the HJ *Musikeinheiten* (music units). A *Spielmannzug* (marching band) was usually composed of twenty-four musicians wearing a traditional form of detachable shoulder ornamentation known as *Schwalbennester* (swallows' nests). Musicians—directed by a *Musikführer* (bandmaster)—played martial and "heroic" tunes with fife, drum and trumpet to give rhythm and bolster courage when the troops were marching. The Hitler Jugend had choirs singing patriotic, sentimental and political songs characterized by heavy tunes and bellicose lyrics. Songs were popular at party and official meetings, as well as throughout daily life. The organization had also more elaborate orchestras performing live concerts in public squares and theaters. In 1943, there were 1,200 HJ bands and orchestras totaling some 36,000 young musicians. Concerts inside Germany were well attended, but the listeners had to be content with an excess of Wagner (Hitler's favorite composer), and the absence of "degenerate" swing and jazz, which particularly in France and Holland became symbolic resistance music.

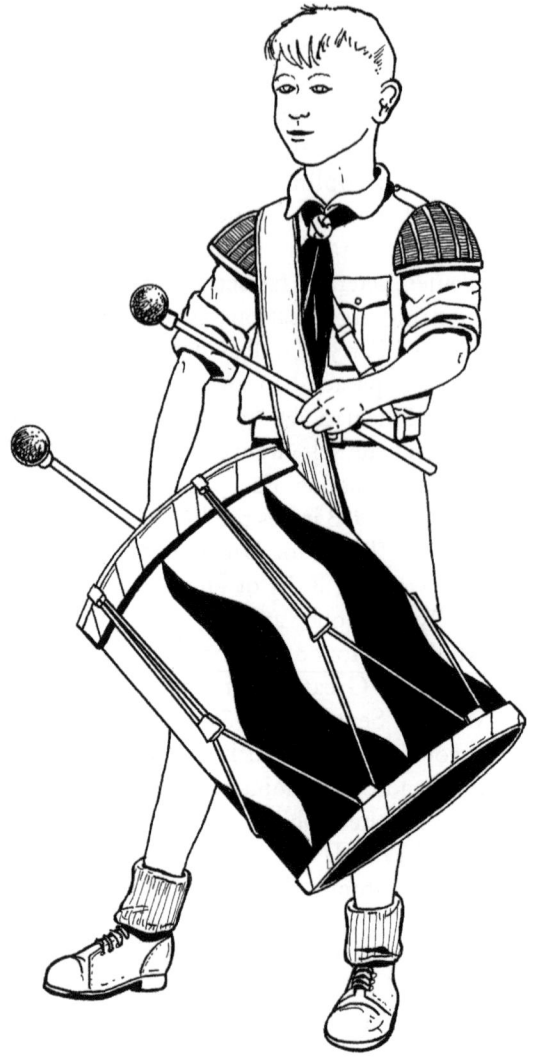

Junior HJ drummer boy

Publications

The Hitler Jugend had several monthly and weekly publications, including the *Sturmjugend* (Storm Youth), *Hitler-Jugend-Zeitung* (Hitler Youth Newspaper), *Junge Front* (Young Front), *Deutschen Jugendnachrichten* (News of the German Youth), *Der Pimpf* (for the junior DJ members, age 10 to 14), *Das deutsche Mädel* (a paper for BdM girls), *Junge Welt* (Young World, for the junior girls), *Wille und Macht* (Will and Power, for the HJ leadership), *Das Junge Deutschland*

(Young Germany, a publication of the social service of the HJ specializing in labor) and *Junge Dorfgemeinschaft* (Young Villagers, intended for young peasants). In 1930, Kurt Gruber created his own publishing company, the *Jungfront Verlag*, which published numerous newspapers, weekly magazines, various Nazi literary works, and countless *Handbücher* (manuals and handbooks) intended for youths, parents and educators. Von Schirach himself wrote a book, *Die Hitler Jugend: Idee und Gestalt* (The Hitler Youth: Idea and Form) published in Berlin in 1934. The book was not a success and was described by his press agent Günther Kaufmann in 1941 as being entirely "outdated in all sections." Schirach himself was not interested in a new edition, because in his own words, "various fundamental questions concerning education will have to be thoroughly looked into after the end of the war."

Keenly aware of radio's propaganda potential, the Nazis broadcast programs especially intended for youth every Wednesday at 8:15 P.M. For this purpose a *Reichsfunkschule* (a school for the training of HJ broadcast personnel) was created in December 1934 in Göttingen. The radio program consisted of martial music, news for young people, and plays based on Germany's past, with the aim of instilling love of heroism and contempt for weakness.

Front page of Der Aufmarsch *(Marching Forward) newspaper for German youths. The* Aufmarsch *was a monthly paper published by the Association of the German National-Socialist Schoolboys founded in November 1929 in Hamburg by Adrian von Renteln.*

Health and hygiene

The HJ training also included an almost obsessive emphasis on health, vigor and hygiene. Ten commandments were issued by the Reich physician to the HJ in 1939, the "Year of Hygienic Duty":

1. Your body belongs to your nation, to which you owe your existence, and you are responsible for your body.
2. Always keep yourself clean and exercise your body. Light, air and water can help you in this.
3. Look after your teeth. Strong and healthy teeth are a source of pride.
4. Eat plenty of raw fruit, uncooked greens and vegetables, first washing them thoroughly in clean water. Fruit contains valuable nutrients which cooking eliminates.
5. Drink fruit juice. Leave coffee to the coffee addicts. You do not need it.
6. Shun alcohol and nicotine. They are poisons which impair your development and capacity to work.
7. Take physical exercise. It will make you healthy and hardy.
8. Sleep at least nine hours every night.

9. Practice first aid for use in accidents. It can help you save your comrades' lives.
10. All your activities are governed by this slogan: Your duty is to be healthy!

These injunctions doubtless applied with special force to girls. Particularly the ninth commandment indicated a sphere of activity admirably suited—according to Nazi ideology—to the "natural" feminine disposition. The Hitler Youth trained 40,000 budding field surgeons and 35,000 girl medical orderlies. Seventeen-year-old BdM girls had to do twelve two-hour classes in nursing and hygiene, after which the best of them could join the Health Service Troop and were entitled to wear, in addition to their uniform, a white kerchief and a white apron adorned with the symbolic *Leben rune* (rune of life).

Youth exchanges

Before 1933 many German youth freely traveled abroad—to Scandinavia, France and Britain, for example—the only limitation being personal budget. After the seizure of power by the Nazis, voyages abroad were forbidden. Hitler wanted German young people isolated, as travel and unsupervised tourism could expose them to what he regarded as bad influences. The only foreign countries where visits were allowed were other dictatorships, like Mussolini's Fascist Italy and Franco's Spain. Relations with European democratic countries were carefully supervised by several Nazi agencies which made contact and organized cultural and political exchanges with foreign "friends." Delegations of young foreign pro-Nazi guests—including adult artists and intellectuals—were invited to Germany and shown the achievements of the new regime. Supervision of cultural exchanges with France, for example, were done by a young enthusiastic, francophile and French-speaking art teacher, named Otto Abetz (1903–1958). After the defeat of France in 1940, Abetz became German ambassador in occupied French territories.

Winter Relief and Agricultural Service

Winterhilfswerk

Before and during the war, the Hitler Jugend was an important component of Winterhilfswerk. *Winterhilfswerk* (WHW—Winter Help) was the official German winter relief organization. Its socialistic aspect struck a chord among many of the poorer Germans who were recipients of the charity campaign. The WHW, launched in the winter of 1933-34—was organized on an annual basis by the *Nationalsozialistische Volkswohlfahrt* (NSV—Nazi People's Welfare Organization). As already described above, the NSV—headed by *SS Gruppenführer* Erich Hilgenfeldt—was devoted to the welfare of party members and their families, especially mothers and juveniles. *Winterhilfswerk* was supported by members of the NSDAP, Hitler Jugend and DAF, as well as by prominent artists, functionaries, and athletes, with the aim of collecting money, food, shoes, blankets, warm clothing and other items for the poorest Germans. With the help of voluntary contributions, the Nazis provided hot meals, warm clothes and comfort for the needy. The Jews and "asocials" were excluded from the benefits of this organization. In winter 1935-36, the WHW collected some 31 million Reichsmarks. In 1937, helping *Winterhilfswerk* was made compulsory. Every worker had to pay a special winter tax (10 to 15 percent of one's salary) from October to March. During the war, the *Kriegs-winterhilfswerk* (KWHW—wartime winter relief organization) continued the activities, and collected donations for soldiers at the front, widows, civilian victims, and those made homeless by Allied air bombardments.

Landdienst

The Nazis had a strong desire that urban youth would commune with the rural folk. Popular slogans were "Back to the countryside!" and "Nature never lies!" In addition to their other activities, Hitler Jugend members were required to help with the harvest each year. Combining the ideologically desirable and the economically useful, this was intended to reduce urban youth unemployment, to harden them, and to ease the rural labor shortage. Some students who had completed their elementary education were encouraged to volunteer for a nine-month stretch in the *Landdienst* (agricultural service), living in camps, working in the morning, and receiving lessons in Nazi ideology in the afternoon. In peacetime this program was concerned with helping to slow the drift of population away from the country into the large, industrialized cities. The agricultural service was based on the theories developed by the *Bund der Artamenen* (Artaman League). As already described, these were a group of young fanatics who believed in the back-to-the-soil movement and the creation of a "racially pure" Germanic peasant class. Members of the *Landdienst* were submitted to a frugal and spartan vegetarian life. They had to abstain from alcohol and tobacco and face up to strict discipline and hard work. It was no easy life. The farm camps were usually military-style barracks with primitive washing and toilet facilities, and the work could be unremittingly hard. A typical day might have looked like this:

5:30—rise
6:00—work in the fields
8:00—breakfast
8:30—work in the fields
Noon—lunch
1:00—political lecture
2:00—sports drill
4:00—political class
5:00—household work
6:00—break
6:30—recreation
7:30—political instruction
8:30—supper
9:00—evening singing with bonfire
9:30—lights out

The youngsters at these camps were allowed no vacations, no leave, no parental visits and no religious services. Originally the *Landdienst* was a small branch of the HJ. In 1935 it totaled only 500 members. In 1936 it involved 6,600 teenagers. In September 1939, there were 11,750 boys and 14,000 girls working for the *Landdienst*. The subjection to authoritarian rule and the exploitation of cheap youth labor were justified by the National Socialist leadership with the claim that everyone's welfare was at stake. Concern with individual needs was regarded as synonymous with irresponsibility. The *Landdienst* was also an important Nazi means of penetration into the peasant world and a way to propagate their ideology in the countryside. At first the German peasantry reacted coolly to the massive arrival of unskilled youth over the land, but their reluctance quickly faded away as they realized the benefit they could get out of the free labor offered by the Nazi state. Volunteers of the *Landdienst* also learned trades, planted trees and flowers in national parks, maintained trails in forests and mountains, and removed snow in winter.

During the war, the *Landdienst* was tasked with the "Germanization" of conquered territories in the East, in Poland and Russia. It was intended to recruit "racially suitable" Germans to colonize wide areas.

Cuff-title of the **HJ Landdienst** *(Agricultural Service)*

The Slavic populations were to be enslaved. This ambitious and inhumane project—which meant death and slavery for millions of people—was taken seriously and widely supported by Heinrich Himmler's SS. The aim was to create an area of "Aryan" farmers, working the land and also providing a defensive buffer zone between Germany and the East.

Conflicts at Home

Some parents harbored doubts about the way their children were treated in the Hitler Jugend. Far from promoting universal health and happiness, the rigorous activities performed by HJ members damaged their health and interfered with their education. Excessive hard work and discipline caused an increase in physical and psychological ailments among the young. Complaints ranged from anxiety brought on by ceaseless bullying to disorders of the feet caused by carrying burdens that were too heavy on marches that were too long.

Generational conflicts did not always produce open resistance, because people were caught in an ideological trap, but a child's participation in the HJ could create tension at home. Clashes between parents and children were—and still are—normal phenomena linked with personality development, but in Nazi Germany they were often aggravated by the "youth leads youth" principle of the HJ. The millions of Germans who had experienced World War I, revolution, inflation, misery, and social confusion, and who had supported Hitler—in whom they hoped to find a solution—were in for a grim surprise. A large majority, attracted like a magnet to the Führer, recognized that achievements had been made with regular pay, reduction of inflation and employment, and a *Heimat* (fatherland) that was again strong, prosperous, respected and influential. Beyond the rapture, however, lay the reality of the Nazi order—a sweeping social revolution that used terror to impose rigid standards of behavior, not only in schools, workplaces and churches but also within the home. From the start, Hitler made it quite clear that no one had any further claim to a private life. The citizens of the Third Reich soon found themselves living in an eerie world of watchers and watched. Neighbors were set against neighbors, wives against husbands, children against parents. Until the end of the Nazi regime in 1945, countless victims of denunciation—merely on suspicion of having committed crimes, offenses or indecencies against the regime, and without ever being brought to trial—were taken into custody, where officials had the right under the law to extract confessions by intimidation, psychological pressure, blackmail, beating and torture. The terrified prisoner could then be carted off to a concentration camp and never be seen again, in accordance with the Nazis' prophylactic methods of repression.

For millions of children, the enthusiasm for the Hitler Youth movement canceled out all other interests. Even when church groups or parents pleaded to them to keep away, they were captured by the uniforms, the songs, the fife and drums, and the example of their peers. The Hitler Youth members lived more and more with their comrades, and they were gradually weaned from their families. In fact the Nazis planned to incorporate all boys and girls by the age of six in children's groups affiliated with the Women's Association. The peaceful phase of the Third Reich proved too short to allow this plan to be put into effect. In the long term, the Nazis intended to reduce the role of parents to their unavoidable biological function. Relegated to the background, parents had often trouble keeping their brown-shirted sons and daughters in line. Some parents who opposed or were not committed to the regime tried to discourage their youngsters from joining the organization, and the generation gap became a battleground in some families. It was difficult—and sometimes dangerous—to forbid a child to do what many children were doing, or to refuse a child the uniform that others so gladly wore. Dissident parents could not safely ignore their youngsters' idolatrous demands to be good Nazis. Conflicts at home were aggravated by the emphasis on authority which the Nazi totalitarian state delegated to the youth. HJ members were systematically turned against their parents. They were encouraged to criticize the conventions of their parents' generation and think of themselves as the hope of the future. "Youth must be led by youth" and "Youth is always right" were slogans frequently used. The Nazis' appeal to youth led to generation problems, as new National Socialist structures replaced values based around the family. Boys and girls of the HJ carried their new confidence and belief into the home and challenged traditional notions of parental control. This could result in conflicts within the household as loyalty to the Führer clashed with the traditional structures of the older generation. Many families were still marked with love, affection and respect, but in many homes the trust between parents and children was severely disrupted. The new creed was accepted with passive resignation and silent anger. For many fathers and mothers, caution and silence replaced candor and guidance. Parents no longer ventured to speak openly in front of their children. The tracking down of subversives and the maintenance of the Nazis' iron grip on the population unleashed a series of forces which sucked children into the most odious deed. Denunciation of parents by their own children to the authorities became one of Nazism's most shocking by-products.

Indoctrination and Discipline

Hitler believed that the survival of his Third Reich for a thousand years depended upon the education and indoctrination of the youth. As we have seen, all non–Nazi youth organizations had ceased to exist. Rival groups had been eliminated by force, fear, and law, but the triumph of the Hitler Jugend left the Führer unsatisfied. German youths had to be radically transformed ideologically by strict indoctrination and discipline.

The main purpose of the HJ was to inculcate discipline and good order in general and to submit young people to strict National Socialist schooling. Liberalism was a thing of the past and so were the days when all could do as they pleased. The order of the day was this: "Believe! Obey! Fight!" Indoctrination, as a long-term process, could be most effectively applied to Germany's youth. Children are, on the whole, vulnerable, malleable and naïve. They are easily fooled, conformist, committed, enthusiastic, spontaneous, and eager to participate in something heroic, great and exciting. Appealing to passion more than to reason, the Nazi system could easily exploit these youthful qualities. As already pointed out, young people who became teenagers after 1936 had no memories of the pre–Nazi days and went through a schooling process steeped in National Socialism. Those who came to adolescence during World War II experienced the most extreme and brutal form of Nazism: conscription and war. Their minds were led step by step through an intensive drill to accept Nazi principles with the aim of turning them into future soldiers and party technocrats. A whole generation of children were fooled by the state and deceived by indoctrination.

During the Third Reich period, the household lost its dominant role in the rearing and training of children. The school became an instrument for the dissemination of racist propaganda, helped to win young minds for Nazism and made children receptive to militaristic practices. Indoctrination through a revised school curriculum was complemented and reinforced by mobilization through the Hitler Youth movement. The organization conveyed ideals that extended beyond the terms of reference of the traditional upbringing. The HJ was a mainstay of the Nazi regime and its influence became all-persuasive in Germany. It was an alternative center of authority, a serious rival to the traditional home, church and school. The HJ was intended to serve as a counter-authoritarian sanctuary; involvement in its activities offered the promise of making a name for oneself, but also growing pressure toward uniformity. This latter feature grew stronger as the Hitler Jugend became more bureaucratic, as its leadership corps grew older, and as the use of coercion to draw remaining young people into the organization increased.

The HJ was a huge organization comprising almost 60 percent of German youth. Discipline, hierarchy, physical training and indoctrination were strictly observed and conducted by Hitler Jugend staff who were trained in a school created for this purpose in Potsdam. By the end of 1933 there were twenty-two schools forming the leadership cadre of the youth organization. In 1935, this had increased to thirty training centers. A young man who desired become a *Gebietsführer* (district leader) had to go through a three-week training. Of the 170 hours of the course, 105 were devoted to *körperliche Ertüchtigung* (physical training, sport, exercises and shooting), and 65 to *weltanschaulichen Schulung* (racial, cultural and Germanic indoctrination).

More than the rest of the German citizens, the boys and girls of the Hitler Youth were subject to a constant flow of indoctrination from the propaganda ministry directed by Josef Goebbels and from the Nazi Party through their officers. Leaders of the HJ totally endorsed the political and ideological aspects of Nazism. HJ-DJ boys and BdM-JM girls had to attend *Heimabende*, a meeting every Wednesday evening for political, racial and ideological indoctrination— and singing. They were politically programmed with distorted theories of Germanic civilization and *Lebensraum*; taught to obey orders blindly, to cultivate soldierly virtues and the love of heroism; instilled with the love of toughness, silence, loyalty and sacrifice; and exhorted to be proud of their remote ancestors' heritage. Great emphasis was put on rituals, racist and anti–Semitic theories, biological notions of vitality, hero worship, the hard-headed dogma of *raison d'état*, the need for the unscrupulous use of force, and the obligation to be brutal and contemptuous of weakness. Great stress was put on the danger of Bolshevism and the rottenness of capitalist, plutocratic democracies and how they wished to keep Germany down. The Hitler Youth taught a whole generation of Germans to defy danger and to glory in the idea of dying heroically in battle. War was seen as normal, violence was legitimated. Hitler's foreign-policy achievements from 1936 to 1939 had accustomed the Germans to regard the combination of violent posturing, risk-taking, and assertion of their "legal right" to wipe out the "shame of Versailles" as a recipe for success. Part of this psychological conditioning was imposed at the huge annual rallies at Nuremberg where tens of thousands marched with banners and music in review before Hitler himself. The spirit of sacrifice was fostered during nighttime neo-pagan ceremonies, verses celebrating death in combat, patriotic songs, and even mock funerals for future "fallen comrades." All morality and intelligence were propagandized out.

Few young people had read Hitler's book, *Mein Kampf*. Some quoted from the book, but easy mottos and simple slogans were constantly repeated. For the boys these included: "Live faithfully, fight bravely, and die laughing," "We were born to die for Germany," "You are nothing, your folk is everything," and "God is struggle and struggle is our blood, and this is why we were born." The popular slogan *"Heute Deutsch-*

land, morgen die Welt" (today Germany, tomorrow the world) illustrated the Nazi drive for political power and world domination. As for the young girls they were always told, "Be faithful, be pure, be German!"

Violence was not an accidental accompaniment to Nazism, it was central to it. National Socialism was presented as an unceasing struggle, a combat against Germany's enemies both internal and external. It was essentially organized hatred, it drew its power and inspiration from the desire to destroy. Hitler was a man at war, a man of hate; his language was the language of conflict. Everything was refracted through the prism of his warlike and racist way of thinking. Members of the Hitler Jugend were therefore exhorted over and over to uphold Nazi Germany's "honor"—as defined by Hitler. Ideological lectures were intended to increase motivation so that boys and girls would know for whom, what and why they were fighting. Young men and women, vulnerable to indoctrination, were encouraged not only to be aggressive, strong and decisive but also to repress all human feeling, to regard Jews and Slavs as *Untermenschen* (subhumans), to feel hatred and to show no pity toward those unworthy enemies.

As young as ten years old, all boys and girls had to swear a pledge of allegiance which was taken very seriously: "*Ich verspreche, in der Hitler-Jugend allezeit meine Pflicht zu tun in Liebe und Treue zum Führer und zu unserer Fahne. So wahr mir Gott helfe.*" (I swear, in the Hitler Youth, always to do my duty with love and loyalty, for the Führer and our flag. So help me God.) There was also an oath which went as follows: "In the presence of this blood banner which represents our Führer, I swear to devote all my energies and my strength to the savior of our country, Adolf Hitler. I am willing and ready to give up my life for him, so help me God." This was the revival of the ancient *Fahneneid*, the medieval soldier's traditional oath, passed down from the knights, which bound warriors to the German emperor. The oath was repeated by HJ members with their right hands raised and their left hands placed on the unit flag. The oath, sworn not to Germany but personally to the Führer, illustrated the pitilessness of the demands upon themselves and others, duty-bound to spare neither their own blood nor that of others.

The heavy HJ training and indoctrination produced a new type of children. From the same mold they emerged as unquestioning automata, physically fit sponges for the official ideology. The HJ boys and girls regarded mothers' darlings and "losers" as poor specimens. They were brainwashed to feel superior, deprived of criticism, made always to obey and never ask questions. The evil Nazi indoctrination implanted new norms of behavior into the young Germans. Teenagers of the HJ were encouraged to denounce their parents or neighbors who listened to enemy broadcasts or spoke against the regime, for example. The indoctrination robbed them of their moral powers of judgment and replaced them with coldheartedness, cruelty, impatience and an excessive, narrow, group egoism. Training and indoctrination contributed in no small measure to the loyal and exclusive comradeship but also to phenomenal cruelty, scorn of enemy lives, and acceptance of one's own sacrifice. As a result there was a feeling of strong and proud *esprit de corps*, along with the arrogant sense of superiority. The children of the Hitler Youth lived in a world far removed from reality. They were always under a strict code of behavior which forbade them any overbearing and inflammatory attitudes toward their leaders but which allowed the worst ruthlessness toward their "enemies." They were instilled with a special arrogance. Repeatedly told that they were the best of the best and upholders of Germany's future, they felt themselves members of a top-class warrior caste or *Sippe* (tribe). They were aware of their worth, with confidence and soaring self-esteem. They often tended to ignore non-members, saw other "common" children as people of no consequence, and even looked down on priests, foremen, teachers and their own parents. Being a member of the organization often provided the chance to engage, sometimes quite aggressively, in conflict with these traditional figures of authority.

The Führer's purpose was to create a violently active, dominating, brutal youth intended to be indifferent to pain, merciless and without weakness. "Knowledge would spoil my young people," Hitler said. "I prefer that they learn only what they pick up by following their own play instinct. But they must learn self-control. I will have them master the fear of death through the most difficult trials. That is the heroic stage of youth. Out of it will grow the stage of the free man, a human being who is the measure and center of the world." And further: "The German youth must learn to do without, to endure criticism and injustice, to be reliable, discreet, decent, and loyal."

The system of indoctrination was perfect: the brainwashing actually started in the cradle. From childhood onward, HJ members were drilled in toughness and blind obedience. The Hitler Youth movement was based on aggressive rivalry between members but discipline was severe. It was meted out by leaders little older than the members. A common spectacle was a twelve-year-old leader bawling out ten-year-old cubs and driving them all over the school playground and meadows. The slightest signs of recalcitrance, any attitude of rational criticism, the slightest faults with the uniform, the slightest lateness on parade, all were punished with extra pointless drills or the interdiction of wearing medals and uniform, or a ban on participating in activities, for example. One of the heaviest penalties, so it was thought, was permanent expulsion from the group.

Discipline and "honor" were only one side of the coin. In many cases HJ members regarded each other as rivals and competitors. The emphasis was on winning at any cost, to be the best physically, the strongest and the most determined. In this context of aggressive competition, members behaved even more drastically in order to show how good and dedicated to Hitler's cause they were. The stricter or meaner the leaders were, the worse the Hitler Youth groups behaved. It was much like a "follow the leader" type of organization. The very name of the Hitler Youth suggests that they existed to follow in Hitler's footsteps and to carry out his ideas as well as his commands.

Thus from the age of ten the young German was subjected to a continual obsessive barrage of Nazi propaganda and ideology. From this tender age, when the personality is easy to mold, the *Führerprinzip* was implanted in young brains as absolute dogma. Indoctrination allowed a human being to be reduced to a state of total subordination, and dehumanization provided an excellent grounding in the Hitlerian creed. In order that a handful of professional murderers might reign over a whole nation and impose its will upon it, children had to be perverted from infancy. Most of the rank and file of the SS, people who were to make all of Europe tremble and who caused the suffering and death of millions, were between 6 and 14 at the time Hitler came to power. All had been subjected to Nazi education from early youth and no one had given them a chance to question the values of these teachings.

Führer worship

The Nazi propaganda created a larger-than-life image of the Führer, both as an idol endowed with superhuman qualities with revolutionary plans, and as a moderate man upholding traditional virtues and guaranteeing peace—at least until 1939. The personality cult was designed deliberately to appeal to the diseased side of the human psyche, above all to the capacity for resentment. It struck a chord with people's widespread disillusionment with the institutions, parties and leaders of the Weimar Republic, and the chameleon Hitler seemed to offer something different to each class of society and pulled them all together with the uniqueness of his own vision for the future. A cluster of myths was created around the leader. Hitler was depicted to his people as a teetotaler, vegetarian, nonsmoker, and asexual bachelor, as a man without human ties of love and friendship, a man with a divine mission using all his energy and skills for the good of Germany. This was intended to appeal to the German people's yearning for greatness.

Joseph Goebbels, minister for public enlightenment and propaganda, led the campaign of national devotion, declaring, "We are witnessing the greatest miracle in history. A genius is building a new world!" And: "He alone is never mistaken. He is always right. He is always like a great star above us."

Other high-ranking Nazi leaders praised their Führer. The deranged Rudolf Hess spoke of his master in biblical terms, approaching hysteria: "And then unto us was born a child in Braunau.... Whatever he does is necessary ... whatever he does is successful. Clearly the Führer has divine blessing!"

Robert Ley, head of the State Labor Service, claimed: "The Lord God has sent us Adolf Hitler!"

Special efforts were made to win the attention of children who were encouraged to worship the Führer. To the HJ, Hitler was presented as the supreme father, an idol, a kind of god. There were Hitler Youth prayers modeled after church prayers:

> Adolf Hitler, you are our great Führer.
> Thy name makes the enemy tremble.
> Thy Third Reich comes, thy will alone is law upon the earth.
> Let us hear daily thy voice and order us by thy leadership, for we will obey to the end and even with our lives.
> We praise thee! Heil Hitler!

> Führer, my Führer, given me by God,
> protect and preserve my life for long.
> You saved Germany in time of need.
> I thank you for my daily bread.
> Be with me for a long time, do not leave me,
> Führer, my Führer, my faith, my light,
> Hail to my Führer!

The leader Baldur von Schirach had sayings of praise which were constantly repeated:

> We do not need intellectual leaders who create new ideas, because the superimposing leader of all *desires of* youth is Adolf Hitler.
> *Your name*, my Führer, is the happiness of youth, your name, my Führer, is for us everlasting life.
> He who serves Adolf Hitler, the Führer, serves Germany, and whoever serves Germany, serves God.

World War II added a new dimension to the Hitler worship. Goebbels extolled the Führer as the greatest and most genius strategist of all time. "*Hitler ist der Sieg!*" (Hitler is victory) was a popular slogan. In this atmosphere of adulation, the most banal clichés, the most ridiculous platitudes, and the most grotesque errors of judgment, if uttered by Adolf Hitler, were accepted as the words of inspired genius.

The impact of indoctrination and Hitler worship is very difficult to evaluate. There were great believers in order, authority, the Führer principle, and a great Germany. There was racial hatred, but Hitler's regime was certainly no sudden break in the continuity of German history, nor was anti-Semitism thinkable without the different kind of anti-Semitism that preceded it. The sources of Nazism were deeply rooted, and could be traced far back in German history. There were convinced Nazis in the Hitler Youth, but were all members passionate and fanatical? Since by definition, young people are inexperienced, naive and easily manipulated, may we admit that their responsibility was limited by pressure, immaturity and ignorance? Perhaps a majority of the HJ members—like the German people in general—muddled along somewhere midway between the devil and the deep waters. Probably a fair number of them supported Hitler as long as the going was good. They were jubilant during the time of the great victories of the Wehrmacht; they became uneasy and despondent when the tide turned; and by 1944 many thought it was senseless to prolong the war, though they obeyed orders as mechanically as ever. Within those limits there was a vast variety of attitudes, and within these attitudes doubtless as many nuances as individuals. In absence of statistics these questions must be left open to discussion.

Herbert Norkus and *Hitlerjunge Quex*

Before the seizure of power by the Nazis in 1933, the principal task of the HJ (and that of the SA) was to impress the public by ostentatious parades through the streets of big cities, but the youth movement also frequently engaged in street fights in which weapons were used. Opponents were attacked and sometimes killed in these brawls, which occasioned some casualties among the Hitler Jugend themselves. The cult of death was part of the Nazi ideology and was instilled in the youth. This cult was illustrated by several shrines. One of these was a street in Berlin where a 15-year-old member of the HJ, Herbert Norkus, had been stabbed to death on 24 January 1932. Norkus was a member of the HJ in Wedding, a suburb of Berlin held by communists, and while posting Nazi placards he was killed by them. Amid memorial wreaths and torches, the Reich youth leader Baldur von Schirach delivered a radio address at Norkus's funeral. Herbert Norkus became a hero of the Nazi cause, an example for other members, and his tragic fate was the inspiration for the propaganda film *Hitlerjunge Quex*, one of the first Nazi films. There were many attempts at making an idealized portrait of Nazi youth, and between 1933 and 1939 about forty films especially intended for a youth audience were produced. *Hitlerjunge Quex* was a novel written by Karl Alois Schenzinger, which was serialized in the Nazi newspaper *Völkischer Beobachter*. A film with the same title, based on the book, was directed by Hans Steinhoff, with the young actor Jürghen Ohlsen in the main role. Both novel and film were based on the story of Herbert Norkus, with the aim being to glorify young people's spirit of sacrifice for Nazi ideals. The film, made at a time when the Nazi dictatorship was not yet firmly consolidated in 1933, is interesting as a document of the prevailing mood of the time, showing Nazi readiness to integrate communists into the national community.

Hitlerjunge Quex was the story of a blond, blue-eyed boy, Heini, who was drawn by his father into Young Communist activities. What he saw of them (drunkenness, disorderliness, boorishness) disgusted him, and Heini wished to enter the clean and healthy ranks of the Hitler Youth. By contrast they were sympathetic, friendly, strong, determined, and forward-looking. Heini was rejected from membership, however, because the Nazis suspected him of being a communist infiltrator. The rejection tormented him as it would any "good" Nazi. Meanwhile, his mother, totally unable to cope in the confusion and hardship of the Weimar Republic, has committed suicide. Heini is finally accepted in the Hitler Jugend where he earns the nickname *Quex* (quicksilver) for his readiness to undertake the most dangerous missions. He goes to distribute pamphlets in a communist-dominated part of the city, is attacked and badly wounded by the Reds. Found by his comrades, Heini dies a martyr of the Nazi cause, whispering the first words of the Nazi Youth song: "Our flag is fluttering before us." Quex dies while seeing a vision of the future—thousands marching in endless procession. His final apotheosis became a Nazi film cliché, with his figure superimposed upon swastika flags and a marching song booming across the soundtrack:

> For Hitler we march through night and dread
> With the flag of youth for freedom and bread
> And the flag leads us into eternity.
> Yes, the flag means more than being dead!

In *Hitlerjunge Quex*—and all other vibrant, passionate, emotional, lyrical, and kitsch Nazi propaganda films—the message was clear: "*Wir sind opferbereit*" (we are ready for sacrifice). Death was a small price to pay for the love of Hitler. One had, at all times, to be ready to sacrifice everything, including parents, relatives, friends and oneself, for the Nazi movement.

Book Burning and *Kristallnacht*

Not surprisingly, the Hitler Youth participated in *Bücherverbrennung* (public book burning). A few months after the seizure of power, a campaign of *Säuberung* ("cleansing") of libraries, bookshops and universities was launched, by making lists of writers whose works were considered by the Nazis as "immoral" or "Jewish" or not in line with Nazi ideology. In fact, the eclectic assortment of forbidden writers had in common only their belief in the dignity of the free human spirit. About 12,400 books were forbidden. The interdiction was followed by public book burning on 10 May 1933 in Berlin and other cities of Germany. The books destroyed by fire included works by some of Germany's greatest authors and thinkers, such as Albert Einstein, Sigmund Freud, Ricarda Huch, Thomas and Heinrich Mann, Carl Zuckmayer, Anna Seghers, Stefan Zweig, and Alfred Kerr, to mention just a few. Foreign authors' books were also publicly burned, including works by Henri Barbusse, John Galsworthy, André Gide, Ernest Hemingway, Jack London, Marcel Proust and Emile Zola, again to mention only a few. These actions were organized by the ministry of propaganda, the *Nationalsozialistischen deutschen Studentenbund* (League of German Students) and the *Kampfbund für deutsche Kultur* (Combat League for the German Culture). They were carried out by students; HJ, SA, and SS members; and other Nazi sympathizers as a kind of public ceremony, with violent speeches denouncing "cultural decadence." The burning ceremonies were sanctioned by the presence of Joseph Goebbels who lauded the arsonists for destroying intellectualism and other "unworthy filth." Goebbels declared: "Today's ceremony is a symbolic act. It will teach the world that the basic morality of the November 1918 Republic has been destroyed forever. From this pile of ashes will rise the phoenix of a new spirit."

On November 7, 1938, in Paris, a young Jewish-Polish refugee murdered the secretary of the German Embassy. As retaliation, the Nazis ordered a night of terror in Germany, the so-called *Kristallnacht* (Night of Broken Glass) on 9 November 1938. Initiated and coordinated by propaganda minister Goebbels, *Kristallnacht* was a large-scale, anti–Semitic pogrom throughout Germany and Austria. With unrecorded savagery, the Nazis (including members of the HJ) sacked Jewish shops, looted Jewish homes, and set hundreds of synagogues on fire. Some hundred Jews were killed, 20,000 were carted off to concentration camps, and a large fine was imposed on the German Jewish community as indemnification. *Kristallnacht* was a first step on the road that would lead to the extermination camps and gas chambers of the "Final Solution."

Education in the Third Reich

Schools

As the Hitler Youth grew, its power and influence increased. It was a propaganda machine and its inculcation was now taking place also in schools. The education system had been nazified by the process of *Gleichschaltung*, applied after the seizure of power in January 1933. Since writing *Mein Kampf*, Hitler had never tired of stressing the evils of intellectual instruction and how vital it was to abolish he called "universal education." Certainly influenced by his own academic failure, the Führer of Germany had views on education which permeated all echelons of the Nazi hierarchy. All learning had to be subject to continuous supervision and selection, as—according to Hitler—knowledge was only an aid to life, not its central purpose. The role of school was reduced to basics—instruction in the alphabet and multiplication tables. Each stratum of society needed to learn what was necessary for its particular purposes, and nothing more. All education was to be under constant surveillance, with the broad mass of the lowest class receiving the "blessings of illiteracy." In each classroom in every school there was a picture of Hitler in the front, and the Nazi flag with swastika was also omnipresent.

Hitler was contemptuous of teachers, academicians, scholars, scientists and intellectuals whom he regarded as dangerous obstacles to the kind of compliant society he intended to build. After the Nazi takeover, the education system underwent an immediate and chilling change. The Führer wanted the youth of the Nazi state to be more virile and strong than intellectually developed.

From April 1934 until the end of the war in May 1945, the school system was headed by Wilhelm Bernhard Rust (1883–1945). After studying philosophy and classical philology, Rust became teacher and provincial *Oberlehrer* (schoolmaster). He had been an infantry lieutenant in World War I, during which he was severely wounded and granted the Iron Cross First Class. He joined the Nazi Party in 1922, was appointed *Gauleiter* (upper leader) of district Hannover-Braunschweig, and—for his steadfast loyalty to Hitler—promoted to Reich minister for science, art education and culture. The mentally disturbed Rust committed suicide in May 1945, but while alive he presided over the sabotage of Germany's intellectual life in the name of racial "purity." Schools and universities were reformed and purged of Jewish and democrat teachers, depriving Germany of famous scientists, Nobel Prize winners, and many other distinguished chemists, mathematicians, engineers and jurists. Teachers were encouraged to join the Nazi Party and all of them had to be members of the *Nationalsozialistische Lehrerbund* (NSLB—Nazi teacher league). The monolithic NSLB, formed in November 1935, rejected the democratic heritage of the Weimar regime, and subjected all teachers to strict Nazi Party control. It had a newspaper, *Der deutsche Erzieher* (German Educator) and took charge of services to the teaching profession. After 1938, teachers were indoctrinated at a special, compulsory, one-month training course of drills and lectures where they learned what knowledge to pass on the pupils. By 1939 the forty-one NSLB training camps had prepared 215,000 members for their educational tasks—these being spirit of militarism, paganism, anti-Semitism, and the cult of the perfect "Aryan" racial type—by means of ideological instruction, propaganda courses, conferences, group travel, paramilitary physical training and field sports. There was also the *Reichslehrerbund* (RLB—Reich Teachers' League), an organization of teachers devoted to the ideals of Nazism, carefully watched by high Nazi officials.

Nazi education was based on the sense of race and emphasized two essential ideas: the preparation to war for the boys and motherhood for the girls. The school curriculum for girls was based on the understanding that few of them would go on to university. Crafts and skills that would make girls good homemakers were encouraged: the course of study for girls was limited to German, history, singing, race study, domestic science, ideology, eugenics and health. The heavy emphasis on race and ideology points to the use of the schools as a major means of inculcating Nazi racial theory.

In Hitler's own words, HJ boys were required to be *"flink wie die Windhund, zähe wie Leder, und hard wie Kruppstahl"* (swift as greyhounds, tough as leather, and hard as Krupp steel). It was no accident that none of these adjectives referred to mental capacity. The rearing of healthy bodies was regarded as more important than gaining knowledge. Reflecting the regime's commitment to war, the time allotted to physical training was more than doubled. Sport received unprecedented attention from the elementary grades to the high schools. The number of weekly physical education classes was raised to three, then five. Boxing and field sports helped to vary the program. School reports attached more and more weight to athletic prowess. Sport was intended to instill team spirit and corporal vigor. It also had an ideological and selective function. Pupils with low performances and those with physical disabilities were barred from admission to centers of higher education.

Internally, school life was also subject to transformation. Corporal punishment was reintroduced; parent and pupil participation was abolished; the introduction of the Führer principle at all levels bolstered the power of head teachers at the expense of the rest; and much time was wasted with a politicized morning assembly and in observing the regime's self-celebratory calendar. For schoolchildren of "non–Aryan" origin (Jewish, Sinti and Roma people), attendance became a living nightmare; they were insulted and harassed by teachers and pupils, and subjected to malevolent injustices. Finally they were forbidden to attend German schools. Schools for backward and handicapped children were subject to particularly disgraceful treatment in the context of Nazi racial policy. They were submitted to funding cuts on the grounds of "false notions of humanity," and gradually abolished.

Education in the Third Reich was completely revised to meet the standard of dictatorship. Fewer hours were devoted to foreign history and literature, and the study of foreign languages was curtailed. Religious instruction was sharply reduced or simply abolished, school prayer was made optional or curtailed, and Christian symbols and images were banned from the classroom. All subjects were completely altered and infused with an extreme anti–Semitism, nationalist, ethnocentric and anti-democratic spirit. Some subjects were upgraded and converted for political purposes, and used to subliminally implant the racial-social values and goals of the Nazi regime in the minds of the young. Students, both male and female, were expected to know about their own history, as revised, however, by the Nazi system: this was generally reduced to a study of the Jews trying to undermine the great achievement of the Germans, World War I, the glory of the *Kampfzeit* (including the Munich Beer-Hall Putsch of 1923), the martyr Horst Wessel, the evils of the Weimar Republic, and the central role assigned to the Führer who had saved the nation from peril and servitude. Thin pamphlets recounting Hitler's life or other edifying tales replaced bulky expositions of history and literature. Biology emphasized Hitler's views on race, breeding, selection and heredity. This subject afforded the best opportunity to preach the supposed distinctions between human races, the German Nordic "superman," and the ignoble and hated *Untermenschen* (Slavs and Jews). Special anti-Semitic primers—such as *The Poisonous Mushroom* and *Trust No Fox*—were issued in order to instill an illogical but passionate hatred of Jews in the very young. The racial theory was simple, not based on science but repetition: Aryans = good; Jews = bad. This was backed in the eugenics classes by models which showed that, as in nature, harmful germs could corrupt the whole body, so, in society, the Jews damaged the whole people. Members of the *Jungvolk* were issued the *Schwertworte* (sword words), a highly compressed synopsis of Nazi dogma designed to cultivate German awareness and the militant approach. This had to be memorized and constantly repeated by the young boys and girls. In geography, ideological indoctrination continued by way of geopolitical and racial theories which justified Hitler's aggressive expansion policy. The *Deutschkunde*, the vague study of a supposedly specific superior German culture, was a required subject in all schools. It stressed Teutonic greatness, the culture-producing northern *Herrenvolk* (master race) opposed to the culture-destroying Jew. It urged familiarization with folk culture including music, literature, customs, heroic Nordic sagas and runes, and it encouraged respect for Aryan heritage and love for the fatherland.

As war was regarded as the most glorious and valiant demonstration of the nation's purpose, mathematics put the emphasis on conditioning for war service with questions revolving around weaponry, artillery trajectories or bomb dropping. A typical question from a lower-grade test: "An airplane flies at a rate of 240 km/h to a place at a distance of 210 km in order to drop a bomb; when may it be expected to return if the dropping of bombs takes 7.5 minutes?" Official math textbooks also contained ideological references such as calculations of the cost to produce lunatic asylums as opposed to workers' housing. On such matters a school manual entitled *Mathematik im Dienst der national-politischen Erziehung* (Mathematics at the Service of National Political Education) was written in 1936 by Adolf Dorner. The Study Group for German History Books and Educational Material was created in 1934, headed by Philip Bouhler (1899–1945) the same Bouhler who was also the chief of the notorious euthanasia program intended to murder the mentally ill.

Curricula of this type were, however, hard to devise, because the outlines of the Nazi ideology were vague and often contradictory. "Race," "blood," and supernatural

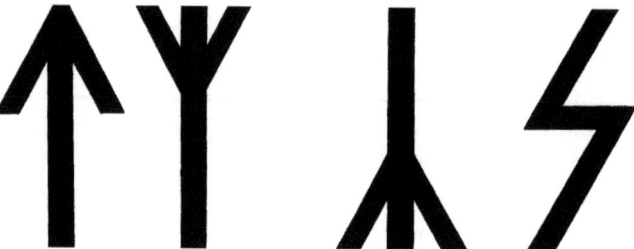

Runes. The runic alphabet was used by ancient German and Scandinavian tribes. Their literature was not very important but runes were carved on gravestones. The alphabet had 24 signs which were used from left to right. The characters also had a magic power and were used for divination and mystical practices. "Rûn" or "runar," in pre–Christian ancient Norwegian, means "mysterious or secret script." The Tyr-rune or Teiwaz (far left) was the battle rune symbolizing the pagan god of war, Tyr. The Leben rune or Algiz—letter Z (middle left), the symbol of life, was used as emblem for the SS **Lebensborn** *Society; it was also used on SS documents and graves to indicate date of birth. The Toten rune—upside-down letter Z (middle right) was the symbol of death, used on SS documents and graves to indicate date of death. The Sig rune or Sowelu (right), symbolic of victory, was the emblem used by the junior boys of the Hitler Jugend. Two Sig runes were the emblem of the* **Schutz-Staffeln** *(SS).*

forces were far too indistinct, but a few things were clear: the rejection of liberalism, materialism, scientific objectivity and intellectualism. The aim, too, was clear: the creation of fighting spirit and physical efficiency. Every individual had to regard himself or herself first and foremost as a component of the community. Passing the once-dreaded examinations became a matter of regurgitating Nazi biological theories, myths about the country's recent history, and other nonsense. The nazification of the school system was pursued beyond the classroom in the Hitler Jugend.

Universities

Universities, too, were purged of Jewish, liberal, and social-democrat personnel after 1933. These were harassed, dismissed, forced into exile and retirement, and even imprisoned. They were replaced by inexperienced and unqualified but reliable Nazi professors. This was a terrible loss for Germany which had held a position of world leadership in science. On the other hand, the purge was a gain for the free world as many scientists, such as Albert Einstein, were more or less forced into exile. University teachers were controlled by the *Nationalsozialistische-Dozentenbund* (NSDB—Nazi Lecturers League), a professional association of university lecturers designed to keep them in line with Nazi ideology. Students had to be members of the *Nationalsozialistischen deutschen Studentenbund* (NSDStB— Nazi Student League). The NSDStB, headed from 1928 to 1933 by Baldur von Schirach, was devoted to the furtherance of the Nazi way of life among students and indoctrination with National Socialist philosophy, and included physical training and military drills. The new curriculum emphasized the basic elements of Nazi ideology: racism, nationalism, Germanic culture, duty, loyalty to the Führer, soldierly spirit, obedience and discipline. Students were often required to put aside their books and spend months in military training and labor camps. With continual rounds of marches, rallies and other party activities, the desperate professors had to ease their requirements drastically in order to graduate sufficient numbers.

The educational reforms instituted by the Nazi regime had catastrophic results. The traditional German humanism was replaced with politico-racial institutions dedicated to militarism, racial hatred and aggressive expansionism. Many young people began to question the value of obtaining the once-prestigious *Abitur*—the graduation certificate needed to enter a university. By the late 1930s, many students were dropping out of school to work as craft apprentices or industrial trainees. Education—from elementary schools to the universities—became merely an appendage of the Propaganda Ministry, intellectual standards declined precipitously and a whole generation was the victim of odious indoctrination.

However, contradictions arose in what appeared at first to be a uniformed program of assimilation. Education experienced overlapping between administrative and party organs. Conflicts arose between Rust, von Schirach and Ley, and those were never fully resolved, with unfortunate side effects. The ideological content of Nazism remained too vague to function as a self-sufficient objective. It was indeed so vague that notions of racial and national arrogance were mixed up with traditional pedagogic humanism. The content of the curriculum was diluted by more traditional influences, the model of the front-line soldier-hero got mixed up with the idea of racial superiority, and profound agrarian German culture and backward-looking romanticism and tradition were mixed up with enthusiasm for modern high technology. Because of the confusion within the schools themselves, many teachers were unsatisfied. Many were probably more confused than deliberately uncooperative.

The Hitler Jugend encouraged challenges to more conservative forms of authority, and gave youths a sense of collective power. The youth movement, the family, and the educational system tended to diverge. This precipitated the disintegration of the home as a place of education, and the decline in the quality of education and school discipline, to an alarming extent. Teachers found themselves confronted with classrooms full of boys and girls who were more and more disobedient and reluctant to do what they were told, and who seemingly regarded intelligence itself as unimportant. Teachers had to subordinate themselves to the Hitler Youth, as it became dangerous for them to maintain discipline in the classroom, give orders or inflict punishment. Activities took precedence over any kind of formal education. Young HJ members were increasingly given time off regular schooling for meetings or attendance at party rallies. Every free moment was monopolized by the HJ. As there were important and exciting things to do outside the classrooms, students—treated as "chaps" instead of children—often missed class to take part in HJ activities. There was a widespread lack of any commitment and keenness, and an increasing of unmannerly behavior and laziness at school. As one student HJ leader said: "We have no respect for the clever monks in their quiet cells!" Things went so badly wrong, and clashes between arrogant HJ members and teachers became so widespread, that the Nazi state created the *Jugendschutzkammer* (Youth Protection Chamber), an official body responsible for adjudicating the rights of the young people of the HJ. The chamber handled such cases as teachers accused of face slapping as a disciplinary measure, for example. Teachers dared not object to the Nazi demand for conformity and its regime of terror. Even a benign objection or remark might be regarded as a crime against the regime. Hitler, who had never got over his poor showing at school, grabbed the opportunity to avenge himself on the teaching profession as a whole.

Special Nazi Schools

Hitler found his administrative, political and military leaders in the existing structures that he had taken over. But undoubtedly this situation was only transitional, as Hitler's Reich was intended to last for a thousand years. After a generation at most, the old leadership would have to be replaced by a new one. Whoever had the children, had the future. From the start, Nazi officials sensed that classical military academies, public schools and universities might not be the best training grounds for the future elite of the Third Reich. The Nazi regime needed military officers, police, civil servants, administrators, and political leaders who were both competent and uncontaminated by subversive ideas. Those qualities could best be inculcated in special schools. In the chaotic fashion of the new order, several agencies—the Reich Ministry of Education, the Nazi Party, the Hitler Jugend, the SA and the SS—vied for the honor of filling the bill. Rust, von Schirach and Himmler found themselves on opposing sides in the struggle to monopolize Nazi "elite" education. The result was two types of rival grammar schools and a romantic university outside the normal education system. These schools were exclusively reserved for boys and young men, as the Nazi Party did not accept women into its top leadership. These new types of schools created by the regime failed on the whole to achieve their aims; in the end—due to wartime conditions—they represented a poor alternative to the traditional education system. The boy who wanted to become a leader in the Nazi system no longer had to worry about his future. He knew that he could rise to the top of an elitist cult. His family usually did not object, out of fear, ambition, or ignorance. Many did not realize until it was too late that a dreadful Pied Piper had taken their boys away from them.

Napola

The first new kind of school was the so-called *Nationalpolitischen Erziehungsanstalten* (national political institutes), known as *NPEA* or "Napola." Created in April 1933, these boarding schools were a birthday present to Hitler from Education Minister Rust. They were established for the purpose of training a Nazi elite for future high posts in the Third Reich. In addition Napolas were intended to restore the type of military education formerly given in the old Prussian academies. The Napolas were roughly equivalent to the *Gymnasien* (high schools), but the academic standards were far below those of the average grammar schools. Athletic prowess and tests of courage weighed more heavily than academic knowledge. The Napolas were officially open to all qualified youngsters regardless of social origin, but in practice priority was given to the sons of the families of loyal Nazis, members of the Hitler Jugend, sons of war dead, and sons of old-line Army officers. Other candidates came from the rural and working-class elements of the population. All *Jungmannen* (cadets) had to be physically fit, intellectually able and—most important—of "untainted" German blood. Preliminary tests and a one-week trial were held to examine candidates' character, physique and intelligence, in that order. Though depending on the Ministry of Education, Napolas were gradually placed under SS tutelage. Himmler gained control insidiously, first offering to supply clothing and equipment, then scholarship and funding. His efforts were rewarded in 1936 when *SS Obergruppenführer* August Heissmeyer was appointed as inspector general. Himmler then pushed for all school staff to be enrolled in the SS. By 1940 the Black Corps had taken full control, introducing SS style uniforms and ranks. Candidates were nominated by high SS functionaries responsible only to Himmler and Hitler. The teaching was greatly influenced by the Nazi ideology, with a strong emphasis on developing soldierly spirit, physical courage, a sense of duty, simplicity, austere conduct, self-discipline, physical fitness, a sense of community, and readiness for service and self-sacrifice, focusing on forming a Nazi personality rather than intellectual development. The curriculum was designed accordingly. Five subjects were obligatory: German, history, geography, ethnology and biology—precisely the subjects predestined for ideological indoctrination. In addition, engineers and officers were available to instruct pupils in technical and military subjects. Morning classes were interspersed with gymnastics, athletics, swimming, ball games, rowing, riding, fencing, boxing and field sports. The boys also went sailing and gliding, activities important to the navy and the air force respectively. Military training included field exercises, maneuvers, route marches with compass and target shooting with various weapons. There were also ceremonies designed to make a romantic impact on youthful participants, held on the Führer's birthday, at solstice and harvesttime, and many other occasions. Teachers and pupils were militarily organized, wore uniforms and were submitted to strict, spartan discipline. The uniform consisted of an earth-gray suit, including a four-pocket tunic and trousers. The shirt was khaki with black tie and brown facings on the tunic collar. This color was repeated in the band of the peaked cap. An SS style eagle was worn on the left sleeve. The shoulder straps were black and bore the initials "NPEA." Students retained their HJ knifes but officers carried a distinctive dagger with an eagle and swastika on the grip; on the blade was displayed the motto *"mehr sein als scheinen"* (be more than you appear to be). To help integrate the pupils in German society, they were employed on farms in the summer.

Originally Napolas were established at the former Prussian cadet schools at Potsdam, Plön and Köslin. There were 15

Napolas in 1935 and 21 by 1938, including four in Austria and one in the annexed Sudeten area of Czechoslovakia. This number grew to 39 in 1943, though the original plan envisaged a hundred of them by 1945. Despite the importance placed in the Napolas by Himmler, only a tiny proportion of Germany's young people ever passed through these schools, and thus their influence on German life was minimal.

Graduates were free to choose their own career. Some opted for civil engineering, teaching and medicine, but many went into the German armed forces and the SS corps, which suited their sense of elitism, and most served during the war. Early in 1944, *SS Obergruppenführer* Heissmeyer praised the heroism of Napola graduates of whom 1,226 had already been killed in action.

Adolf-Hitler-Schulen

The second type of new school was the so-called *Adolf-Hitler-Schulen* (AHS—Adolf Hitler schools). The first school was opened in April 1937 at Krössinsee—once again, on Hitler's birthday—by the party's director of organization, Robert Ley, and by Hitler Youth leader Baldur von Schirach. From the start there was a ferocious rivalry about who was to control and direct the new AH schools. Having long sought to gain control of Ministry of Education Rust's Napolas—vainly, as Rust favored the SS—Robert Ley proceeded to open his own elite academies with Hitler's blessing. Ley gleefully, rudely rejected Rust's attempt to trespass on his new preserve, and appointed his colleague Kurt Petter as inspector-general. The *Adolf-Hitler-Schule* were secondary boarding schools expressly designed to train the future NSDAP and Hitler Youth leaderships. Each *Gau* (region) was supposed to have its own Adolf Hitler School, but the expense proved too big a drain on party funds and the NSDAP treasurer Franz Xaver Schwarz stopped short.

There was also a shortage of teaching staff. Only ten of the schools existed in 1939, and eleven by 1942. The AH schools were free of charge and intended for the brightest of the 12-year-old Hitler Jugend boys. Candidates were sons of petit-bourgeois and provincial, lower-middle-class tradesmen, shopkeepers and white-collar workers. During their second year in the *Jungvolk*—the junior branch of the HJ—potential candidates for the AHS were examined for their racial background and then sent to a youth camp for two weeks for final selection. A main criterion of selection was a good record during the first two years of membership in the HJ, plus physical appearance: any fair-haired, blue-eyed boy had a better chance to be selected. With a curriculum lasting six years, the AH schools were established to create a new generation of Nazi followers, and meant to turn out a technically and ideologically trained elite. The inspiration was ancient Sparta, the British public schools and the Jesuit education system. Here again the emphasis was on the five ideological subjects including history—which was distorted in a way serving Nazi aims—and biology, which included "scientific" proofs intended to develop racism. The stress, too as usual, was the forming of Nazi cadres by physical training, not intellectual development, and with pre-military training and service within the community. There were five periods of physical training each week and one half period of study. Pupils wore uniforms and were structured into military units. Teachers watched their charges at every moment, even overseeing bedmaking, deportment, and personal hygiene. Squads competed with one another and were judged collectively instead of by individual examination. Students were graduated at the age of 18 and then, after military service in the Wehrmacht, were considered qualified for entrance to a university or to one of the *Ordensburgen* (see below). Because of their isolated and specialized education, young people in the AHS knew nothing about practical life, while, on the other hand, their arrogance and conceit about their own abilities were boundless. It is significant that most of the high NSDAP functionaries did not send their own children to such schools. Graduates with favorable political reports formed cadres of parvenus and careerists of varying respectability and effectiveness in the NSDAP structure. The best graduates could also attend two other schools: the Superior School of the NSDAP (established at Chiemsee), and the National School of the NSDAP (established at Feldafing). Both schools provided high-ranking Nazi leaders for the future.

Ordensburgen

The third institution intended to form future reliable and fanatical Nazi generations—was the *Ordensburgen* (literally "castles of knightly order"). These were the finishing schools, the highest residential academies for the training of the future Nazi elite. United in narcissism, mysticism and fanaticism, those chosen formed a kind of NSDAP university, an institutional core of Nazi brothers, the best of the SS elite. Hitler once declared:

> My teaching is hard. Weakness has to be knocked out of them. In my *Ordensburgen* a youth will grow up before which the world will shrink back. A violently active, dominating, intrepid, brutal youth—that is what I am after. Youth must be all those things. It must be indifferent to pain. There must be no weakness or tenderness in it. I want to see once more in its eyes the gleam of pride and independence of the beast of prey. In this way I shall eradicate the thousands of years of human domestication. Then I shall have in front of me the pure and noble natural material. With that I can create the New Order.

The *Ordensburgen* received their name from the medieval fortresses built by the Teutonic Knights, and they attempted to recreate a medieval order of chivalry. Four castles were established in out-of-the-way, romantic, scenic settings, at Krössinsee (Pomerania), Sonthofen (Upper Bavaria), Vogelsang (Eifel), and Marienburg (East Prussia). Each castle accommodated about 1,000 students called "Junkers." Supervision was in the hands of no fewer than 500 instructors, administrative staff, cooks, porters, orderlies, athletic and military trainers, ideology teachers, grooms and other personnel. Each school was carefully separated from the outside world. It had its dormitories, refectories, classrooms, chapel, meditation cloister, athletic accommodations, private cemetery, and a library comprising all the literature connected to Nazism. The executive official was Robert Ley, head of the *Deutsche Arbeitsfront* (DAF—German Labor Front), who set its standards. The *Ordensburgen* were, however, gradually placed under control of Himmler's SS. Entrants were chosen from among those who had spent six years, from age 12 to 18, at the *Adolf-Hitler-Schools* or Napolas, two and a half years in the *Reichsarbeitsdienst* (RAD—the state labor service), and another four years in full-time party activity. The candidates were thus in their mid-twenties when chosen for the order castles. The selection of candidates was controlled by high party and SS functionaries. Most candidates were of humble origin, sons of party provincial officials, farmers and artisans. Those who were chosen were usually of limited intelligence but regarded it as a distinct honor. As might be expected, intellectual standards were very low and attendance to the *Ordensburg* did little to foster education. Students went to each of the four castles for a year at a time. At the academy at Krössinsee, the first year, the stress was on the study of racial science, athletics, boxing and gliding. Great attention was given to horse riding because that gave the Junkers the feeling of being able to dominate a living creature. The second year, at Sonthofen, the emphasis was on athletics,

parachute jumping, mountain climbing and skiing. The third year, at Vogelsang, the students received political and military instruction, and physical training. One of the tests that year was the *Tierkampf*, combat with bare hands against wild dogs. The fourth year, at the prestigious Teutonic castle Marienburg, the Junkers were expected to obtain their final military formation, and political and racial indoctrination.

All through their education and training, the Junkers were subjected to a rigorous discipline and expected to be obedient and respectful. The finer points of social etiquette were also cultivated assiduously. The slightest infractions were severely punished. Live ammunition was used in war training. Graduates entered the highest echelons of the Nazi Party, the SS corps and the German army as well-drilled functionaries and docile executives but most of them had not acquired the many qualities of a good leader. In contrast with the Napolas, the castles were not linked with German military traditions, and the system failed miserably. The *Ordensburgen* never attracted a full complement of students despite the financial inducement and the prestige of attendance. According to some estimates, half the available places remained vacant. Even in the most fanatical NSDAP circles, the product of the *Ordensburgen* were occasionally considered too ruthless and arrogant.

During World War II, the *Ordensburgen* were characterized by a further emphasis on the military. They were then placed under tutelage of the SS. They became a part of the *Amt XI* (branch 11) of the *SS Führungs-Hauptamt* (SSFHa—the headquarters of the *Waffen SS*) created in August 1940 and headed by *SS Gruppenführer* Jüttner. The *Amt XI* was charged with the training of *Waffen SS* senior officers; the *Ordensburgen* were used for this purpose.

NSDAP **Gemeinschaftsleiter** *(Ordensburgen teacher)*

The *Amt XI* had two other schools/training places at Bad-Tölz (Bavaria) and Braunschweig (Brunswick in Lower Saxony). The SS ensured that those marked for high office by attendance at the SS school at Bad-Tölz had bloodied their hands during a practical period in the Dachau concentration camp. The Junkers were then "solid chaps"—part of the SS apparatus of terror.

The Junkers' original uniform was designed after the SA and NSDAP model. It included a khaki tunic and trousers with a brown belt. The cap had a brown peak and band, and a sleeve displayed the name of the attended *Ordensburg*. Later during the war, when the institutions were taken over by the SS, the uniform was strongly influenced by the new leaders, with black suit, military dress and SS insignia.

SA school

An SA school for boys was situated in Feldafing on the Starnbergersee south of Munich, *NS Deutsche Oberschule Starnbergersee* (National-Socialist German High School Starnbergersee). This school, opened in April 1933, was intended to train future SA leaders. The selected pupils were mostly sons of SA veterans, and known as *SA Jungmannen* (Young Men of the Storm-troops). The main educational aims went without saying: ideological reliability and physical fitness. The standard of education was pitiable. It never proved difficult to find enough pupils. The final examination consisted of essays on optional subjects and an oral test by members of the teaching staff. Graduates could enter the SA corps with the rank of *Truppführer* (staff sergeant). In February 1936 control of the school passed from the SA to Nazi Party hands, although the headmaster remained an SA officer: *Obergruppenführer* (Lieutenant-General) Julius Görlitz. In 1941 all connection with the SA was severed. Pupils were enrolled in the Hitler Jugend, and the staff in the NSDAP.

Special Units (*Sondereinheiten*)

To the casual observer, the Hitler Youth seemed like the scouting movement that flourished in other countries—tanned boys hiking, camping and lifting their voices in song. But the HJ was not an innocent youth movement at all. In fact the Hitler Youth was providing the Nazi Party with a new generation of believers and with cannon fodder for the war. It was a government-dominated organization dedicated to making fervent Nazis, producing obedient citizens, and molding savage warriors for the Third Reich. Everything in the HJ stressed the martial and physical. There was a strict discipline reflected by oath, rituals, regalia, uniforms and ranks. The training's overriding purpose was to fill the ranks of the regimented labor force, the national *Wehrmacht*, and Hitler's private army, the *Waffen SS*.

After the bloody purge of 30 June 1934

Schiessauszeichnung *(Hitler Youth shooting award for proficiency in firing small-bore weapons). The highest level of marksmanship was considered to be 90 percent accuracy hitting the target from 50 meters with half the shots made in the prone position.*

the SA did not disappear, but their size was drastically shrunk, and they were completely deprived of political power, relegated to a backseat role, assigned mundane tasks and turned into a veterans' association. Until the end of the war in 1945, the SA—headed by the loyal and colorless SA *Obergruppenführer* Viktor Lutze—continued to exist as Nazi propagandists, fund collectors, a sporting organization, and as pre-military training units to the SA Reserve and the boys of the Hitler Jugend. For this training purpose, *SA Wehrmannschaften* (defense teams) were created in January 1939. During the war, the SA *Wehrmannschaften* functioned as home-front auxiliaries for civil defense and police work. The pre-military training of the Hitler Jugend was increasingly taken over by the SS administration.

As the threat of war came closer, HJ activities were even less focused on fun and leisure, while militarization was drastically increased. Under SA (later SS and army) supervision, the *Kern* HJ members, age 14–18, attended camps for one month where they were engaged in physical exercises, parading, war-gaming, close-order drills and maneuvers. The training included running, swimming, and other athletic pursuits, campfires, cookouts, and adventurous field trips. To these were added navigation training with map and compass, the use of camouflage, and arms drills, as well as learning and practicing semaphore, and the operation of communications apparatus and cryptography devices. Young men were accustomed to wearing steel helmets and gas masks, familiarized in the use of hand grenades, and trained with pistols, carbines, rifles and machine guns in order to acquire sharp eyes and steady hands. In 1938 the HJ possessed over 15,000 small rifles, and a *Schiessauszeich-*

Training with pistol firing

nung (sharpshooter's badge) was awarded for accurate shooting and precision sniping. In 1939 alone, some 51,500 of these badges were granted to HJ members.

Children who became proficient at such tasks were given rewards such as a ceremonial sharp knife and prestigious medals which were worn with immense pride. For the purpose of training future officers, the Hitler Jugend opened two training schools in Obermassfeld (Thuringe province) and Middelburg (Mecklenburg province). Officers and NCOs of the German army also participated in the training of the Hitler Youth. One of them—in 1937—was none other than *Oberstleutnant* Erwin Rommel, who later became the legendary "Desert Fox," head of the famous Afrika Korps and Generalfeldmarschall of the Reich.

In addition, the Hitler Youth had several *Sondereinheiten* (special units) which were for direct preparation for war, providing needed military skills and useful qualifications. The special units were more attractive to older boys than was monotonous service in the general Hitler Youth. Indeed, signs of boredom could be observed among

Training with hand grenade

Training with light carbine

older members of the HJ. Devotion to duty crumbled under the onset of teenage problems and outside interests. The special paramilitary units were meant to maintain the interest of the teenagers by putting the emphasis on adventure and modern technology which had a great appeal to the youth. The courses were also of great interest to the armed forces and *Waffen SS*, who gladly supported the training of potential recruits and aided by supplying equipment and instructors.

Marine-Hitler-Jugend

The *Marine-Hitler-Jugend* (Navy Hitler Youth) was created in 1935. This special branch of the youth organization was very popular. It had 50,000 members in 1938 and 62,000 in 1939, mainly in the northern regions close to the North Sea and Baltic Sea, around the towns of Kiel and Hamburg, but also inland, as Germany has many lakes, canals and rivers. The Marine-HJ had two *Reichsseesportschulen* (schools for sea sport) in Prieros (province Brandenburg), and in Seemoos near Bodensee Lake. Both schools were originally created for and managed by the special navy branch of the storm troops (*Marine-SA*, formed in 1934), for training in physical exercises, swimming, rowing, navigation, navy armament, signaling and other communication. After their intensive training the members of the Marine-HJ were sent on practice cruises in small boats in the North and Baltic seas. Every year there was a national championship meeting held at Kiel where the best teams paraded and practiced. The highlight of the naval training was a cruise in the Baltic Sea aboard the prestigious Kriegsmarine's training ships *Horst Wessel* and *Georg Fock*. In 1940, as a display of skill in inland navigation, a Marine-HJ party sailed from Passau in Lower Bavaria to Vienna and Budapest.

Members of the Marine-HJ wore the rather expensive traditional uniform of the

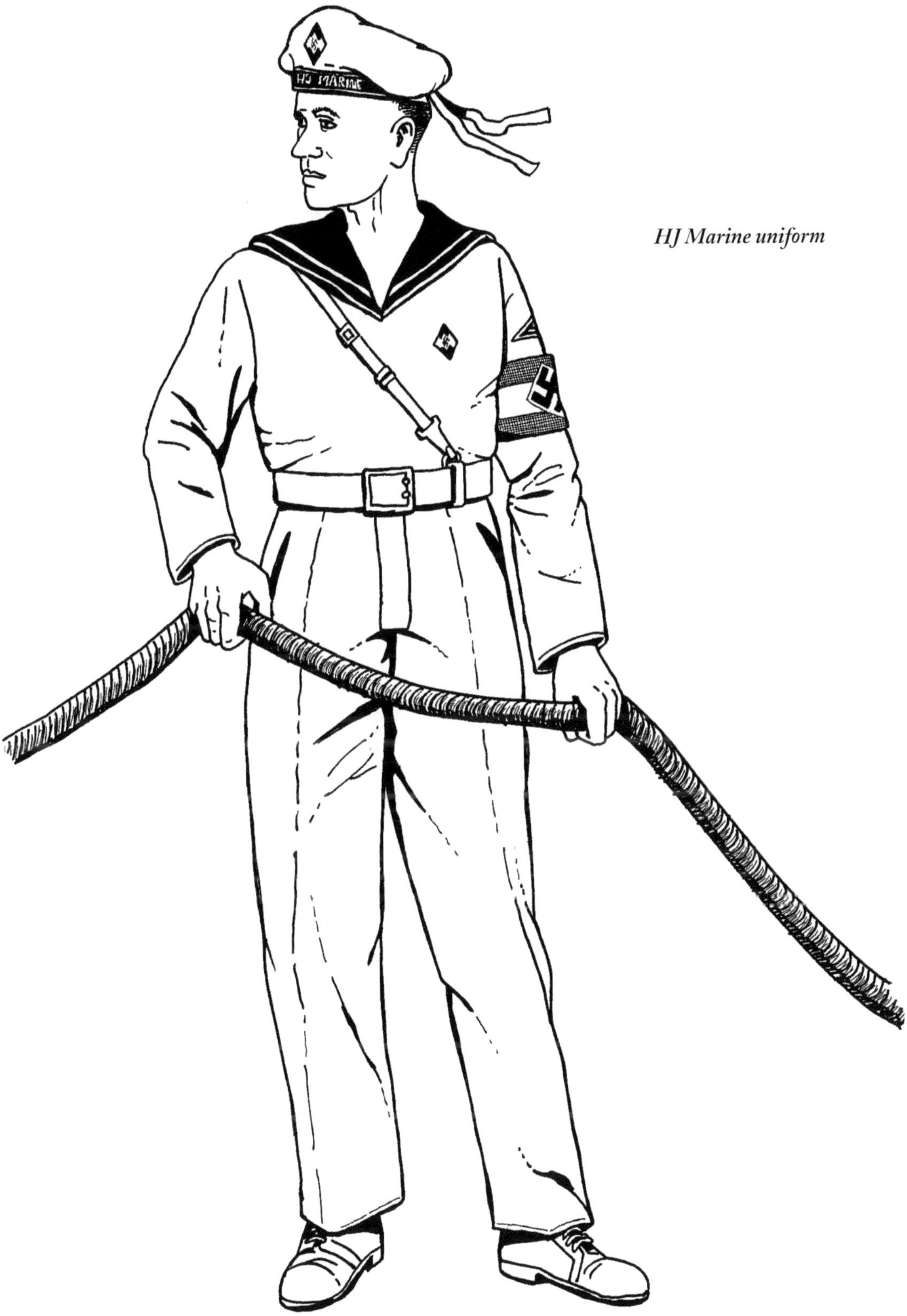
HJ MARINE

HJ Marine uniform

German navy. There was a double-breasted jacket with navy-blue trousers and a peaked cap. During seagoing exercises, they wore a white moleskin smock and trousers, and a navy-blue forage cap. The *Waffenfarbe* (arm of service color) of the Marine-HJ was blue and displayed in the form of piping on the shoulder straps and hats. After 1936, Vice-Admiral *ausser Dienst* (retired) von Trotha was *Ehrenführer* (honorary leader) of the Marine-HJ. Many of the members became sailors of the *Kriegsmarine* (German navy) during the war.

Flieger-Hitler-Jugend

Members of the HJ could also be seduced by the exciting *Flieger-Hitler-Jugend* (Hitler Youth Flying Association). According to the stipulations of the Treaty of Versailles in 1919, Germany had no right to possess a military air force, but no clause forbade gliding. In the late 1920s and early 1930s, gliding was a national German sport which was encouraged by the Nazi Party as a patriotic activity. Germany had been a pioneer in gliding; the inventor and aeronaut Otto Lilienthal (1848–1896) was the first to establish gliding as a science. He made over 2,000 flights before being killed in a glider accident, and left a valuable book on glider techniques. Model airplanes and gliders were thus very popular among the German youth. The purpose of the *Flieger-HJ* was to learn the basics of flying, the first step to training pilots for the *Luftwaffe*. Members spent their first two years building model gliders and learning the theory of flight. Simple winch-launched gliders gave youthful pilots their first experience of flight and produced a powerful propaganda image of a modern nation taking to the skies. Glider proficiency badges were issued in the form of seagull. There were three classes: third class, with one seagull; second, with two; and first, with three. The *Waffenfarbe* (arm of service color) was light blue. Then they would attempt to earn their glider certification. Training was also provided in radio signaling, anti-aircraft activity and air-raid operations.

The Youth Flying Association had close contact with the *Flieger-SA*, the flying branch of the storm troops created in 1930, and the *Nationalsozialistische Flieger-Korps* (NSFK—Nazi Flyers Corps). The NSFK organization was founded in 1932 under future chief of air force Hermann Göring; it was headed by a certain Ziegler who had been Göring's colleague during World War I. The NSFK corps was intended to promote interest in and development of air sports, notably gliding and ballooning. The NSFK managed to rally World War I–veteran pilots for propaganda aims. Heroes such as Bruno Lörzer and Ernst Udet joined and played a significant role in the creation of the *Luftwaffe* in 1935. The Corps was semi-civilian but militarily organized. As with every other Nazi organization, members of the NSFK wore a uniform. Service dress was *Luftwaffe* gray with a pale blue shirt, black tie and SA-type kepi. The right sleeve had a striking motif, a winged man above a swastika. Ranks were similar to those of the SA, and displayed on collar patches. The summer uniform included a khaki shirt, black tie, swastika armband, black leather belt, and gray trousers. The mission of the *Flieger-HJ* and the NSFK was to channel energy, to exploit youth enthusiasm, to train potential pilots for the *Luftwaffe*, to continue post-military training of reservists and to further consciousness of aviation among the German population at large. For the latter purpose there was also the *Luftsportverband* (LSV—League for Aeronautic Sport), a consortium of aviation clubs and associations devoted to civilian flying and gliding. The *Luftwaffe* supported close relationships with these highly popular organizations as they developed future combat pilots for fighters and bombers, as well as ground personnel for technical and administrative duties. Members of the *Flieger-HJ* were taken to visit aircraft man-

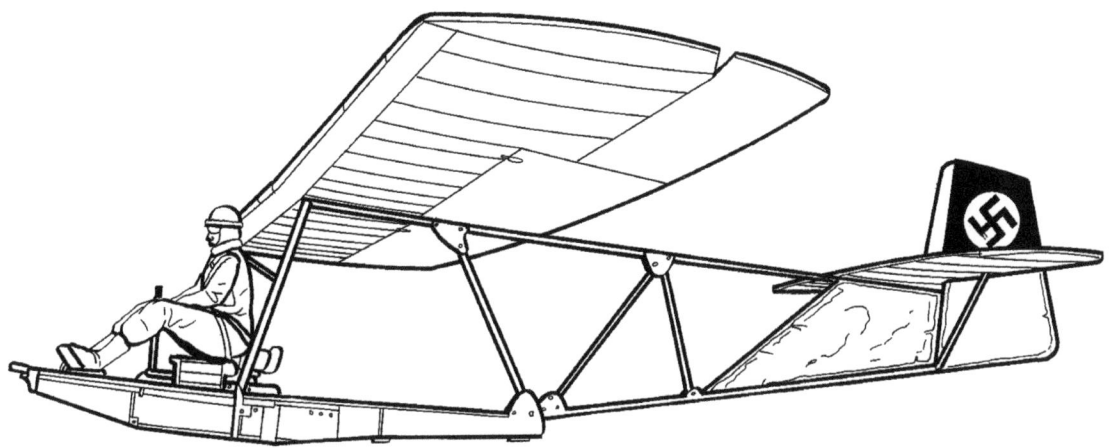

Stamer Lippisch SG 38 glider. The SG 38 training glider, designed by engineer Alexander Lippisch, was the standard for the basic instruction of the Luftwaffe student pilots. It had a total length of 6.28 m (20.604 ft), a wingspan of 10.41 m (34.154 ft), and an empty weight of 110 kg (242 lbs). Maximum speed was 115 km/h (71 mph).

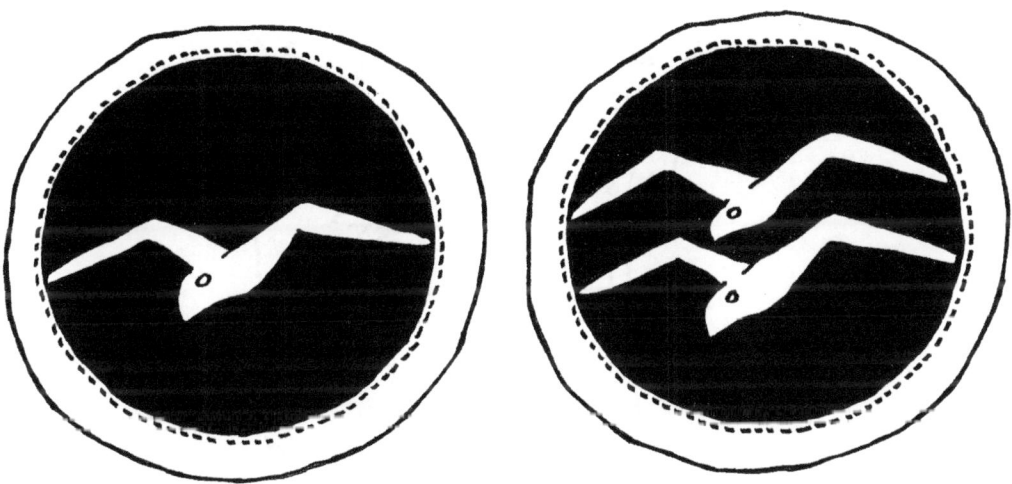

HJ glider proficiency badges

ufacturers, and *Luftwaffe* airfields, where they had the opportunity to have a close look on the air force's newest airplanes. A few of them even had the honor and pleasure of flying as passengers in transport and bomber aircraft. In addition, the *Flieger-HJ* and the other flying associations provided future *Fallschirmjäger* (paratroopers, including glider-borne troops) and *Flakhelfer* (anti-aircraft gunners and searchlight personnel).

The *Flieger-HJ* was one of the largest of the special units. In 1938 it had about 78,000 members, of which 15,000 had graduated, gaining a gliding brevet. Teenagers of the *Flieger-HJ* who showed promise were made future *Fähnrich* (officer cadet) in the *Luftwaffe*. This was to ensure that when the boys became old enough for military service, no other branch could take them.

German pilot Unterfeldwebel *1939*

Paratrooper. Developed by General Kurt Student, the German **Fallschirmjäger** *(paratroopers) were a part of the* **Luftwaffe.** *They were a small elite force that played a noteworthy role during World War II. Using both gliders and parachutes, the carefully selected and highly-trained German airborne units achieved remarkable successes in Belgium and Holland in 1940. The casualties suffered by the landing in Crete the following year, though leading to the capture of the Greek island, were judged too costly by Hitler for him to permit a repetition. Paradoxically, as the likelihood of another large-scale airborne operation receded, the parachute forces expanded, earning a reputation as formidable fighters as they attracted a steady flow of young volunteers of the highest caliber from throughout the German air force, army and Hitler Youth.*

Motor-Hitler-Jugend

Young men interested in mechanics and driving trucks, motorcycles and cars could join the highly popular *Motor-Hitler-Jugend*. When a boy reached sixteen, the age at which a driver's license could be procured, he could petition for entrance. The Motor-HJ had a close connection with the *Nationalsozialistische Kraftfahrer-Korps* (NSKK—National-Socialist Driver Corps). The NSKK originated from the *Nationalsozialistischen Automobil Korps* (NSAK—National Socialist Automobile Corps) that was founded in 1930. The NSAK included wealthy car owners who sympathized with the Nazis and put themselves at the party's disposal in their free time, and formed a group of mechanics and drivers to transport Nazi Party leaders. The *Sturm Abteilung* (SA) had its own transport service, called the *Motor Sturm Abteilung* (MSA). Both MSA and NSAK were inspired by Mussolini's *Squadristi* and played a significant role during the *Kampfzeit*, the troubled period before the Nazis took over power in Germany. After the purge of the SA in June 1934, the Motor-SA was disbanded and its members were transferred to the NSAK which was then reorganized and renamed *Nationalsozialistische Kraftfahrer-Korps* (NSKK) in November 1934. The Nazi Party gave a great deal of attention to modern means of transport. Hitler was keen on cars and planes. After the seizure of power in January 1933, a wide *Autobahn* (motorway) network was launched and the Führer ordered engineer Ferdinand Porsche to design a cheap popular car, the future Volkswagen. Until the end of the Nazi regime, the NS Driver Corps was an important official *Gliederung der NSDAP* (Nazi Party organization) directly placed under Hitler's authority. The NSKK—counting 500,000 members, headed by Major Adolf Hühnlein in 1938—was progressively more militarily organized and divided into structured units with ranks similar to those

Haupttruppführer *Motor SA 1933*

of the SA. The members of the NSKK had not only a logistical role, driving and maintaining vehicles, they were also high-technology specialists in military matters, having close contacts with the army, notably with the armored forces headed by Heinz Guderian. They gave mechanical advice and driving lessons to lorry and tank driver candidates in Wehrmacht *Fahrschulen* (driving schools). The technical efficiency of the motor corps was a major trump card, considering the formation of tank crews and the development of *Blitzkrieg* (lightning war) which gave Germany tremendous victories in 1939–41. Closely connected to the Nazi Party, Motor-HJ and NSKK members were often politically active. They participated in party rallies and ceremonies, dispensed Nazi ideology via lectures, and organized visits to factories for propaganda purposes. It was no coincidence that Adolf Hühnlein was both *NSKK-Führer* (chief of the motorized corps) and *Ehrenführer* (honorary leader) of the Motor-HJ. In late 1937 the association opened a *Reichsmotorschule* (driving school) at Bad Gandersheim, north of Göttingen, where members learned all the requirements of driving and maintaining vehicles. Members of the Motor-HJ had to log their driving hours like pilots. Eighty hours of driving a year were required for continued membership. They also had to know international road signs and have at least 105 hours of workshop mechanic experience. The Motor-HJ special unit's *Waffenfarbe* was pink, the same as the armored force. The corps was very popular and counted 18,000 members in 1935. By 1938 this had increased to 90,000 members. In 1937, 10,000 driving licenses were obtained

NSKK arm eagle cloth badge

Member of the Motor-HJ. The young man's head is protected by a leather motorcycle crash helmet. On the left sleeve of his shirt he sports the triangular badge of his district, the white/red HJ diamond with black swastika, and the round driving badge.

NSKK Truppführer *(sergeant) 1939*

by Motor-HJ members; in 1938 that number was up to 28,000. Drivers and mechanics were later incorporated in the NSKK, in army transport units, and in the army and *Waffen SS* motorized combat formations.

Nachrichten-Hitler-Jugend

Members of the HJ who were interested in modern communication technology could join the *Nachrichten-HJ* signal unit whose *Waffenfarbe* (color of service) was yellow. The Germans were quick to see the full potential of radio communication. As early as 1935, Heinz Guderian (chief of armed forces) encouraged the development of simple and reliable radio for modern warfare. The HJ transmission units benefited of the experience of the *Nachrichten-SA*, the signal units of the storm troops, formed in 1930. There was also a high-tech school in Berlin that trained selected young men in the use, maintenance and repair of signal lamps, Morse code and telegraph devices, field telephones, teleprinters and teletypewriters, and wireless telegraphy.

Radio in the late 1930s was still largely an affair of bulky devices, clumsy accumulators, complex tuning systems, tinny loudspeakers, headphones, crystal rectifiers and short receiving ranges, and so more traditional means of communication were also used, such as messengers on foot, bike or horseback, as well as pigeon and *Meldehunde* (messenger dogs). During World War II, radio communications—in spite of limited technology—revolutionized how armies fought on the battlefield. They played an important role in the development and success of the German "lightning war" in the period of victory, 1939–41.

Reiter-Hitler-Jugend

Although ill-suited for modern warfare, the military horse did not disappear during World War II. Throughout the war, the mobility of the German army as a whole largely depended on horses. The animals demanded specialized troops. Created in 1938, the *Reiter-HJ* (Hitler Youth cavalry) was in the beginning a relatively small unit with a snobbish, elitist character, with wealthy members of riding clubs providing their own mounts. With the rearmament program and the preparation for war in the late 1930s, the *Reiter-HJ* was greatly expanded to agricultural communities and no longer relied upon private horse ownership. Its purpose was preparation for service in the army cavalry. Its participants fed, watered, cleaned and exercised horses and maintained harnesses and other equipment. Cavalry personnel of the HJ were generally formed by the *Reiter-SA*, the equestrian corps of the storm-troops, created in 1930.

HJ health service

In addition to all the other branches described above, the HJ had its own health service. In 1939 there were 36 regional units and 608 regimental health units employing some 4,000 doctors, 800 dentists and 500 pharmacists, supported by 40,000 auxiliary workers and 35,000 sanitary orderlies recruited from the girls of the BdM, all of whom were trained to move on into nursing, providing basic medical assistance and emergency help.

The German Labor Front and the Labor Service

Deutsche Arbeitsfront

The *Deutsche Arbeitsfront* (DAF—German Labor Front) was a Nazi organization of professional associations and guilds directed by Robert Ley (1890–1945). Workers' rights and trade unions were abolished in June 1933 and replaced by the *Deutsche Arbeitsfront*. Membership in the DAF was voluntary, but any person who was an employer or an employee in any area of German industry or commerce was more or less a member by default. The concept of the DAF was that it conciliate rather than advance workers' demands, in order to ensure political stability and smooth operation of all German industry, business and commerce.

The DAF was a major political player during the Third Reich, challenging both government ministries and industry, striving to become a kind of Nazi superagency. It was a gigantic bureaucratic edifice composed of several sub-branches, such as the *Kraft durch Freude* (KdF—Strength Through Joy). This sub-organization was tasked with providing activities such as trips, cruises, concerts, and cultural activities for German workers. These events were specifically directed toward the working class. It was through the KdF that the NSDAP hoped to bring to the "common man" the pleasures once reserved only for the rich. By opening the door for the working class to afford more leisure activities, it was hoped that workers could be lulled into being more flexible and productive.

Reichsarbeitsdienst

Another important sub-branch of the DAF was the *Reichsarbeitsdienst* (RAD—German Labor Service), headed by Konstantin Hierl. The Reichsarbeitsdienst, with the motto "*Arbeit adelt*" (work enobles), was formed in June 1935 as the official state and party labor organization. Service in the RAD was compulsory for all Germans between the ages 18 and 25. It was divided into two sections. The *Reichsarbeitsdienst Manner* (RAD/M) was set up for men, and the *Reichsarbeitsdienst der weibliche Jugend* (RAD/wJ) for females. The initiation of this young-labor corps was born of economic necessity, and the service had far-reaching economic benefits. The young people of the RAD learned devotion to German ideals and formed at the same time a huge labor

Emblem of the **Reichsarbeitsdienst** *(RAD—German Labor Service), badge for men. The emblem of the RAD was a spade blade surrounded by two corn ears.*

resource which did not need paying. The organization was construed as a form of "honorary service" to the national community, its object being to train young people in a "true approach to work." The reward, supposedly, was the health of community life, the betterment of the fatherland, and the right (at later rallies) to march in mass formations with spades glinting like rifles. The RAD had a huge number of unpaid workers, conscripted young men and women who were organized in uniformed, disciplined battalions. RAD workers were housed in tent camps, temporary buildings and hastily erected huts. Their life was grim, strictly supervised, with bed-making, locker and kit inspection, camp discipline and indoctrination classes. Work was the focal point of Nazi life and it was supposed to be done joyfully. Propaganda materials showed nothing but smiling faces, radiant expressions, and youthful, sun-tanned, joyous vigor. Shouldering their shovels like weapons, with a lot of marching and singing, RAD workers were taken to various projects demanding hard physical labor, making them very fit. Their workday could be as long as nine hours, frequently even longer, and they were expected to work efficiently. RAD women were often employed as auxiliary farmworkers, nurses, maidservants and other occupations deemed feminine. The RAD male units were used for such labor projects as harvests, reclamation of marshland for cultivation, and construction of canals, bridges, dykes and roads, as well as drainage improvement work, vast tree removal operations, and the reclamation of fallow or inundated land. They were also involved in military projects, such as the construction of the *Westwall* (a fortification line built along the western German border between 1938 and 1940).

During the war the DAF and the RAD supported the army. Individual *Reichsarbeitsdienst* units were transferred in full as auxiliaries to the *Wehrmacht*, to form the basis of the new *Bautruppen* (construction troops). The construction troops would go on to build roads, clear obstacles, dig trenches, create fortifications and airfields, and take part in all manner of military construction duties. As the war proceeded, some RAD *Abteilungen* (battalions) were incorporated directly to the *Heer* (German ground force). With the addition of older, untrained army reservists, they were formed into a series of regiment-sized units. They helped repair damaged roads, built and repaired airstrips, constructed coastal fortifications, loaded and unloaded supplies and ammunition, laid minefields, and even manned fortifications.

Throughout World War II, the RAD continued to serve its originally established duty of training Hitler Jugend young men prior to their service

RAD **Obervormann** *(conscript, private first class)*

RAD officer with dagger

in the *Wehrmacht* by providing construction and agricultural work for the nation. But also throughout World War II, the RAD increasingly took part in more militarized roles in supporting the troops by helping to ensure that supplies continued to reach the front over clear roadways. After 1942, many RAD units were forced into frontline combat, while other units were drafted directly into military service on the spot. Security operations and police work also became an increasingly common duty of the RAD units. On the eastern front, RAD units took up arms to fight off Soviet partisan forces. Service was not limited to the multitude of combat-support roles listed above. Hundreds of RAD units were trained and later used as anti-aircraft gunners under the control of the *Luftwaffe*. In October of 1944, at least 60,000 RAD troops are known to have served in *Luftwaffe* Flak batteries.

Youth Opposition

Dissidence and resistance

With the consolidation of the Hitler Jugend as a large-scale bureaucratic organization, with the gradual aging of its leadership cadres in the course of the 1930s, and with several purges in response to allegedly "anti-German" behavior, the movement's attraction to young people began to decline. Not every child thrived under the indoctrination program. The more intelligent and individualistic must have found it unbearable to be watched like prisoners, and laughable to hear the crude lies fabricated by the Nazis. These young persons who did not succumb to the brainwashing had to be extremely cautious, however. Innocuous conversations were recorded by eavesdroppers, and they had to be careful to whom they said what they really thought.

Deviant behavior among German youth during the Third Reich was much more common than once thought. The belief that the HJ successfully mobilized all young German people is faulty. The growing political and ideological influence of the Hitler Jugend was accompanied by a clear diminution of its attraction to many young people. It was a mass organization but it was not totally homogeneous. The HJ had absorbed many non–Nazi youth associations, and the originality and particularities of these groups had not been eradicated overnight. The leaders of these former youth associations were not all convinced Nazis, and when they had remained in charge, they felt like immigrants in a new and unknown continent. They tended to flock together within the Nazi order. Some tried to create undercover islands of resistance, or at least preserve and infuse the HJ with something of their own spirit and tradition. No doubt this was a hopeless struggle against the effectual *Gleichschaltung* that ironed out all independence. Deviations from Nazi norms were soon detected, disciplinary measures taken to eradicate "bad" influences, and many would-be reformers were arrested, expelled or transferred to positions of no consequence. There could be no reforming of the HJ from within.

Although there are no means of verifying this phenomenon, there is good reason to believe that a fairly high proportion of upper- and middle-class young people, and also youth from former religious associations were not completely nazified. The youth who had been induced to join the HJ, undoubtedly had not always had the aspirations of the ideal fanatical Nazi type. To this must be added that Germany had never been a united nation until 1871, and even till 1933 it was a federation of states, large and small, with several independent Hansa cities, originating from a medieval trade league. The people of East Prussia were quite different from those living along the Rhine river in the West. The Protestant Germans of Hamburg in the north had little in common with the southern Catholic Bavarians. Regional and local particularisms (e.g., religion, accents and dialects, attire, traditions, and other cultural markers) were still very strong and different. Behind a façade of uniformity, the HJ was a patchwork which mirrored the variety of the ancestral and traditional Germanies.

The conduct of some of the younger people illustrated how the Nazi code of behavior could disintegrate. The more the Hitler Jugend arrogated state powers to itself, the more obvious became the examples of deviant behavior among teenagers, but the records of resistance to Hitler's regime present complex problems to historians. There is a very wide definition of resistance. A German resisted Hitler by continuing to buy from a Jewish shop despite a boycott organized by the Nazi Party or by giving bread to one of the millions of starving slave laborers brought to Germany from all over Europe during the Second World War. Resistance might entail the refusal to join a Nazi organization. A variety of courses of action were open to a German who was opposed to the Third Reich and who wanted to do something about it, but how many of these really amounted to resistance? One could distinguish dissidence (the spontaneous voicing of anti–Nazi opinions) and opposition (actions only directed against limited characteristics of the Hitler state) from full-scale resistance. The latter might be defined as the "active participation in organized attempts to work against the regime with the conscious aim of undermining it or planning for the moment of its demise." According to this view, resistance was about action not words. It entailed organization and planning, not spontaneity. It meant the rejection of everything Hitler stood for, not just part of it. Resistance was nothing less than a meaningful contribution to the destruction of the Third Reich. But how many ordinary Germans could ever have hoped to destroy a whole modern state? Some tried to do so. While no small number of Germans at some time or other made signs of defiance toward the Third Reich as they went about their daily round, others were filled with such a passionate desire to oppose Hitler that resistance became the whole purpose of their lives.

Given the nature both of resistance/opposition and of the police state, it is doubtful whether it will ever be possible to know the full scope of German struggle against Nazism. Not everyone who was arrested for interrogation by the Gestapo was a committed enemy of Hitler's dictatorship. Roughly speaking, three types of resisters can be identified: those who had become disillusioned with the Third Reich; those who acted out of necessity (Gypsies and homosexuals, persecuted with more and more savagery, and particularly German Jews); and a few people who could have conformed but courageously resisted because of political, religious or moral principles.

The decision for a German to become a true resister often was neither easy nor straightforward. This was shown clearly in the cases of a number of teenagers. From 1934 on, reports compiled by the police in the Ruhr and Rhineland described the existence of groups of largely working-class youths who dressed distinctively (often in cheesecloth shirts and leather shorts), who went on outings together and who were at loggerheads with the Hitler Jugend. These groups, which will be discussed further, were called Kittelbach Pirates, Navajos and, most famously, Edelweiss Pirates. According to historian A. Kenkmann, most of the teenagers involved here originally had been happy to join the Nazi youth movement. They only became "pirates" when the Hitler Jugend proved unable to meet their needs. Often there were very personal reasons for this. For instance, some teenagers had had arguments with their leaders, others had been refused promotion within the organization, others again belonged to families which quietly had political reservations about Nazism. The example of Hans Steinbrück is particularly interesting. He was a member of an Edelweiss Pirate group during the Second World War, and as a result was hanged in November 1944. Originally, however, he had been a leader in the Hitler Jugend and in due course tried to join the secret political police in Düsseldorf. Stupidly he started passing himself off as a secret policeman before his application had been approved and as a result he was not only rejected, but put in prison for a short while. Only after his release did Hans begin a career of resistance to the Third Reich. It culminated in his leading attacks by armed gangs on government buildings in war-torn Cologne. In summation, Steinbrück rejected the Hitler state only after it had first rejected him.

Compulsion and the requirement of absolute obedience were found unpleasant by some young people. As the years went by, the whole structure of the Hitler Youth became more bureaucratized and less imaginative. Some of the earlier attractions began to wear off. The HJ came to be seen increasingly as part of the establishment rather than rival to it. The initial wave of enthusiasm for the Nazi cause at certain schools and university campuses gave way to apathy and outright rejection. On some occasions, attendance at party meetings and rallies lagged. The involvement of the youth ceased to be on a voluntary basis, particularly after 1936, but was rather the consequence of a stream of ordinances. Many young people became disillusioned, recalcitrant and rebellious, and they reacted to the onset of compulsion in various ways. Young people, who, according to the official doctrine, were supposed to satisfy their needs by joining the national youth organization, the Hitler Youth and its numerous affiliates, were forming groups of their own. Young people had a patent urge to associate independently, not only outside the organizations prescribed and controlled by the system, but in opposition to them.

And so alternative, even oppositional, cultures and groups developed among the German youth. Officially recorded cases of juvenile delinquency were more than twice as numerous in 1941 as they were in the peacetime year of 1937. By the late 1930s, a few rebels began to defy authority openly. Youth rebelliousness was multiform as we have seen, but—to oversimplify for the sake of clearness and brevity—there were two major groups of young people more or less opposed to the Nazi system, the *Swing Jugend* and "pirate" gangs.

Swing youth

Within the upper-middle-class youth developed the so-called *Swing Jugend* (Swing youth) developed, a group whose values and focus helped them defy cultural indoctrination. These boys and girls were predominately adolescents with enough schooling to be able to use the English language, large homes to organize parties when their elders were out and enough money to have a gramophone, go out in clubs and buy English-looking fashionable clothes. Remarkably similar in dress and look to the American zoot-suiters and the French *zazous* of the 1940s, the young German "swing" men wore jackets that came down to the middle of their thighs and pants that were narrow, with cuffs that gripped the ankle. Their shoes were large and heavy, with thick, crepe soles, and deliberately unpolished. The round collars of their shirts were held together by straight stickpins under linen or wool neckties or showy scarves. Their full, bushy hair shone, not from pomade—which had long disappeared from the counters—but from salad oil. Like the boys, the girls wore their hair below the collar, but theirs was in large curls. They wore turtleneck sweaters under fur coats, regardless of the weather, and striped stockings, flat shoes, and very short, pleated skirts. They carried large umbrellas, which remained resolutely closed even in the rain. Their eyebrows were penciled, they wore lipstick and their nails were polished. Where in the midst of the severe clothing shortages did they find the Swing dress style they insisted on? At a time when the average housewife was finding it extremely difficult, if not impossible, to find a pair of cheap black stockings, even if she had the coupons, and when men were turning their suits inside out and having them recut, the Swing youth were able to obtain their exaggerated long jackets and narrow pegged trousers. The money undoubtedly came from doting parents, and significant chunks of that obtained from black-market operations.

These groups of extravagantly dressed teenagers proceeded to display their contempt for the conventions and the hypocrisy of their elders, but on the whole they had no political beliefs and no real orthodoxy other than jazz, the fabulous syncopated music of Benny Goodman, Tommy Dorsey, Duke Ellington, Louis Armstrong and other giants of the golden age of American swing. These malcontents rejected the Hitler Youth and took every opportunity to avoid *völkische* German culture and music. They used humor as a tonic for coping with everyday frustrations, and poking fun at ranking Nazis became a popular, if dangerous, pastime. Malicious gossip, puns, lampoons and jokes were told, such as these "Mottoes of a True German":

> Be prolific like Hitler
> Simple like Göring
> Loyal like Hess
> Silent like Goebbels
> Sober like Ley
> And beautiful like Scholtz-Klink!

The Swing youth adopted British and especially American influences. They listened to the BBC (more for the music than for information and news), but this was nonetheless a capital crime. A relaxed regime in their parents' home, or lack of nighttime supervision, offered ample opportunity for going out, drinking and gaining sexual experience. These young men and women had a more liberal attitude to pornography, sexuality and homosexuality than the Nazi state liked. (Unrestrained sexual pleasure was denounced by the Nazis as moral degeneration). The Swing youth gathered at urban clubs to flaunt their long hair, spoke English and French, smoked cigarettes, and danced to the highly syncopated American swing music. This was particularly provocative to the authorities, as American jazz and swing were denounced and banned by Nazi propagandists as "Negro" culture, and regarded as un–German "degenerate" music. Diametrically in conflict with what was expected in the BdM, Swing girls used make-up, affected an air of sophistication and displayed their physical charms with nonchalance. The Swing youth had no taste for military service, were opposed to war and doubted the veracity of glowing military communiqués. They mumbled a vague "*Gut'n tag*" (Mornin') instead of greeting anyone with a crisp *Heil Hitler!* The latter was often replaced by a mockery: *Drei Liter!* (Three liters!). Swing youth had fun and accepted Jews into their groups—another outrage for the Nazis. Public jazz concerts were banned and the Swing movement shifted to informal groupings, illegal clubs and private parties where hard liquor flowed freely in the largest cities such as Hamburg, Kiel, Berlin, Stuttgart, Frankfurt, Dresden, Halle and Karlsruhe.

The Swing youth were not anti-fascist in a political sense. Their behavior was emphatically nonpolitical. What they wanted was simply to be left in peace, particularly by the HJ with its boring organized events. They laughed at patriotism, and believed only in themselves, dancing, and the good life—now. They were, on the whole, individualistic and elegant "dandies" refusing Nazi uniformity. They sought their own counter-identity, and were to be found along the borderline between passive insubordination and active effrontery. Their "unpatriotic, degenerate and reactionary behavior" carried, however, an inherent rejection of the system's regimentation and uniformity. Playing and dancing to the enemy's music was an act of open rebellion, an affront to the regimented Germanic folk music favored by the regime. The Swing youth were an abomination to the Nazi Party and the Hitler Youth, who denounced them viciously. They clearly deviated from Nazi social acceptability and were a deadly insult to Hitler's order. To be overtly a Swing youth was thus not without danger. On numerous occasions, the Hitler Youth and police swept through the bars and dances where the Swing youth amused themselves, provoking fights. The Swing youth were threatened, if caught, to have their hair cut short as a public branding, and to be beaten up. After World War II began, punishments became draconian, with punitive drills and even prison or forced labor in concentration camps. Despite repression, the oppositional Swing youth movement was attractive to many adolescents, especially after the membership in the HJ had been made compulsory.

Only a small fringe of the Swing youth had any interest in politics, made contact with opposition circles, or engaged in political activity.

Some of the middle-class dissident groups were to a certain extent a revival of the old *Wandervogel* movement. Indeed some former members of the now forbidden non–Nazi youth movement had kept together in groups, large or small. Some did so at neutral meeting grounds, such as sports clubs, mixed choirs, or literary societies. Some of them continued their excursions, arranged lectures, and went together to theaters and concerts. They carefully refrained from any public demonstrations, but meetings and correspondence took place between such groups of friends. The ban on non-Nazi youth groups from the 1934 *Gleichschaltung* had to be officially repeated in

February 1936, May 1937 and again in July 1939, showing repeatedly that sections of the German youth did not conform.

Edelweiss Pirates

Social deviance was most apparent among younger Germans, especially from the working class, and pointed to the deficiencies of the Hitler Jugend as a channel of indoctrination. Working-class youngsters spontaneously formed gangs that roamed the streets and brawled with Hitler Youth detachments. Less cultural and more militant than the Swing Youth in their emphasis were various urban youth groups such as the Navaros, centered largely in Cologne, the Kittelbach Pirates from Oberhausen and Düsseldorf, and the Dudes from Essen. These were more or less sub-groups within the larger Edelweiss Pirates, although a coordinated central movement never emerged. The *Edelweiss Pirates*, mainly originating from the urban areas of the Rhineland and the industrial Ruhrgebiet, arose spontaneously in late 1942. Other gangs were the Buschwölfe and Charliblase from Munich, the Bärenbande from Kassel, the Klub der Goldenen Horde, Schlangenklub and Shambeko Bande from Düsseldorf, the Goldene Vierzehn and the Schreckensteiner from Hamburg, and the Blauer Dunst from Wismar.

The Pirates were composed mainly of students and working-class youth. They did not meet in clubs but gathered in bars, cinemas, parks and street corners, outsides the confines of the home yet within a neighborhood territory. They belonged together because they lived or worked together. Some rebellious gangs had the characteristics of illegal, secret sects, evolving their own rules, electing leaders and treasurers, adopting badges and code names. These deviants often developed a rebellious sort of humor and a remarkable knack for rewriting song lyrics and used them as protest. Aged between 14 and 18, members of gangs (called *Clique, Klub, Horde, Meute* or *Schar*) typically consisted of about a dozen boys and a few girls. The presence of girls at evening get-togethers and on weekend trips gave them a relatively unrestricted opportunity for sexual experience. As with the middle class Swing youth, the working-class Pirates were antagonistic to authority, hierarchy and militarism, they tried to get as much space as possible between themselves and their everyday conditions. They tried to avoid the educative incursion of adults, and tried to withdraw from the pressure of the Nazi society. They displayed behavior that deviated from the social norms imposed by Hitler's National Socialism. The younger generation entered a sort of vacuum, especially during the war years, and binding standards of behavior ceased to exist. The result was that many youths kicked over the traces in a manner which cast doubt on all the maxims and claimed successes of Hitler's totalitarian system. Young people had a patent urge to associate independently, not only outside the youth organizations prescribed and controlled by the regime but in opposition to them. Their recalcitrance was only random, took the form of juvenile delinquency, and brought an increasing number of clashes between them and the authorities. The offenses were of moral nature, and latent in these eruptions of adolescent instinct was protest, not only against rules in general, but also against the specific constraints of the Nazi system. There were also youthful acts of violence and offenses committed for profit—muggings, theft, black market sales, burglary, and prostitution. Alarming reports flooded in from all over the country in such numbers as to suggest that the National Socialist educational system was at risk. Visible cracks appeared in the laboriously cultivated image of public morality, as the organization of power structures was outpaced by the spread of wartime disorganization. In many cases, families were disrupted; fathers and uncles were at the front, younger brothers and sisters were evacuated, and mothers were overburdened with work and material difficulties. As the war dragged on, there was a decrease of parental control, and this reduction of supervision of juveniles led to some moral dissolution, a collapse of "normal" social behavior, and increasing criminality. More and more the youth movement became opposed to Nazism. One of the slogans was: "Eternal War to the Hitler Jugend!" Prudently calculating their own strength, they either sought to avoid the HJ, or they ambushed HJ members and beat them up. They defied war restrictions on movement by undertaking weekend hikes. The communist and socialist youth organizations were the earliest to be banned. There is, of course, a difference between interdiction and eradication, and local groups continued to carry on various clandestine anti–Nazi activities. Collaborating with Catholic and Protestant opposition, the most determined fringe gradually got involved in active anti–Nazi resistance work by writing graffiti, editing and passing out flyers and leaflets, and distributing pamphlets denouncing the Nazi regime. Some supported the Allies by hiding downed airmen, feeding prisoners, and offering help to German army deserters, political dissidents, and escapees from camps and prisons. One noteworthy case study is the White Rose, a group of students at Munich University in 1942–43. Its nucleus consisted of Sophie and Hans Scholl, Willi Graf, Christoph Probst, Alexander Schmorell, and professor Kurt Huber, who used pamphlets to arouse a university movement against the regime. They were denounced in February 1943, summarily tried, and executed.

Repression

The activities of the Swing movement, Pirate gangs and other deviants were seen as a serious risk—the criminal, moral and political subversion youth. In all cases the Nazi authorities were puzzled and seriously concerned, but frequently did not know what to do. Some state functionaries regarded the offenses as childish pranks, a result of the degeneration of youth and stress caused by the war. Other high-ranking Nazis sensed a large-scale, Jewish-Bolshevik conspiracy, and looked for secret organizations, projecting their own morbid obsessions and sick fears onto a movement they did not understand. The only response was repression, ranging from individual warnings to raids with beatings, arrests, and shaven heads, corrective education, and referral to labor camps. Juvenile delinquency was regarded as "criminal biology" and a police agency (Disciplinary Company of the HJ) was created as early as July 1934 to deal with it. In July 1935, Gestapo branches throughout Germany were advised to prepare lists of all persons formerly active in the forbidden *bündisch* youth movements to check their infiltration of the HJ and to prevent separatist, illegal and subversive activities. Himmler placed the Disciplinary Company of the HJ under the authority of the SS police in 1938, and a special *Jugendstraflager* (punishment camp) was established at Moringen, near Göttingen, for rebels under the age of 20. The camp was headed by the SS doctor Robert Ritter, director of the Criminal-Biological Institute of the RSHA (the SS Main Office of Security of the Reich). There, on the basis of highly dubious pseudoscientific criteria, deviant youth were divided into groups of "community aliens" according to their alleged socio-biological characters and perceived reformability. Some were regarded as reeducable and later given a chance to prove themselves through the *Reichsarbeitsdienst* and military service in disciplinary battalions. Others were considered nuisances, "persistent failures" or "incapable," compulsorily sterilized and sent to "adult" concentration camps on their eighteenth birthday. Similarly a youth custody camp for females was established in the immediate vicinity of the women's concentration camp at Ravensbrück. A further camp exclusively for young Polish "criminals" was established at Lodz. From 1939 to 1943, it is estimated that about 700,000 youth were "reeducated" by the SS. In March 1940 a curfew decree was issued, forbidding youths under the age of 18 to be on the street after 9:00 P.M. Two laws introduced by the Ministry of Justice in October 1939 and November 1943 reduced the age at which a death sentence might be received to 14; a sentence depended on a judge's assessments of an offender's "criminal attitude of mind" and on the specifically "antisocial" nature of the offense, if any. In reality the judges were politically influenced, in the simple sense of supporting the interests of their boss, the state (i.e., Hitler), and were forced into a position where they allowed police (i.e., Himmler) to predetermine their verdicts.

In 1944, another concentration camp especially intended to detain young deviants was established at Neuwied-am-Rhein. Like other concentration camps, these youth penitentiaries were managed by the *Amt IV* of the SS Central security office (RSHA). Himmler's vicious reaction to juvenile offenders culminated in November 1944, when 13 members of the Edelweiss Pirates from Cologne were arrested and—without trial—publicly hanged by the Gestapo as an example to other youth. One boy was sentenced to death and executed for trying to build an illegal short-wave radio transmitter.

Measures taken by the state against anti-Nazi youth did not eradicate rebelliousness. On the contrary, the persecution, savagery and harshness provoked further protest and resistance. Juvenile crime statistics continued to increase, although it was the Nazis, of course, who decided what was criminal in the first place. The activities of the deviant youth groups lacked the political organization to be anything more than an embarrassment to the regime. The isolation of these groups and individuals, their total lack of support from the majority from their compatriots ensured that social youth deviance would never amount to serious political opposition. The plain fact is that too many people in Germany were unable or unwilling to differentiate between right and wrong. The acts of resistance by the youth were for the most part aimed with utopian and illusory expectations, and very often were merely spontaneous hopeless gestures, lacking unifying leadership to guide or coordinate them. When the Catholic student conspirators of the White Rose, Hans and Sophie Scholl, were arrested and executed, this was followed by a demonstration of 3,000 students eager to express their loyalty to the regime.

However, subcultures such as White Rose demonstrated that the Nazis—even after years in power—still did not have a complete grip on German society. Nazism—offering only military discipline, an anachronistic and criminal ideology and a stifling bureaucracy—unintentionally paved the way for later manifestations of modern youth culture in the late 1940s and 1950s. Youth opposed to Hitler should perhaps be regarded as precursors of the "teddy boys" from the 1940s who rebelled against military drills and other compulsory activities.

Those opposed to Hitler—whatever their motivation and no matter how modest their actions—deserve remembrance, understanding and the utmost respect. They were a few bright lights in the darkest period of German history.

4

Hitler's Boy Soldiers, 1939–1945

Hitler Jugend at War

Arthur Axmann

On 1 December 1936 *Jugenddienstpflicht* (youth conscription) was decreed but it was not until 25 March 1939 that HJ service was made compulsory (only for 17-year-old boys) and not until 12 September 1941 that it was made compulsory for boys and girls from the age of 10. In 1936, Baldur von Schirach's enemies had started a campaign of vilification against him. Jokes about his effeminate behavior and his allegedly white bedroom furnished in a girlish fashion, the cult of his personality, and his plump appearance became a national pastime. His position was undermined by the intrigues of Martin Bormann and other rivals and enemies, and von Schirach's popularity declined. When World War II started in 1939, the control of the HJ was increasingly slipping out of his grasp. Many HJ leaders had entered the army, and the supervision of the HJ passed in practice to the Nazi Party. At the beginning of 1940, von Schirach himself enlisted in the German army, serving in France for a few months as an infantry officer and receiving the Iron Cross First Class. Afterward, Hitler did not want him any longer as *Reichsjungendführer der NSDAP*. Hitler's reasons remain unclear. Maybe he thought von Schirach was no longer the right man for the job, or maybe he feared that von Schirach would become too popular and too powerful. Whatever the reason, in mid-1940, Baldur von Schirach was dismissed, and appointed *Gauleiter* and Reich plenipotentiary in Vienna, a much less important post. He was replaced as head of the HJ by one of his deputies, Arthur Axmann, a man who had a long history with the organization.

Arthur Axmann (1913–1996) had studied law, became a Nazi in 1928, and founded the first Hitler Youth group in Westphalia. A convinced and determined Nazi with real organizational skills, he was promoted rapidly and in 1932 was called to carry out a reorganization of the HJ. A year later he became chief of the Social Office of the Reich Youth Leadership, and one of von Schirach's close collaborators. In 1939 and 1940, Axmann fought in Poland and France. Later the new head of the HJ returned to the army to take part in the invasion of Russia where he remained until he lost his right arm below the elbow in December 1941. Until the end of the war Arthur Axmann remained *Reichsjungendführer der NSDAP.*

Behind a façade of health, fitness and comradeship, there were more sinister purposes to the Hitler Jugend. Even before the outbreak of the Second World War, disciplinary and surveillance measures to enforce youth service concentrated increasingly on war preparation and pre-military drills. When the war broke out, several laws were passed for the *Kriegseinsatz* (mobilization) of the Hitler Jugend, and new tasks were defined and given priority by Arthur Axmann. HJ boys and BdM girls had to uphold the Nazi spirit on the home front. They went from door to door to collect metal scraps for industry, and bones, bottles and paper which were recycled for the war effort. They collected furs, blankets and warm clothes for troops at the front. Gradually, they were committed to keeping the war economy going. As many peasants and workers were drafted, HJ members had to fill the vacancies. Eight million HJ boys and girls were available to replace the mobilized soldiers. HJ boys and BdM girls then became auxiliaries in all branches of social life—from industry and agriculture to public transport and administration. During the war, three million girls and women worked in the weapons factories as much as 60 hours per week. Some BdM girls were employed in the mail service, and others assigned to help care for wounded soldiers in hospitals. They also helped in kindergarten as well as assisting in households of large families. They worked in refugee camps, and stood on railway platforms, offering encouragement and refreshments to army troops departing for the front.

Following Allied bombing raids, HJ members assisted in neighborhood clean-up. They helped locate bombed-out civilians. They knocked on doors, looking for unused rooms in undamaged houses or apartments. Occupants refusing to let in new tenants were reported to local police, and they most likely would receive a visit from the dreaded Gestapo. HJ members were also used to carry messages. Every free hour of theirs was monopolized for the NSDAP and the war effort, children scarcely had a moment for themselves and their families. During the last two years of the war, the average German family was dislocated. Fathers, elder brothers and uncles were drafted, taken prisoner, dead or missing, mothers were more and more involved in war production in bombed factories, and younger brothers and sisters had been evacuated safely to the countryside.

Kinderlandverschickung (KLV)

In September 1940, the Nazi regime decided announced the *"Kinderlandverschickung"* (KLV—"sending of children to the land"), the evacuation to the countryside of children from the cities at greatest risk of bombing. Initially the evacuation was to apply only to children of school age from Berlin and Hamburg who lived in suburbs and parts of the cities which did not have sufficient air-raid shelters. The project soon became more extensive as the Allies stepped up their bombing campaign. In April 1942, there were already 850,000 evacuated boys and girls. The KLV was a large program carried out by the *Nationalsozialistische Volkswohlfahrt* (NSV—Nazi welfare organization) and many girls of the BdM became involved in the care of children. Evacuated children were housed in homes, youth hostels, farms, monasteries, holiday camps, pensions, and special camps. These camps, approximately 5,000 of them, were located mainly in the rural regions of East Prussia, the Warthegau section of Poland, and Upper Silesia, as well as Slovakia. The camps varied in size, anywhere from 18 children to over 1,200. Each camp was run by Nazi-approved teachers and a Hitler Youth leader. These camps began replacing many urban grammar schools, most of which had been

closed due to all the bombings. The operation was supervised by the HJ and the Nazi Party. The KVL policy also served the purpose of removing children from their family environment which made it possible, to some extent, to implement indoctrination and militarization. The KLV camps prepared German teenage boys for deadly encounters with Allied soldiers in the rubble and ruins of Hitler's Germany. Parents were reluctant to send their children away to the camps, but those who refused to give their children permission to leave were denounced as unpatriotic. Parents were discouraged from visiting the KVL camps and homes in order not to intensify homesickness and also to avoid a strain on the public transportation system. From 1940 to 1945, over 2.8 million German children were sent to the KLV camps.

Military auxiliary forces

After Germany's invasion of Eastern Europe, Hitler decided to send young men and women of the HJ to the occupied territories of Poland and Western Ukraine to ease the shortage of teachers. Between 1941 and 1943, about 30,000 HJ members were sent out after three months training. The improvised teachers often found that they were teaching "Germans" who hardly spoke any German at all.

The HJ was doomed to get more and more involved in military activities. By the end of 1940, the National Youth Directorate required target practice and terrain maneuvers for boys aged 10 and older. Soon Axmann declared that one million boys were practicing with live weapons and that 31,000 of them were first-class marksmen. The shortage of bodies meant that the Hitler

Girl of BdM/KLV. This teenage **Bund deutscher Mädel** *member was serving as a child-care auxiliary of the KLV, as indicated by the black cuff title.*

HJ **Flakhelfer**, *1944. The anti-aircraft crew helper (left) wears the* **Luftwaffe** *blue-gray uniform consisting of a* **Fliegerbluse** *(a short battle-dress-style blouse) and long, blue-gray trousers gathered at the ankles. A blue-gray greatcoat (right) and an M1935 steel helmet were part of this uniform.*

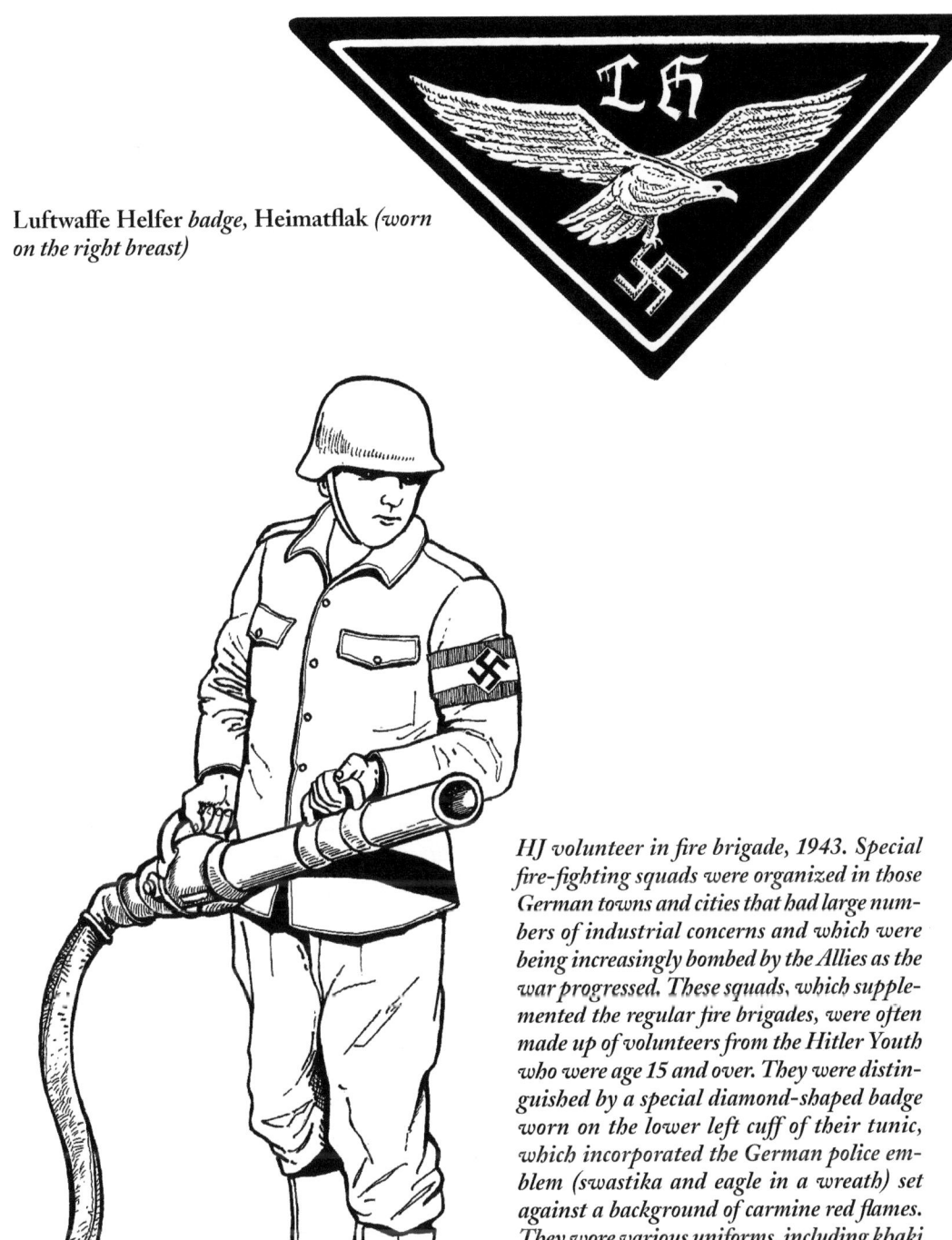

Luftwaffe Helfer *badge*, **Heimatflak** *(worn on the right breast)*

HJ volunteer in fire brigade, 1943. Special fire-fighting squads were organized in those German towns and cities that had large numbers of industrial concerns and which were being increasingly bombed by the Allies as the war progressed. These squads, which supplemented the regular fire brigades, were often made up of volunteers from the Hitler Youth who were age 15 and over. They were distinguished by a special diamond-shaped badge worn on the lower left cuff of their tunic, which incorporated the German police emblem (swastika and eagle in a wreath) set against a background of carmine red flames. They wore various uniforms, including khaki or brown jacket, HJ dark-blue tunic, or air force **Fliegerbluse**, *a short, double-breasted, blue-gray tunic, often with HJ armband. Headgear included a black side cap on which was displayed a police-eagle cap emblem, as well as army or* **Schutzluft** *(Civil Defense) steel helmet.*

Youth were also called on when the Allied bombardments began to strike Germany. HJ boys became a military auxiliary force. They were issued army uniforms and equipment, trained to serve in the *Feuerwehren* (fire brigades), and the *Feuerschutzpolizei* and *Luftschutzpolizei* (emergency rescue squads and air-raid police units). German youths were encouraged to enlist in the *NSKK* (transport squads) and the *Technische Nothilfe* (TeNo—Technical Emergency Service), the latter created in 1919. As the war progressed, the youthful loyalty of the HJ members was ruthlessly exploited. By mid-1943, a new *Luftwaffe* flak artillery branch was created, called *Heimatflak* (homeland anti-aircraft artillery). The Hitler Jugend was drafted to serve in it as *Luftwaffe-Helfern* (air-force auxiliaries) for anti-aircraft duties, to operate search-light batteries, and to carry ammunition supplies, and dispatches.

The Hitler Jugend members were also encouraged to volunteer for the *Streifendienst*, a patrol/police auxiliary service staffed, trained and equipped by the SS. Created in 1938 by an agreement between Baldur von Schirach and Heinrich Himmler, the *Streifendienst* was originally responsible for policing youth meeting and rallies, so the

Hitler Youth in **Streifendienst** *1943. The Hitler Jugend* **Streifendienst** *was a special patrol service consisting of older members of the Hitler Youth. It was set up for the purpose of policing the Hitler Youth, but during the latter stages of the war years it became an armed body of fanatical youth members who assisted the police and the SS in hunting down escaped prisoners of war, allied aircrews who had bailed out of their aircraft and anyone else that was suspected of evading the authorities or were considered as enemy agents working against the Nazi regime. They wore the standard-pattern HJ dark-blue uniforms with HJ armband. They wore a cuffband with the label* **Streifendienst** *and—when on patrol service—a special* **Streifendienst** *gorget. They were trained to use small arms and rifles, and carried rifles when on duty.*

HJ was not only "led by the youth" but also repressed by it. The members were trained to the age of 18 by officers of the SS. During the war the patrol service was employed to see that curfews and black-outs were observed. They were used as raiding squads and informers. They also formed pursuit detachments intended to hunt escapees from prisons and camps, and capture Allied airmen shot down above Germany. The claim of legal power and the ruthlessness shown by the unscrupulous HJ patrols provoked some indignation among the population. Heavily indoctrinated in Nazi values, anti–Semitic, elitist, and already accustomed to repression and SS practices, many of these HJ members had eventual membership in the SS in mind. In fact the Hitler Jugend as a whole—but more particularly the *Streifendienst*—was regarded as a prerequisite for entrance into the SS.

Waffen SS

The *Waffen SS* were combat formations from the *Schutz-Staffeln* (SS). Originating from a tiny group of highly selected and loyal bodyguards intended to protect Adolf Hitler, the SS became a huge organization within the Nazi Party, a private army within

Private of the TeNo. The **Technische Nothilfe** *(TeNo—Technical Emergency Service) was a corps of specialized troops for rescue and repair, created in 1919. Its original purpose was to make sure that vital services such as electricity, gas and communication would continue to function in the event of strikes. The potential value of the TeNo was fully recognized by the Nazis. The service was continued after 1933 and became a part of the* **Ordnungspolizei.**

the *Wehrmacht* and a state within the state. Headed by *Reichsführer* Heinrich Himmler, the *Schutz-Staffeln*'s tasks were numerous: maintenance of the Nazi order, control of the German population, intelligence, and physical elimination of enemies of the Reich, and the removal of people to concentration and extermination camps, just to name a few.

The SS had its own permanent armed branch which was organized after 1935. The military SS were highly selected, militarily trained and organized, wore uniforms and lived in barracks. Originally called the *Verfügungstruppen* (SS VT—reserve or task troops), the elite corps grew to a huge force during World War II. Himmler was determined that the SS military branch should become the nucleus of a postwar German national police and army service. In July 1940, the *Verfügungstruppen*—reinforced with *Totenkopfverbände* (Death's Head concentration camp guards) and members of the police who were drafted—were renamed *Waffen SS* (armed SS). By exploiting the law to suit himself, ruthlessly confiscating Jewish property, and recruiting Germanic foreigners, Himmler built and equipped his private armed forces. Although the regular army watched the SS with dislike and distrust, and although the generals tried to obstruct him, *Reichsführer* Heinrich Himmler managed to constitute a formidable force which had grown to 38 divisions at the end of the war.

The *Waffen SS* is still a controversial unit today. It built up a reputation as hard-fighting soldiers, but these were not ordinary combatants, nor were they merely a fourth service of the *Wehrmacht*. They were, on the whole, ultra–Nazi, fanatical SS troops who committed numerous atrocities and war crimes, both on and off the battlefield. The *Waffen SS* was declared a criminal organization by the tribunal at Nuremberg in 1946. The corps was organized by *Verfügungstruppen* General-Inspector Paul Hausser and divided into units similar in strength to those of the German ground army. The private Nazi Party SS army was militarily commanded by Hitler himself and administered by Himmler who carried the official title of *Reichsführer der SS und Chef der deutschen Polizei*.

After 1940, the *Waffen SS* was opened to *Volksdeutsche*. These "racial" Germans from northern European Germanic lands (Denmark, Holland, Flanders, and other) were considered people of "similar blood." Where power was at stake, even a perfectionist like Himmler could abandon racial quality for quantity. After 1942, the *Waffen SS* was open to "unpure" volunteers from western and eastern Europe (France, Wallonia and other lands). Even Russian mercenaries and Muslims from the Balkans were welcome. The *Waffen SS* was virtually a private army with its own staff (*SS Führungs Hauptamt*); it was organized separately from the regular *Heer* and had its own badges, ranks and emblems. The SS and the HJ had tight relationship, and Himmler and Axmann a fruitful collaboration. The *Waffen SS* was very popular among the HJ, and many young men were attracted—some fascinated—by the new corps. Many of those who enlisted were already indoctrinated in National-Socialist values, brainwashed, militarized and over-disciplined by their time in the Hitler Jugend and in the compulsory *Reichsarbeitsdienst*. For many youth, the step from Hitler Jugend to *Waffen SS* was a normal and inevitable procedure.

The final move toward complete militarization of the Hitler Jugend was made in 1943. Arthur Axmann encouraged HJ members to join in the *9th Waffen SS Panzerdivision Hohenstaufen* and in the *10th Waffen SS Panzerdivision Frundsberg*, both formed early that year. In spite of protest from the church and parents who had no wish to see their sons killed in battle, Himmler allowed the creation of a special *Waffen SS* unit composed of volunteering HJ boys born in 1926.

The 12th *Waffen SS* Division *Hitlerjugend*

Creation of the division

As the war progressed and military losses necessitated more soldiers, the age for military service was lowered, and more and more youths volunteered for the *Waffen SS*. In January 1943, Allied leaders met at Casablanca and made several agreements, one a far-reaching decision: they declared their determination to fight Germany into unconditional surrender, excluding any political or diplomatic end to the war. This galvanized German youth who believed that the war now had to be won no matter how. A recruitment campaign was launched by the SS, notably by *SS Gruppenführer* Gottlob Berger, who was chief of the *Waffen SS* Recruiting Office. The response from the Hitler Youth was tremendous, and thousands volunteered. Many of the boys had not yet turned seventeen. From the start it was intended to form a truly elite unit, and only the best candidates (about 20,000 boys) in top physical condition and with a sufficient degree of Nazi fervor and unswerving loyalty to the Führer were accepted. One of the provisions was to call for the RAD (Work Service) to release candidates. For infantry duty, candidates had to have a height of at least 1.70 m (5 ft. 7 in.); for the other branches of the division a minimum of 1.68 m (5 ft. 6 in.) was required. The *Hitlerjugend Waffen SS* unit was officially created on 23 June 1943. Then at Antwerp (Belgium) on 20 July 1943, the *SS Panzergrenadier Division Hitlerjugend* was formed, a motorized infantry division. This was redesignated on 30 October 1943 as *12th SS Panzer Grenadier Division Hitlerjugend* and it became an armored division equipped with tanks. The elite character was accentuated by the cadre of the 12th Division Hitler Youth, officers who were drawn from the *Leibstandarte SS Adolf Hitler* (LSSAH—Hitler's personal bodyguards). About 1,000 experienced officers and NCOs were transferred from the LSSAH, including such top soldiers as Fritz Witt, Max Wünsche, Kurt Meyer, Wilhelm Mohnke, and Gerhart Bremer. The patronizing of the 12th Division by the prestigious First *Leibstandarte SS Adolf Hitler* gave the unit both political, ideological zeal and excellent military training, and this was further enhanced by the choice of the emblem. The 12th Division's insignia was composed of the *Leibstandarte* pass key ("*Dietrich*," in German, which was the name of the LSSAH commander—Jozef "Sepp" Dietrich) and the Hitler Jugend emblem: the Sieg rune

Emblem of the 1st Division **Leibstandarte** *(left) and 12th Division Hitler Jugend (right)*

(letter S), symbolizing victory. The 12th Division's motto was that inscribed on the HJ ceremonial dagger: *Blut und Ehre!* (Blood and Honor). Of all the *Waffen SS* units, the *1st SS Division Leibstandarte Adolf Hitler* was the most prestigious. The *Leibstandarte* originated from a tiny group of highly selected body-guards which became a ceremonial unit. Soon after Hitler seized power in January 1933, the guard unit was upgraded into a fighting regiment called *Leibstandarte Schutz-Staffeln Adolf Hitler* (LSSAH) and later upgraded to an armored division. The LSSAH was entirely composed of selected "untainted" Germans, the fittest and the toughest, strictly disciplined and highly trained, the cream of the *Waffen SS* volunteers. The LSSAH had a remarkable combat record, taking part in all the major battles of the Third Reich on all fronts after 1940: Poland, France, Greece, Ukraine and Italy.

Training

Each *Waffen SS* division had an administrative training home depot called *Ausbildungs- und Ersatzbataillon*, followed by the name of the division. This was a *Kazerne* (barracks) in a German town (e.g., "*Ausbildungs- und Ersatzbataillon Klagenfurt*" for the 5th division *Wiking*) where recruits were formed, equipped and trained. That of the 12th Division *Hitlerjugend* was *Ausbildungs- und Ersatzbataillon Kaiserlautern*, situated in the province Palatinate. During the war, lightly wounded men were returned after hospitalization to the divisional *Ausbildungs* depot where they were trained anew to form fresh fighting units. The personnel of the 12th SS HJ division were trained for a whole year, partly in Kaiserlautern, but also in Mailly (France), in Hasselt and in Beverloo (Belgium). Though they were very young and most of them not fully grown, members of the 12th Division were treated exactly like the other soldiers of the *Waffen SS*, with one exception: all boys under 18 received a sweet ration in lieu of the usual cigarette ration for older soldiers. Nazi indoctrination of the HJ continued within the 12th Division, with the emphasis on courage, loyalty and self-sacrifice. The boys were compared to the heroes of German history: Siegfried, who killed the dragon; Arminius, who defeated the Roman Legions; Kaiser Barbarossa, who conquered the Holy Land; Hermann von Salza and the Teutonic Knights who expanded the Germanic world to the lands of the pagan Slavs. The intense training and indoctrination were intended to form warriors. The HJ-SS boy soldiers had to kill without hesitation and die without fear. They acquired military rigidity together with a desperate seriousness, and their self-assured, grown-up manner alternated with childish behavior. Allied soldiers observed that when HJ-SS young wounded were captured, many refused blood transfusions if they could not be certain of the donor's racial purity, preferring to die instead. *Waffen SS* troops were intended to be rapid, mechanized, storm infantry, small but determined assault troops of tough, ruthless, recklessly brave, and self-disciplined young men. Armed to the teeth, they were for leading swift penetration of enemy lines and making cunning outflanking moves with speed and aggressive attack. The aim was to produce a homogeneous whole that would work together as a team as no other army had ever done before. Great emphasis laid on esprit de corps, comradeship and physical fitness. All *Waffen SS* men had to complete the same, comprehensive, extremely rigorous and physically challenging training program. Regardless of the candidate's class background and upbringing, NCOs and officers had to work their way up through the hierarchy, to serve two years in the ranks before proceeding to officer-training schools. No SS leader was to ask his men to do anything that he would not willingly do himself. As with the Hitler Jugend, officers had to submit themselves to the same demanding and ruthless training as their men. Knowing that their leaders had been through the same conditions created a feeling of reliance, trust, and respect among the ranks. The SS command realistically believed that a respected officer would be blindly obeyed. In many SS formations—and particularly in the 12th Division—the leader was both a trusted commander and a respected friend for whom his boys were ready to suffer, risk their lives and die. They were also to obey without arguing over the sense or suitability of orders. This fostering of *Bruderschaft* (brotherhood or camaraderie) between ranks was the result of training in the HJ; it was probably the most distinguishing feature of the 12th Division Hitler Jugend. The *Waffen SS* authorities paid little attention to the recruits' educational background, arguing that it was training, bravery and merit which made a good fighter, not necessarily a good education. A gallant *Waffen SS* private could quickly rise to the rank of NCO. A meritorious and competent subaltern officer could be made a colonel, even a general. The NCOs were the backbone of the SS army. Many of them were young, and the main principle of the HJ—"youth must be led by youth"—was continued in the 12th Division. As a rule, SS middle-ranking and senior officers shared the hardships and meager rations endured by the men, lived in trenches and engaged in combat with them. Officer casualties were therefore very high, due to this tendency to lead from the front. Fritz Witt (the 12th Division's commander) and Erich Olböter and Karl-Heinz Prinz (two main senior officers) were killed in action in Normandy. Other prominent senior officers of the 12th Division were killed in combat in the last months of the war: Hans Waldmüller, Arnold Jürgensen and Bernhard Krausse.

Sports played an important role in the very tough training. This included strenuous physical exercise, cross-country runs, and aggressive *Wehrsport* (contact sport, such as boxing and fencing) to increase speed and ferocity in combat, as well as to test aggression and overcome the fear of being hurt. The HJ-SS teenagers learned how to fire, strip, clean and reassemble all kind of weaponry, they were taught all aspects of tactics and taken into the field to put theoretical teaching into practice. The tough battle training reached a high degree of realism in order to create determined soldiers, super-fit, athletic young men well muscled and with iron nerves. In all weather, by day or night, on the most difficult terrain, *Waffen SS* young men were repeatedly submitted to grueling contests, route marches with heavy loads, and military obstacle races to develop endurance. They had to march for miles, with full pack, to move swiftly and efficiently, to dig foxholes, crawl, run, charge with fixed bayonet, clear mines, assault infantry positions, attack armored vehicles with various techniques and all sort of weapons. Instead of learning the parade "goose step," they were taught to kill as wolves. Of course, a lot of attention was paid to shooting, target practice with all kind of firearms. Training with live rounds and real artillery was common. This was intended to familiarize the HJ-SS teenagers with the sight, sound and dangerous conditions of a real battle. Casualties and fatalities were not unknown, but the efficiency of this method prepared Hitler's boy soldiers for battle like no other training program could, and probably saved many lives on the battlefield. Individual training continued but increasingly gave way to unit training at the squad level and gradually broadening into the company, battalion and regimental levels to create a team spirit. Each *Waffen SS* soldier was trained to take over for his immediate superior if that person was wounded or killed, to assume his mantle and carry on with fulfilling the mission.

The *Waffen SS* always had priority for supplies and weapons. They were issued plenty of good weapons, camouflaged uni-

*SS sport kit. As in the Hitler Youth, sports played a central role in the training of the **Waffen SS**. Each young man was therefore issued a sport kit. The SS sport kit was the same as the HJ one. It consisted of a white singlet bearing the SS emblem, black shorts, and black shoes worn without socks.*

forms, armored troop carriers and the best tanks. However, the build-up of the 12th Division went much more slowly than Fritz Witt wished. This was due to the lack of training personnel, the difficulty in obtaining equipment, uniforms, arms and ammunition, and the shortage of artillery, tanks, half-tracks and trucks. By 1944, the German military economy was strained, disorganized and exhausted by four years of war effort, and gasoline was in short supply. In many ways, the organization of the 12th Division had an improvised character. For example, during the training period at Mailly, the armored unit of the 12th Division had only eight tanks, including four SdKfz 171 Panthers and four SdKfz 161 PzKfw IV (Mark IV), tanks which were illegally "borrowed" from other German armored formations. A shortage of uniforms required some of the boys to train in their Hitler Youth uniforms, and some tank crewmen wore black leather navy U-boat uniforms instead of the regular Panzer suit. There was also carelessness at the top administrative level and bureaucratic clumsiness at the SS headquarters, which infuriated Fritz Witt and his staff. When it was garrisoned in France, right before D-Day (6 June 1944), the 12th Division was submitted to a triple hierarchy. Tactically, it depended on General von Salmuth, the commander of the 15th Army which was a part of Army Group B headed by Field Marshall Erwin Rommel. At the instructional, training level, it depended on the *Panzergruppe West* (Armored Group West) headed by General Geyr von Schweppenburg. Administratively the unit was placed under control of the *SS Führungs-Hauptamt* (SSFHa—the SS military headquarters). In March 1944, the 12th Division conducted a training exercise, observed by *Generalfeldmarschall* Gerd von Rundstedt (Commander-in-Chief West), and *SS Obergruppenführer* Sepp Dietrich (then Commander of 1st SS Panzer Corps). Despite critical shortages, the division earned praise for their combat skills and state of preparedness.

Composition, units and ranks

In spite of many organizational difficulties and material shortages, the 12th SS *Panzerdivision* was a remarkable force when it was engaged on the western front in June 1944. Totaling some 20,000 boy soldiers, it was composed of four combat *Standarten* (regiments) and various support units. The SS Panzer Regiment 12 was an armored regiment divided into two armored *Abteilungen* (battalions): the *SS Panzer Abteilung* I and *SS Panzer Abteilung* II. The armored personnel of the 12th Division had been trained in a camp at Mailly, situated near Reims. Both *Panzer Abteilungen* were equipped with modern tanks, mainly Panthers and Mark IVs.

The 12th Division had two infantry regiments: the *SS Panzer Grenadier Regiment 25 Hitlerjugend* and the *SS Panzer Grenadier Regiment 26 Hitlerjugend*. Each regiment had three *Sturmbanne* (battalions); each battalion had four combat *Stürme* (companies); each company included three *Scharen* (platoons); and each *Schar* was divided into three *Rotte* (squads). Both infantry regiments 25 and 26 were motorized. The soldiers were transported by armored half-tracks, troop carriers, and trucks—mostly captured from the Italian army and prone to breakdown, often making them useless.

The 12th Division had a powerful artillery. The *SS Panzer Artillerie Regiment 12* had three battalions (*SS Panzer Artillerie Abteilungen* I, II and III, armed with field guns, howitzers and SPGs Wespe and Hummel). It included the *SS Flak Artillerie Abteilung 12* (anti-aircraft), the *SS Nebelwerfer Abteilung 12* (rocket launchers), and the *SS Panzerjäger Abteilung 12* (self-propelled anti-tank guns). Additional combat units were the *SS Panzer Aufklärungs Abteilung 12* (reconnaissance), divided into two companies, one for each infantry regiment, and equipped with armored cars; and the *SS Panzer Pionier Bataillon 12* (engineers).

Logistic services included the *SS Panzer Nachrichten Abteilung 12* (signal battalion) and the *SS Versorgungs Einheit 12* (medical unit). In addition there was a motorized transport unit carrying ammunition, supplies and fuel, and a field workshop for vehicle recovery, maintenance and repair. There was also a small unit of *Propagandakompanie* (PK—war reporters) and a unit of *Waffen SS Feldgendarmerie* (military police) for maintenance of discipline, traffic regulation, and escort services for the headquarters.

The 12th Division was commanded by *SS Brigadeführer* Fritz Witt and—after Witt's death on 16 June 1944—by *Standartenführer* Kurt "Panzer" Meyer. Both commanders originated from the 1st Division *Leibstandarte*.

The units of the *Waffen SS* were copied from those of the regular German army. The following table shows the *Waffen SS* units from the smallest to the largest, with U.S. equivalent and composition.

Waffen SS Units from Smallest to Largest, with U.S. Equivalent and Composition*

Rotte	squad	ten soldiers
Schar	platoon	3 or 4 *Rotten*
Sturm	company	3 or 4 *Scharen*
Sturmbann	battalion	3 or 4 *Stürme*
Standarte	regiment	several battalions
Kampfgruppe	combat group	various units
Division	division	several regiments
Panzerdivision	armored division	several armored units
Panzerkorps	armored corps	several divisions

The units of the Waffen SS *were copied from those of the regular German army.*

Waffen SS Ranking System, Abbreviations, and Equivalent in the U.S. Army*

Waffen SS	U.S. Army
Anwärter	Candidate

NONCOMMISSIONED RANKS

Schütze or *SS Mann*	Private or rifleman
Grenadier (Gren)	Private or rifleman
Sturmmann (Strmm)	Private first class
Obergrenadier (Ob. Gren)	Private first class
Rottenführer (Rttf)	Corporal

NONCOMMISSIONED OFFICERS

Unterscharführer (Uscha)	Sergeant
Scharführer (Scha)	Staff Sergeant
Oberscharführer (Oscha)	Technical Sergeant
Hauptscharführer (Hscha)	Master Sergeant
Stabsscharführer	First Sergeant
Sturmscharführer (Stuscha)	Sergeant Major
Junker der Waffen SS (Ju.d.SS)	Candidate officer

Standarte-Junker (Std.Ju)	Candidate officer
Standarten-Oberjunker (Std.Ob.Ju)	Candidate officer

SUBALTERN OFFICERS

Untersturmführer (Ustuf)	Second Lieutenant
Obersturmführer (Ostuf)	First Lieutenant
Hauptsturmführer (Hstuf)	Captain

MIDDLE-RANKING OFFICERS

Sturmbannführer (Stubaf)	Major
Obersturmbannführer (Ostubaf)	Lieutenant Colonel
Standartenführer (Staf)	Colonel

SENIOR OFFICERS

Oberführer (Obf)	Brigadier General
Brigadeführer (Brigf)	Major General
Gruppenführer (Gruf)	Lieutenant General
Obergruppenführer (Ogruf)	General
Oberstgruppenführer (Orstgruf)	General of Army
Reichsführer der SS (RfSS)	no equivalent (Himmler's rank)

Ranks in the Waffen SS were taken over from the SA and SS, which preferred the term Führer (leader) to Offizier (officer) as is shown in the SS rank terminology.

Insignia

The *Hoheitszeichen* (Nazi official national emblem) was composed of an eagle holding a swastika. It was worn on the left upper arm in the *Waffen SS* instead of on the right breast pocket as in the army.

The *Waffen SS* had its own badges of ranks and emblems. The notorious *Siegrunen*, double SS victory rune, commonly described as the "double lightning flash," was worn on the right collar patch. The left collar patch carried the rank, indicated by stars, bars and oak leaves. In mid-1942, SS units (and all other units issued camouflage suits, such as paratroopers) were issued a more distinctive system of rank insignia used for NCOs and officers. These were intended for wear on special combat clothing, camouflage gear, anoraks, wind jackets, denim overalls, winter suits and other clothing without collars and shoulder straps on which ranks were usually displayed. These new *Dienstgraden* (badges of rank), with relatively low visibility, were simple patches (10 cm wide) with bars and stylized oak leaves, worn below the left shoulder seam; they were printed in green (yellow for senior officers) on black cloth backing.

The *Totenkopf* (Death's Head) was worn on headgear in miniaturized form by the regular army tank troops, by the SS and by the *Waffen SS*.

Specialist badges were worn by *Unteroffizieren* (NCOs) who were trained to a specific task. These were indicated by an embroidered yellow symbol (or gothic letter) on a dark-green, round cloth background. The badge was generally worn on the lower right sleeve of the tunic. For instance, a gothic letter S indicated a *Schirrmeister* (motor maintenance sergeant, or harness sergeant if horse outfit), a gothic letter F indicated a *Feuerwerker* (a pyrotechnician, dealing with explosives). Many *Waffen SS* units were allowed to wear a thin black *Armelstreifen* (cuff-band) on the left lower sleeve of the tunic, indicating regimental or divisional title, written in silver Gothic lettering. That of the 12th Division carried the designation "*Hitlerjugend*."

The prestigious insignia, SS runes on collar patches, badges, divisional names, emblems and cuff-titles created a strong emotional bond between the men and their units. The regalia emphasized their pride, loyalty, professionalism and involvement.

Uniforms

All *Waffen SS* uniforms were designed and controlled by the *Reichszeugmeisterei* (RZM—central ordnance office of the NSDAP) and by the *Amt VII*, the logistic department of the SS *Führungs-Hauptamt* (SSFHa). Uniforms and accoutrements were issued through the SS *Wirtschafts und Verwaltungs Hauptamt* (Main Office for Economy and Administration), and production was carried out by SS factories using slave labor and prisoners in SS concentration camps, notably at Dachau and Buchenwald, where Jewish tailors, seamstresses and cobblers were ruthlessly put to work. The uniform worn by the *Waffen SS* comprised a *Feldanzug* (field/combat uniform) exactly like that worn by the army. It included a shirt, a four-pocketed *Dienstrock* (tunic) with turned-back collar, and fairly baggy *Hose* (trousers) held up by a belt or braces. The tunic and trouser color was *Feldgrau* (gray-green) but there were some variations in its actual shade depending on its age and amount of cleaning.

The *Mantel* (overcoat) was a standard pattern throughout the German army. It was worn by NSDAP members, SS men, *Waffen SS* soldiers, army soldiers, NCOs and others with only detail differences to account for rank and insignia. In style the *Mantel* was a very long double-breasted garment reaching to the wearer's calves. Mostly field-gray in color, it had two rows of six gray metal buttons (gilded for generals), deep turned back cuffs and two slash side pockets. The *Mantel* had to be buttoned up to the neck and the collar could be worn turned up around the wearer's neck in cold weather. Holders of a cross were allowed to fold the lapels back in order to show the neck decoration attached to the tunic. There was also a thicker, lined version especially intended and issued for sentry duty in the field.

Although the *Waffen SS* never saw action in northern Africa, the *Tropenanzug* (tropical service uniform) was greatly appreciated in the summer campaigns. The tropical uniform, originally designed for the Afrika Korps, was composed of an olive-green field tunic with khaki shirt, drill shorts, knee-length stockings and canvas-topped lace-up boots. There were also alternative long trousers in khaki drill which were worn full length, gathered in at the ankle into normal army boots. Colors tended to vary quite considerably as the bleaching effect of the sun was severe. After some period of service, they faded to lighter shades of brown and green; in many cases they ended up the color of the natural fabric. Headgear included various items. The *Stahlhelm M35* was standard issue for all fighting units of the Third Reich (with the exception of the airborne troops, who had a lighter version). Very well designed, offering good protection to face, ears and neck, the German helmet was pressed in one piece of steel. Its markings were a swastika on the left side and a white shield with the black SS runes on the right side. These insignia were often missing after 1943 until the end of the war. The helmet could be camouflaged with a canvas cover with patterns of various shades of green and brown. Officers and NCOs wore a wool or canvas service cap (stiff or soft) called *Schirmmütze*; this had a field-gray top, a dark blue-green band, and a shiny patent black peak. Its front included a chinstrap carrying *Waffenfarbe* (arm of service) pipings, a metal or embroidered *Totenkopf* (death's head badge) and the eagle/swastika emblem. All SS ranks wore the very popular

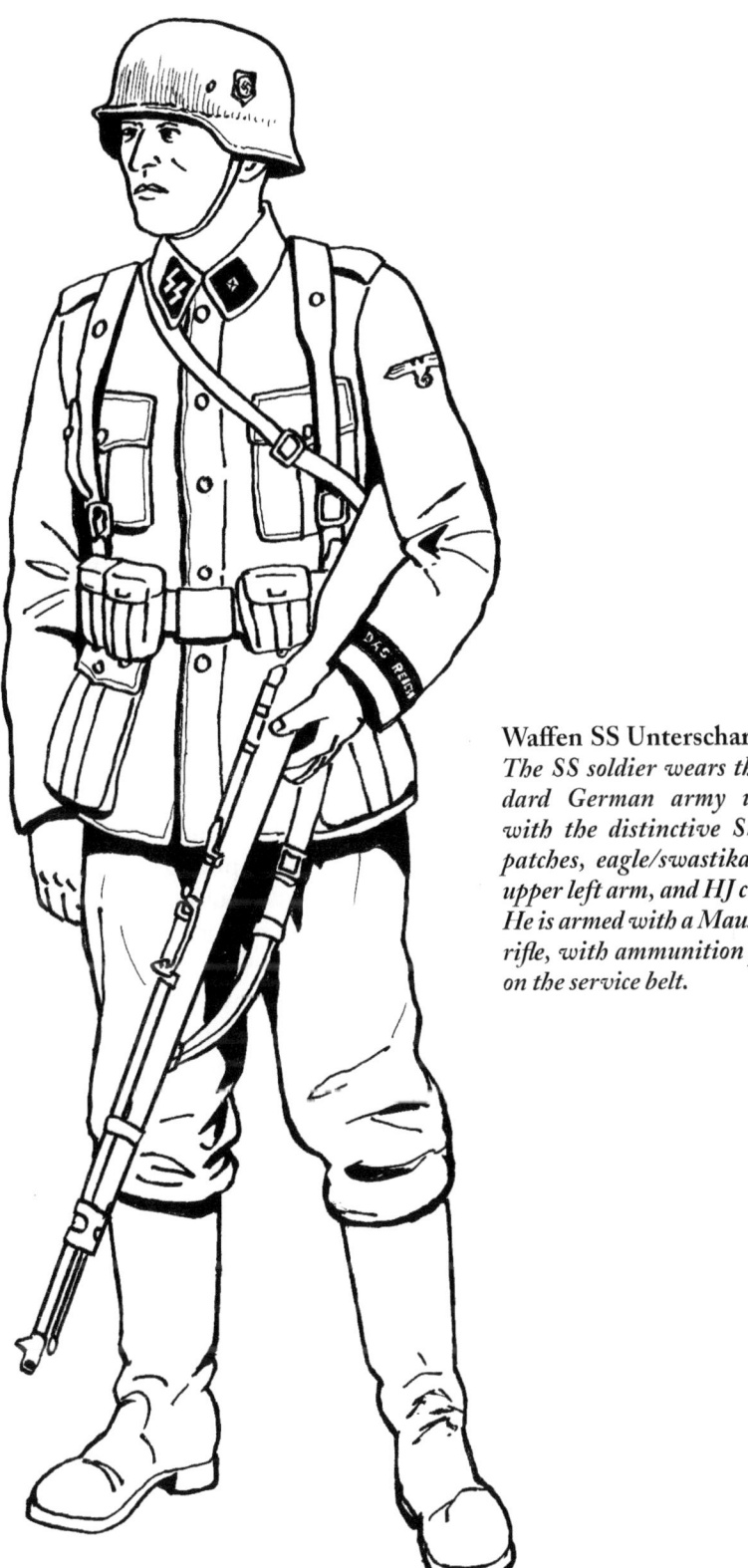

Waffen SS Unterscharführer. *The SS soldier wears the standard German army uniform with the distinctive SS collar patches, eagle/swastika on the upper left arm, and HJ cuff title. He is armed with a Mauser K 98 rifle, with ammunition pouches on the service belt.*

service *Feldmütze* (forage cap). This was a peakless garrison cap made of gray material, designed so that it could be worn under the steel helmet. It existed in various styles and qualities. Some were designed to allow the sides to be pulled down and buttoned around the wearer's ears. In June 1943, a new peaked field cap was introduced, called *Einheitsfeldmütze*. This was based closely on the style of peaked cap worn by mountain troops and Afrika Korps soldiers. It was very convenient and popular; subsequently it became the most widely worn type of headgear in active service. The *Einheitsfeldmütze* had a semi-stiff peak, and was made of canvas for warm climates and wool for cold lands.

Footwear included three-quarter-length, strong black *Marschstiefel* (leather jackboots) with hob nails, hoof irons, toe plates and studded soles. Their finish was either pebbled or smooth. After 1943, leather became scarce and marching boots were gradually replaced by heavy shoes usually worn with old-fashioned puttees, canvas or leather leggings, anklets or gaiters fastened by buckles.

The main distinct feature of the *Waffen SS* was the addition of various camouflage smocks. The typical *Waffen SS Tarnjacke* (camouflage tunic) was a collarless, pullover smock made of closely woven spun waterproof rayon/cotton duck. It was reversible in order to adapt not only to different types of countryside but also to seasonal changes. The smock had an irregular, mottled pattern of red/brown/pink/gray/yellow/tan on one side for autumn wear, and a similar pattern featuring mainly green and brown on the other side for spring and summer wear. A similar reversible helmet cover in matching patterns was issued with the smock. The *Tarnjacke* was elasticized at the wrist and waist in order to give protection from wind; it was generously cut for ease of movement and had a baggy appearance. The collarless neck opening was secured with a lace strung through ten eyelets; the field tunic—worn under the *Tarnjacke*—had its collar generally worn outside the smock, proudly showing the double SS runes. Earlier patterns had no pockets but only two vertical slits with button flaps to gain access to the uniform underneath. As the war progressed, modifications were made to the smock and the camouflage pat-

Waffen SS *early pattern camouflage smock, worn here by a* **Hauptscharführer**

Waffen SS *machine gunner*

Waffen SS Scharführer *1944*

Waffen SS *one-piece camouflage suit, 1943–44, for tank and SPG crew; rank patch of an* SS Hauptsturmführer

terns and colors. A more comfortable version was issued with a longer "skirt"; two proper side pockets with button flaps were added; buttons replaced the neck draw-string; and thin loops and strips of material were sewn on the upper arms and shoulders so that leaves, foliage and twigs could be inserted for additional camouflage in the field. The smock was worn over the field uniform and in cold weather it was sometimes worn over the greatcoat. As the German-made *Tarnjacke* always seemed to be in short supply, captured Italian camouflaged shelters were used to make a variety of jackets, trousers and overalls. The introduction of the new camouflage field blouses in 1943–44 saw an end to the production of the *Tarnjacke* but wartime photographs show the smock being worn right up to the end of the war. In 1944, a complete camouflage suit, including cap, jacket and trousers—called *getarnte Drillichanzug M44*—was introduced for the *Waffen SS* and became widely worn in the last year of the war. As a rule no insignia was worn on camouflaged smocks but in practice rank insignia and *Hohenzeichen* were often sewn on the left upper sleeve.

Field equipment

All personal equipment issued to the *Waffen SS* were exactly the same as the army's. Each SS infantryman carried with him combat, survival and personal equipment to make himself a single unit. This included a waist belt and an adjustable accoutrement made of leather or canvas straps and suspenders fitted with metal hooks intended to carry various items. Ammu-

Getarnte Drillichanzug *M44 (camouflage suit, model 1944)*

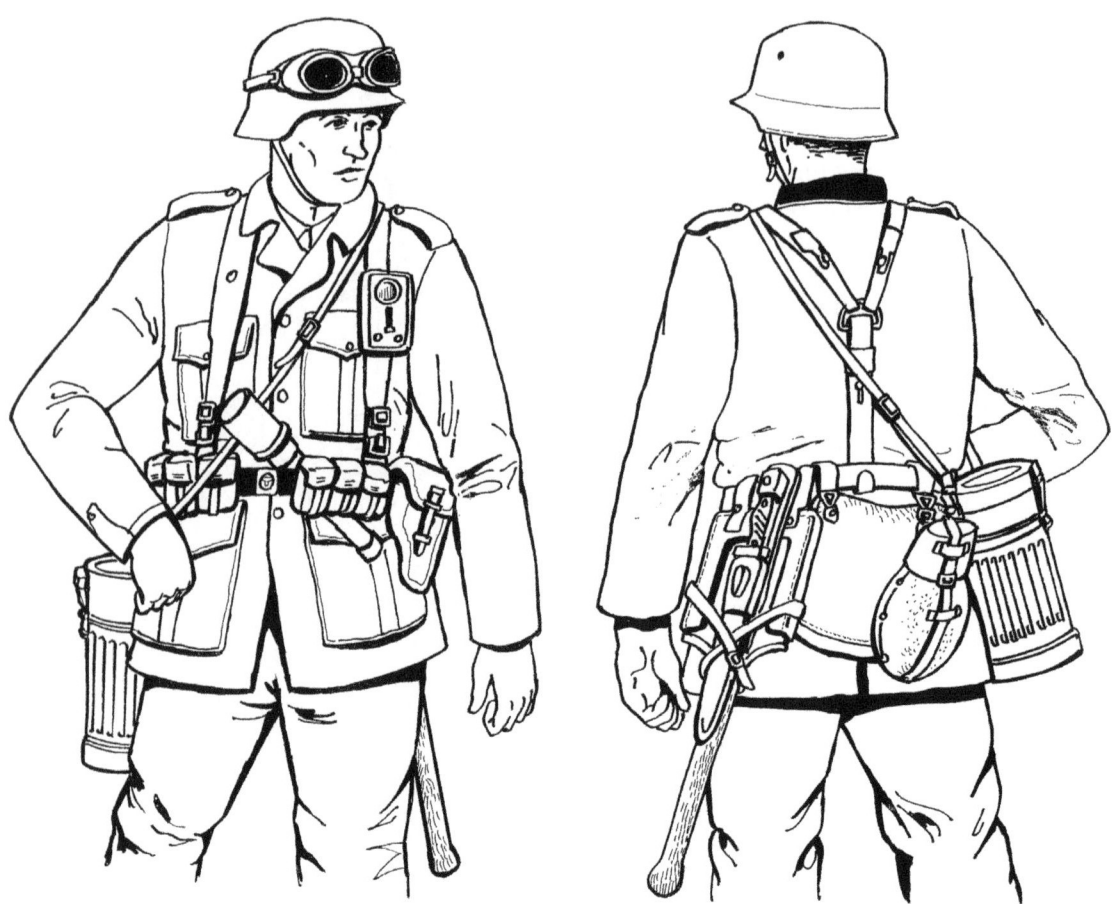

Accoutrements: front and back

nition pouches for the rifle were attached to the belt, those for a submachine gun or assault rifle were hooked on the suspenders. The aluminum *Feldfasche* (drinking bottle), holding 0.8 liters, was oval, with one attached cup. There was a *Kochgeschirr* (a mess kit) and a canvas *Brotbeutel* (bread bag) for rations, provisions and any other oddments. Each man was issued a *Schanzzeug* (entrenching tool); this was a short-handled shovel with a square steel blade riveted to a hardwood handle with a pronounced ball end. The bayonet in a scabbard was generally attached to the waist belt and fixed on the entrenching tool. Each soldier was issued a wooden-handled fighting *Messer* (knife); the knife scabbard was furnished with a spring-loaded hook to fit onto any

part of the equipment. All German soldiers on duty always had a gray, fluted, cylindrical tin canister containing a *Gasmaske* (gas mask); this container was not attached to the webbing but hung on a shoulder belt across the small of the back or was slung around the neck when riding a motorcycle. As gas was not widely used in World War II warfare, the gas-mask canister was a convenient container for various personal items or additional ammunition. Also part of the individual equipment was the *Tarnkappe*, also called *Zeltbahn*. Universally issued throughout the German army and *Waffen SS*, this was a green-and-brown pattern, camouflaged triangular cape, being 203 × 203 × 240 cm in size. It was manufactured from tightly woven, water-repellent cotton drill. In its center it had an opening which could be pulled over the wearer's head and thus it could be used as a poncho for protection from wind, cold and rain. Four or more of these capes could be attached together to form a small tent for bivouac. The cape could also be used as a stretcher to evacuate a wounded man or as shroud for burying a dead soldier.

The use of *Schutzbrillen* (sunglasses and protective goggles) was widespread for drivers, motorcyclists, and gunners, but also for all infantrymen in the open. Officers and NCOs were equipped with such additional items as a *Stoppuhr* (stopwatch), *Feldstecher* (binoculars with leather case and straps, usually hung around the neck), *Karten* (maps contained in a leather map case, generally hung from the waist belt), *Kompass* (compass), and *Pfeife* (whistle).

Weapons

All individual and collective weapons, ammunition, artillery, and vehicles issued to the *Waffen SS* were the same as the army's.

The German rifles of World War II were largely confined to the Mauser, originating from the 1890s and in service since 1904. The standard German infantry rifle was the traditional *Mauser Modell 1898* (Kar 98), manually operated and using bolt action, facilitating rapid loading and ejection of spent cartridges. It could fire about ten shots per minute. A breakthrough in weaponry was the lightweight, self-loading, 7.92 mm automatic assault rifle *Maschinen Karabiner 43 (MK 43)*, also called *Maschinenpistole 43 (MP 43)*. Designed and manufactured by the Erfurter Maschinefabrik Haenel und Suhl (Erma), the MK 43 was an all-metal rifle (except for a wooden butt). It weighed 5.1 kg and the detachable magazine contained 30 rounds. In 1944 the MK 43 was slightly improved and renamed *Sturmgewehr (StG) 44* or *MPi 44*. This proved an excellent assault weapon.

The German did not produce revolvers, preferring the automatic pistol's advantages. There were many types spread among the whole German army, with three predominating models: the Parabellum M08 Luger, Mauser C96 and Walther P38.

The German forces used various models of submachine guns, such as the pre–World War II *Maschinenpistole MPi 28/II* and the Danish-designed *Bergmann Maschinenpistole MPi 34*. The most used submachine gun was the formidable *Erma Maschinenpistole MPi 38*, designed and manufactured by Erma, firing about 500 rounds per minute. The MPi 38 was slightly modified in 1940 by the German weapon designer

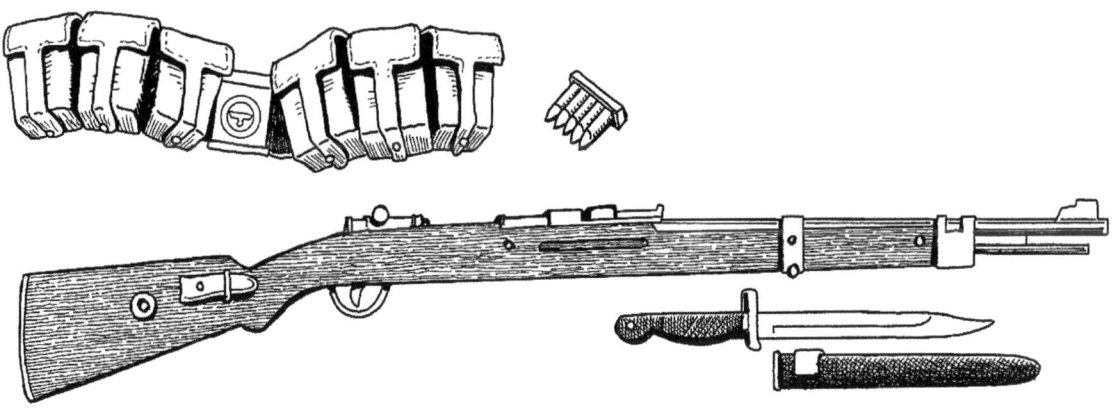

Gewehr *24 Mauser (7.92 mm)*

Hugo Schmeisser, who made it easier and cheaper to produce. The result was the *Maschinenpistole MPi 40*.

Designed in 1915 but used until 1945, the German *Stielhandgranate* (stick grenade or "potato masher") was one of the most characteristic items of weaponry associated with the World War II German soldier. Several types were used for various effects: smoke or tear gas, offensive (giving a strong blast), or defensive (exploding in a hail of lethal fragments within a range of up to 20 meters from the burst). There was also an anti-tank grenade, known as *Panzerwurfmine (L)*, with a hollow-charge warhead fitted with a finned tail for stabilization and guidance. Weighing 1.35 kg (2.98 lb), the grenade was a difficult and dangerous weapon, requiring some skill for use in an effective manner. Its range largely depended on the strength of the thrower (maximum 30 m—32.8 yards), but it could knock out even the heaviest Allied tanks. These grenades were not a general-issue item but mainly issued to specialist, close-in tank-killer squads.

During World War II, the Germans did not produce separate heavy or light machine guns but used the dual-purpose, air-cooled MG 34 and MG 42 that one man could carry and operate. The *Maschinengewehr MG 34* weighed 12 kg and shot about 800 rounds per minute. Though a complicated weapon, demanding a lot of effort to make, and sensitive to mud, dust and snow, production of the MG 34 continued until 1945, concurrent with the later, heavier MG 42. The *Maschinengewehr MG 42* was probably the most famous machine gun of World War II. Intended to be produced in wartime, the MG 42 used the fewest possible machining processes and made the greatest possible use of stamping and pressing, resulting in its very different finish from the MG 34. It was a rough weapon, much more resistant to dirt and ill-treatment than the MG 34, and earned a good reputation in reliability even in the worst combat conditions. The MG 42 weighted 11.5 kg and it could fire automatically up to 1,300 rounds per minute.

The German infantry and the *Waffen SS* were also equipped with various mortars. The standard light mortar was the 5-cm *Granatwerfer 36*. This was trigger-fired, had a crew of three, a maximum range of about 500 m, weighed about 15 kg, and broke into two parts (barrel and baseplate) for carrying. The standard medium-infantry mortar was the 8-cm *Granatwerfer GrW 34* which had a maximum range of 1.8 km. The GrW 34 broke in three parts for transportation

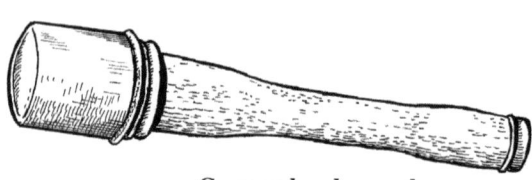

German hand grenade

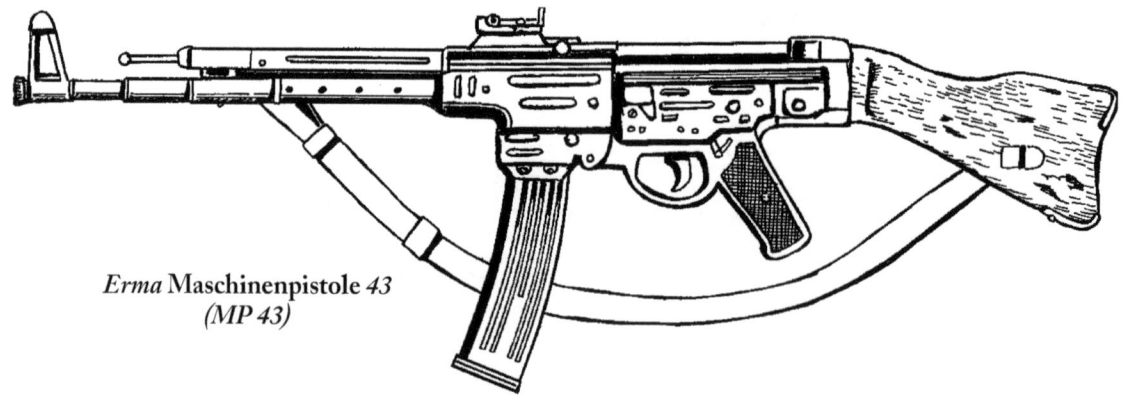

Erma Maschinenpistole *43 (MP 43)*

(barrel, bipod and baseplate). Another German bomb-launcher was the heavy *Granatwerfer GrW 42* (ranging up to 6 km).

The *Flammenwerfer* (portable flamethrower) began to see active service in World War I. Carried by a single operator, it was composed of a canister filled with a fluid fuel (thickened gasoline), with a tank of pressurized nitrogen to propel the liquid which was ignited as it left the launcher. The World War II German *Flammenwerfer* had a limited range (about 30 to 40 meters) which made the operator quite vulnerable, but it had a terrifying effect as well as a formidable physical effect.

The *Panzerfaust* ("armor fist"), designed by Dr. Heinrich Langweiler, was a genuine breakthrough in hollow-charge weaponry and anti-tank warfare. A one-man, disposable missile launcher, it was compact, light and effective at a short distance.

The German anti-tank 8.8-cm *Panzerbüchse 43 Panzerschreck* (literally "tank terror," but also known as the "Stovepipe") was

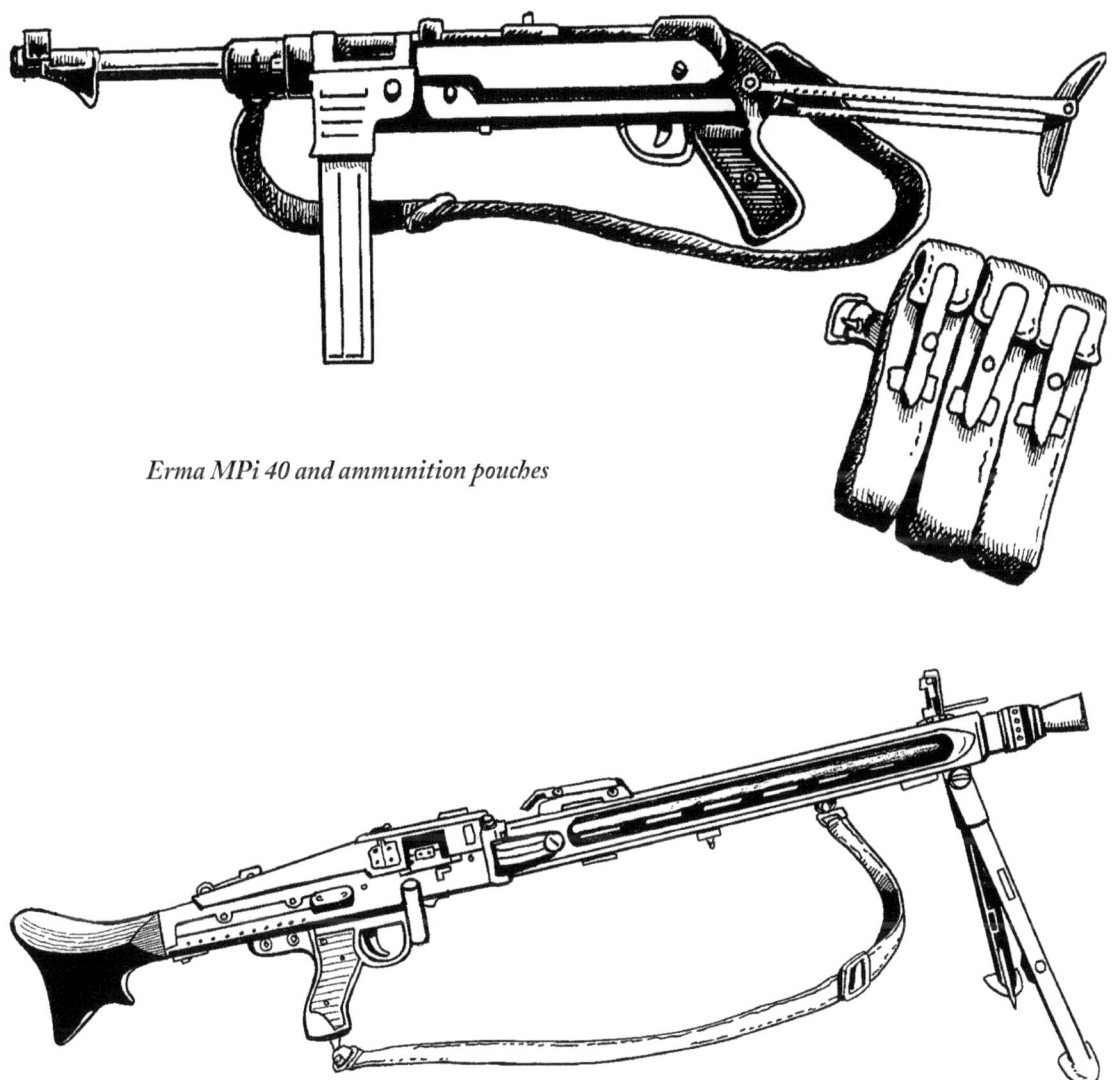

Erma MPi 40 and ammunition pouches

Machinengewehr *MG 42*

a 5-foot-long, smooth-bore barrel firing a 3-kg-charge projectile powered by rocket propellant. It was in effect a direct copy of the American "bazooka," a specimen of which was captured in the desert in 1943. The *Panzerschreck* was a two-crew weapon. The shooter aimed and fired from over the shoulder and the loader put the projectile in the back of the tube. Both *Panzerfaust* and *Panzerschreck* were effective at short range, with devastating effect on armored fighting vehicles. They required nerves of steel to operate, but were ideal weapons in defensive ambush and urban warfare which the Germans found themselves in during the last two years of the war.

The *Waffen SS* also had large stocks of anti-tank and anti-personnel mines, such as the *AT Riegel Mine 43*, the *Tellermine 35* (containing 5.4 kg TNT), and the *Tellermine 42*. Mines were slightly buried underground, and violently exploded when vehicles drove on them or when a man on foot stepped on one. They could also be used as boobytraps.

By the end of the war, the Germans were employing new types of mines. These were mounted in wooden or glass containers, and could not be located by the electronic metal detectors then in use. To locate these mines the Allies had to resort to the hazardous expedient of prodding for them with long-hafted pitchforks.

The Campaigns of the 12th Division

Battle of Normandy

In June 1944 came the move which signaled the impending end of the Third Reich. Since the summer of 1942, the Germans had been preparing to meet and defeat an invasion across the English Channel, and the European coasts had been fortified (with the so-called Atlantic Wall). Yet the arrival of D-Day found them with no clear campaign plan, for the difference of opinion between

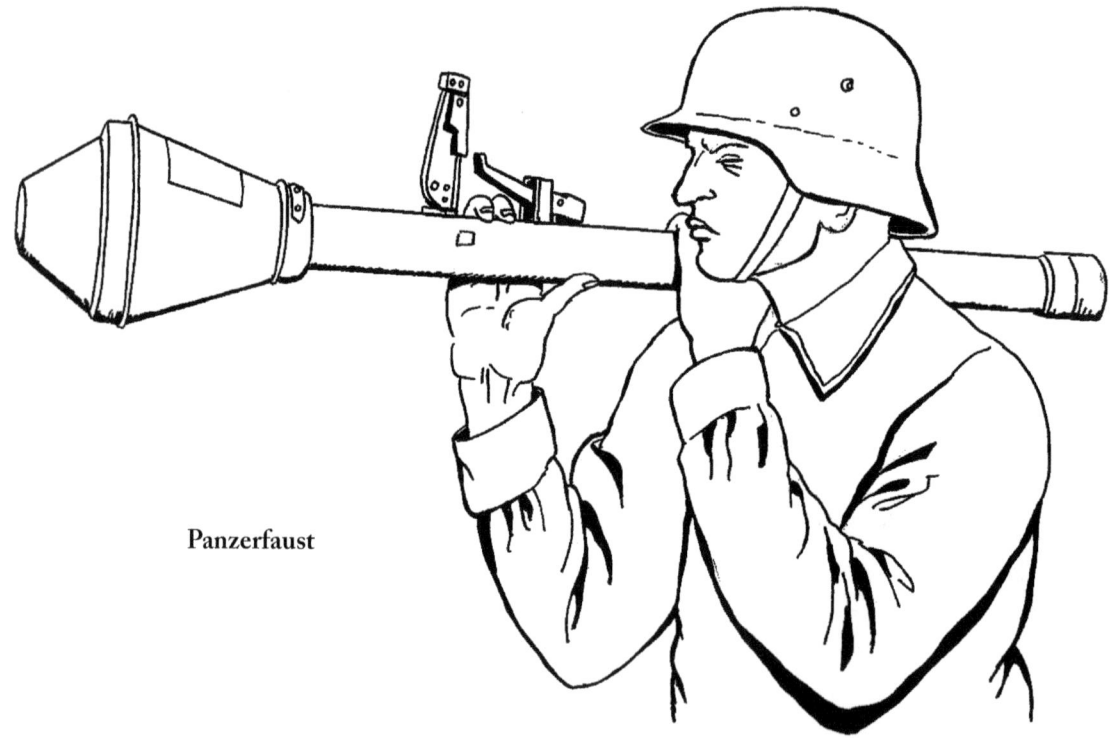

Panzerfaust

Marshall Rommel (Commander of Army Group B deployed in Bretagne, Normandy and Northern France), Marshall von Rundstedt (Commander-in-Chief West) and General Geyr von Schweppenburg (head of armored forces) regarding the employment of the armored reserves was still unsettled.

By April 1944, the 12th Division was regarded as ready for combat operation, and the regiments were transferred to Normandy by train for their appointment with destiny. In May, the 12th Division HJ was stationed in the south of Rouen, and east of Paris as Hitler's counterinvasion strategic reserve. It was part of the *1st SS Panzerkorps* (with the *1st SS Panzer Division Leibstandarte* and the army's crack *Panzer Lehr Division*). The 12th Division was garrisoned at Evreux, Bernay, Vimoutiers and Argentan. According to Marshall Rommel, it had 177 tanks and 28 motorized assault guns, but this striking force had strict orders not to be committed to battle without the sanction of Hitler himself. When the Allies landed in Normandy on 6 June 1944, the German high command was totally surprised and unprepared, as Hitler thought the Normandy landings were a diversion for a real invasion in northern France near Calais. However Normandy proved to be the real thing and in the resulting confusion the 12th Division HJ was issued contradictory orders of march and counter-march to Lisieux, resulting in waste of precious time. Finally, at 3:00 P.M., the order was given for a counterattack northwest of Caen for the next day.

For the 12th Division, the Battle of Normandy was beginning. Kurt Meyer was bursting with confidence. His troops, the pick of the Hitler Youth, would soon throw the Allies back into the sea. But Allied air superiority hampered all movement on the ground, and by the time they reached Lisieux, they had already suffered 83 casualties. On 7 June the Canadian forces launched an attack in the direction of the airfield of Carpiquet. Regiment 25 of the 12th Division counter attacked near the Ardennes Abbey. From the start, the 12th Division was nicknamed the "Baby Division" by the Allies. The blond-haired, pink-faced, hate-filled "babies" fought very well, enduring like men the thousand bomber attacks, the powerful shells, and the tide of tanks that were always replaced no matter how many they managed to destroy. In their innocence they had been apprenticed to evil and now fought till they dropped in the disintegrating European fortress their Führer had built. The Nazi order was crumbling but the "babies" were ferocious. During the combat, a group of Hitler Jugend/*Waffen SS* young men committed the unsoldierly and ugly murder of Canadian prisoners on the battlefield at the Ardennes Abbey. These atrocities were not merely caused by battle stress on untried young soldiers but the result of years of indoctrination. Held responsible for this massacre, the commander of the 12th SS Division, *Brigadeführer* Kurt Meyer, was condemned to death after the war. Pardoned in 1954, Meyer died in 1965. He was ultimately more fortunate than most of his boys who died during the battle.

On 8 June 1944, the Allies broadened the beachheads and took Bayeux, the first French city to be liberated, while the 12th Division was deployed west of Caen for a counter-offensive to Bretteville. This took place during the night of 8–9 June, but the 12th Division was repulsed, resulting in many casualties and a withdrawal to the village of La Mue. By 9 June, the Allies had won the battle on the beaches and mastered the coast of Normandy between the river Orne and river Vire. On 10 June, the Americans took Isigny-sur-Mer and met up with the U.S. paratroopers dropped on Sainte-Mère-Eglise four days before. The German high command ordered a wide-scale counter-offensive with three armored divisions, including the *Hitlerjugend*; but the field command post of the 12th Division was destroyed by a bombardment, with some officers killed. Through confusion and disorganization, the counter-attack was postponed. In the meantime, in southwest France, the 2nd SS division *Das Reich* butchered the entire village of Oradour-sur-Glane allegedly in retaliation for a maquisard ambush.

On 12 June, the city of Carentan was captured by the Americans, the 12th Division took defensive positions, and the first V1s (flying bombs) fell on London. On 13 June, the British—marching from Balleroy and Caumont—attempted a wide encircling movement in the south of Caen. At Villers-Bocage, the 501st *SS Panzer* battalion intercepted a British armored column and destroyed it completely.

On 15 June, General De Gaulle visited Bayeux. The Allies had by then a half million soldiers on French soil. On 16 June, *Brigadeführer* Fritz Witt was killed in action. He was replaced at the head of the 12th Division *Hitlerjugend* by *Standartenführer* Kurt Meyer who established his command post at Verson. On 17 June, the Americans reached Barneville, and marched in the direction of the port of Cherbourg. The 12th Division was engaged in skirmishes near Tilly-sur-Seulles. On 18 June, British forces conquered the village of Tilly-sur-Seulles, while the Canadians concentrated their attack on Fontenay-le-Pesnel, held by the Regiment 26 headed by Wilhelm Mohnke, belonging to the 12th SS Division HJ. Combats was particularly furious in the park of Boislonde, continuing until 21 June, when the Americans took Valognes. Between 22 and 25 June, Fontenay was evacuated and the front held by the 12th Division remained rather stable. This was to change on 26 June when the British and the Canadians, supported by 600 tanks, launched an offensive south of Caen. Meyer and Wünsche established their headquarters at Vernon, while the advanced elements of the 12th Division were engaged in terrible fights at Rauzay. On 27 June the Americans managed to neutralize the Fort du Roule defending Cherbourg. The Canadians established a bridgehead on the river Odon, the 12th Division withdrew and Meyer installed his headquarters at Caen. On 28 June the Allies accentuated their movement on the Odon River. Violent fights took place at hill 112 southwest of Caen which dominated the main road from Caen to Falaise. The 12th Division was reinforced by the 1st *Panzerdivision Leibstandarte* and the 2nd SS armored corps, including the elite SS divisions Hohenstaufen and Frundsberg. On 29 June, the Allies conquered hill 112, and managed to repulse a counter-attack launched by the SS. On 30 June, the Germans recaptured hill 112. On 1 July Montgomery increased the offensive around Caen. Hitler declared: "Caen will be defended until the last German soldier!" and the 12th Division was officially charged to hold the town.

By 2 July, the Allies had landed nearly one million men in Normandy. From 3 to 8 July the battalion commanded by Krausse (150 soldiers from the 12th Division) managed to hold the airfield of Carpiquet. After heavy air bombing and a general offensive, the pivotal Caen fell to the Allies on 9 July. The units of the 12th Division, having paid a heavy price (20 percent killed and 40 percent wounded), withdrew to defensive positions on the river Orne. On 12 July what remained of the SS HJ Division was relieved by other *Wehrmacht* units. The *Hitlerjugend* Division was then divided into two *Kampfgruppen* (combat groups) headed by Krausse and Waldmüller, with the headquarters established at Potigny, north of Falaise. On 15 July, American forces had conquered the Cotentin peninsula and launched an offensive to the south at La-Haye-du-Puits. On 17 July, Marshall Erwin Rommel was severely wounded in an air strike and evacuated to Germany, while the remnants of the 12th HJ Division were placed in a defensive position. On 20 July, Hitler was lightly wounded at Rastenburg in a failed assassination attempt directed by several senior

German officers. From 25 July to 6 August the Allies launched an offensive in a southern direction and to Bretagne. This was marked by the capture of Coutances, Granville, Avranches, Pontaubault, Dol, Dinan, Rennes, Thury-Harcourt, Vannes, Redon, Vitré and Laval. On 8 August, the Canadians moved in the direction of Falaise; the *Kampfgruppe Waldmüller* was charged to hold the front at Cintheaux. On 9 August the Americans conquered Quimper and Le Mans. The whole province of Bretagne was liberated and the front was turned by the south of Normandy. On 12 August, the Free French (headed by General Leclerc) took Alençon, while the Americans reached Nantes and Saint-Malo. On 15 August the Canadians attacked hill 159, while the Poles put the pressure on the villages of Jort and Perrières to cross the river Dives. By that time the combatants of the 12th Division did not number more than 500 soldiers, and they were put in defensive positions on the river Ante, north of Falaise. On 17 August the Americans had reached Dreux, Chartres and Orléans. On that day Marshall von Kluge committed suicide and was replaced by Marshall Model as head of the German troops on the western front. The town of Falaise, defended by a handful of SS, was assaulted by the Canadians. On 18 August, the survivors of the 12th SS Division established a defensive position south of Falaise between the river Dives and the village of Nécy.

On 19 August the liberation of Paris began while Leclerc's Free French 2nd Armored Division moved to the capital of France. The Americans took Argentan and Trun. Patton reached the river Seine at Mantes and Vernon. By that time, the Germans were pocketed around Falaise, and the only escape was through a narrow gap at Chambois where they were bombed and systematically picked off. On 20 August the survivors of both *Kampfgruppe Krause* and *Waldmüller* managed to break through between the villages of Saint-Lambert and Chambois. Max Wünsche was taken prisoner and the 12th Division had no tanks left. On 23 August the Allies reached Evreux, Meaux and Sens. On 25 August the German garrison of Paris surrendered: the capital of France was liberated and General De Gaulle established the provisory government of the French Republic. On 26 August *Brigadeführer* Kurt Meyer received the Iron Cross with Swords. The survivors of the 12th Division could only offer token activity and fought one last battle in the forest of Londe before withdrawing over the river Seine. Eventually a few *Waffen SS*/HJ young men managed to break away, but the others died or were taken prisoner, and all heavy equipment and weapons were lost. On the 29 August, the Battle of Normandy was over. The ill-fated Mortain counter-offensive and the Falaise pocket brought the greatest disaster to the *Wehrmacht* since Stalingrad. The Germans had 240,000 killed and wounded, 210,000 taken prisoner, and 1,800 tanks destroyed. By that time the debris of the 12th Division regrouped at Beauvais, then retreated to Hirson, and finally moved to the Ardennes mountains. Field Marshall von Rundstedt said: "It is a pity that this faithful youth is sacrificed on a hopeless situation."

Battle of the Bulge

In September 1944, the remnants of the 12th SS *Panzerdivision Hitlerjugend* retreated to the River Maas in Belgium. The unit was then sent for rest in Sauerland and refit in Germany (Bremen) in autumn 1944. New equipment and weapons were issued, officers were drawn from the *Luftwaffe* and even from the Kriegsmarine, a new commander was appointed (*Standartenführer* Hugo Krass, aged 33), and twenty thousand new HJ boys replaced those fallen in Normandy. As the new generation of HJ boys volunteering for the 12th Division *Hitlerju-*

gend were hastily trained, the unit could never make up those lost. They swore their oath of loyalty to Hitler in November 1944 at the *Ausbildungs- und Ersatzbataillon* (home depot) in Kaiserlautern in the presence of Himmler and Axmann. The last German success was the battle of Arnhem in south Netherlands. In September 1944 the overstretched Allies attempted to secure a Rhine bridgehead by taking Dutch bridges on the rivers Waal, Maas and Rhine by parachute assault at Arnhem, in order to advance in North Germany before winter. They were held up by German troops reacting decisively and the liberators' momentum was halted. The failure of Operation Market Garden marked the end of Allied hopes for victory over Nazi Germany before the end of 1944.

The new 12th SS Division HJ was placed in reserve in the sector west of Cologne before participating in the ill-fated Ardennes offensive (the Battle of the Bulge) in the winter of 1944-45. The Ardennes (a wooded, hilly region in southern Belgium) was chosen by Hitler as the location of a last-ditch offensive. In the lull in fighting which followed Montgomery's abortive drive to the Rhine and the failure at Arnhem, Hitler exploited the opportunity to launch an ambitious counter-offensive which he believed might snatch back the iniative on the western front. Hitler's intention was to split the British from the American armies and to capture the port of Antwerp, thereby cutting the Allies' main supply port. His aim was to gain time and to force a separate peace on the British and Americans, after which he would turn his forces against Russia and win the war. Hitler lived in a world of dreams, and when the dreams faded he looked around for scapegoats.

The offensive begun on 16 December 1944. Army Group B, comprising 25 German divisions, commanded by Field Marshall Walther Model, struck the unsuspecting American forces. Amid a spell of bad weather that kept the Allies' awesome air force at bay, the Germans overran their lines. The 12th Division, placed in the northern sector of the battlefield, had as its immediate task to drive through the Bütgenbach Gap to Malmédy and Stavelot. The troops animated by a strong spirit of vengeance and patriotism, fell upon their unsuspecting opponents as dawn was breaking from a leaden sky. The unit met tremendous difficulties moving forward west of the village of Krinkelt because of bad weather. By 20 December, the 26th regiment of the 12th Division had managed to seize the villages of Büllingen and Bütgenbach. However two major road junctions remained held by the Americans, at Saint-Vith and Bastogne. Stubborn and heroic U.S. resistance and swift reinforcement by both American and British troops, as well as a fuel shortage and bad weather, halted the German advance south of the river Meuse on 26 December. Two days later, the HJ-SS unit launched an attack in the sector of Sambrée, but Hitler's boy soldiers were repulsed. By 31 December, the 12th Division had lost three-quarters of its establishment in furious battle at hill 510, north of Bastogne. In early January 1945, the Allies counter-attacked, and Hitler's last gamble turned into a general withdrawal. The massacre of American prisoners at Malmédy by *SS Obersturmbannführer* Joachim Peiper's *Kampfgruppe* further tarnished the reputation of the *Waffen SS*. Some 160 American soldiers had been taken prisoner and, as they were an "embarrassment" to Joachim Peiper's SS men, they were lined up and machine-gunned. At least 142 were killed. The rest, after feigning death, escaped by night to tell the grim story of the "Malmédy Massacre." Incensed by this outrage, the American forces entered the fight thirsting for revenge. The short-lived Ardennes offensive had cost the Germans 100,000 casualties, 1,000 airplanes and large quantities of weapons and equipment which the Reich was unable to replace. Only a few remnants of the 12th Division, as badly decimated as during the Battle of Normandy managed to withdraw to Cologne after 10 January 1945. The German army and the *Waffen SS* were now reduced to a piecemeal collection of variously equipped units, all far under regular strength.

The end of the 12th Division

The new year 1945 saw mighty Russian offensives, with decisive advances into Silesia, East Prussia and Hungary. Meanwhile the western Allies had crossed the Rhine and pushed across Germany. In early February 1945, the 12th Division, still under command of Hugo Krass (now promoted to the rank of *SS Brigadeführer*), was refit again at Cologne with new HJ volunteers aged 15 and 16. Part of the VIth Panzer Army, headed by Sepp Dietrich, the 12th Division was engaged in the region of the Plattenzee (the Balaton Lake) in Hungary, with the objective of recapturing Budapest. Fighting against heavy Russian resistance and the spring thaw, the offensive ground to a halt. After hard and hopeless battles in Köbölkut, Muzla, Puszta and Stuhlweissenburg, the 12th Division was forced to withdraw to Dudar and Zirc. By 31 March 1945, the unit was encircled in Raab. After a costly escape from the pocket, the decimated unit retreated to the region of Hirtenberg in Austria. In the beginning of April 1945, the division was only the shadow of its former self, still fighting hopeless rear-guard battles while retreating to Tradigist. Finally after a long forced march to escape capture and certain death at the hands of the Soviets, the 455 survivors of the once proud, dreaded and powerful 12th SS *Panzerdivision Hitlerjugend* (totaling 23,244 men in December 1944) crossed the River Enns in Austria and surrendered to the U.S. Seventh Army on 8 May 1945 after a last parade and inspection by *SS Brigadeführer* Hugo Krass. As a final token of arrogance, no white flag was hoisted by Hitler's last fighters when they surrendered.

Volkssturm

During the last months of the war, the Hitler Jugend became an important part of the *Volkssturm* and during the Battle of Berlin many teenagers were committed to the front line on which few survived. The *Deutscher Volkssturm* (popular army) were home defense units created in September 1944. The idea originated from plans made by General Heusinger from the *Oberkommando des Heeres* (OKH—Germany's Army High Command) to raise a territorial army in East Prussia. The plan was first put into action in summer 1944 by *Gauleiter* Koch who raised all able men to form a small army called *Ostpreussen Volkssturm*, fighting with some success in Goldap and Gumbinen. With the military situation worsening and the fighting getting perilously close to German soil, and pushed by Goebbels, who saw a propaganda opportunity, Hitler decided to develop the *Volkssturm* on a national scale. All able-bodied men between 16 and 60 were drafted for the defense of the *Heimat* (homeland) in four levies of men born between 1884 and 1928, intended to total six million. Authority over the *Volkssturm* was mixed; it was equipped and armed by Himmler's SS, but it was recruited, organized, politically led and commanded by the Nazi Party under Martin Bormann's authority. The *Volkssturm* was actually intended to be Bormann's private army, and it escaped Himmler's control. The members of the *Volkssturm* were poorly trained, however. They were not issued regular uniforms, but used a great variety of gear. The only standard identifiable item was an armband indicating "*Deutscher Volkssturm Wehrmacht.*" Weapons and ammunition too, consisted of whatever could be found in army stores.

The recruits of the *Volkssturm* were

either very young or old enough to be veterans of the World War I. Kids and grandfathers found themselves on the front line of the war. It goes without saying that the *Volkssturm* represented an ill-prepared, poorly armed, heterogeneous body composed of old civilian men and young boys with little desire to fight. Not only were they far too young or too old, but they had little training and no experience with the few weapons left for these improvised soldiers to protect themselves with. The *Volkssturm* also included girls of the BdM and women from the *NS Frauenschaft* (Nazi Women League) who provided rear-echelon support such as logistics and medical care. In March 1945, some girls and women were issued weapons and participated actively in the hopeless defense of their towns, facing Allied armies that were determined to win the war regardless of the lives that it might cost. It was very tough on the *Volkssturm* troops. The glamour of being a member was gone, many units were never even formed and the few that were involved in combat were destroyed on the front lines. The *Volkssturm* showed Hitler's determination to fight to the last person. It was a final crime, the expression of complete despair, the "*Götterdämmerung*" of legend, the total collapse of the Third Reich that had sent to death so many German people. Hitler remained true to his original program, "*Weltmacht oder Niedergang*" (world domination or downfall), and considered that if Germany lost the war, that would mean that the nation had not passed the test of strength and in that case it deserved no better than to be destroyed.

The *Volkssturm* was deployed to the front line in early 1945 and the hour of the Hitler Jugend's final sacrifice was at hand. As the HJ members had been receiving military training for ten years, they were the backbone of the *Volkssturm*. Anti-tank battalions (*Panzerschreckabteilungen*) were formed in late March 1945 from HJ personnel. Each special tank-hunter team consisted of nine boys, six trained and armed with anti-tank weapons (e.g., *Panzerfaust*) and three providing covering fire with automatic weapons. As many officers and older HJ leaders were dead or captured, younger boys were promoted fast. It was not uncommon for a 16-year-old *Gefolgschaftsführer* to have command over a group of 800 boys. Girls operated anti-aircraft guns, and youths shot with *Panzerfäuste* on barricades, while children, women and old people were drafted to dig anti-tank ditches and erect other obstacles. The Hitler Youth members continued to take an active part in the defense of their cities as the Allies swept over Germany. Children fought until killed rather than surrender. The HJ fought fanatically because they believed Goebbels' propaganda that the Russians would kill them all anyway. The total number of casualties is not precisely known. About 175,000 members of the *Volkssturm* were listed as missing in action after the war.

In Berlin in April 1945, a detachment of about 600 HJ teenagers—aged 15 and 16—was desperately holding the Wannsee bridgehead on the river Havel awaiting the arrival of General Wenck's 12th Army, by that time a decimated force. Wenck's troops were fighting a pointless rear-guard struggle on the river Elbe southwest of Berlin and never reached the besieged capital of the dying Third Reich, Hitler's final obsessive hope as he shut himself away in the deep concrete bunker under the Chancellery building where he committed suicide. The sacrificed HJ unit was commanded by Axmann who had established his command post at 86 Kaiserdamm until 26 April, and from then until 30 April in the cellar of the Nazi Party Chancellery at 64 Wilhemstrasse. Hitler's last public appearance, on 20 April 1945 (his 56th birthday) on the grounds of the ruined Reich Chancellery, was to decorate HJ members, the youngest only twelve, with the Iron Cross. By then even ten-year-old junior *Deutsches Jungvolk* were serving at the collapsing front. Children were being thrown into the cauldron all over Germany to fight in a meaningless war of annihilation.

In the last months of the war, Hitler Youth members were also intended to crew the new jet-propelled He-162 A-2 Salamander, also known as *Volksjäger* (people's fighter). This airplane, one of Hitler's last hopes, had a wingspan of 7.05 m (23 ft 7½ in), a length of 8.90 m (29 ft 8 in), a weight of 3,000 kg (5,480 lb) and a top speed of 940 km/h (522 mph). It had a crew of one and was armed with two 20-mm cannons. In the field of jet aircraft, the Germans were years ahead of the Allies, but the high command, and Hitler first of all, were slow to realize the potential of revolutionary designs. The old story of "too little, too late" applied to all German jet aircraft production—the He-162 was never used operationally.

Hitler committed suicide on 30 April 1945 in his bunker under the Chancellery in Berlin. His body and that of his wife Eva Braun were burned in the garden of the Chancellery by Hitler's SS adjutant Otto Günsche. Hugh Trevor-Roper, who carried out a thorough investigation of the circumstances surrounding Hitler's death, inclines to the view that the Führer's ashes were collected into a box and handed over to Arthur Axmann, the leader of the HJ. It would have been a logical act to pass on the "sacred relics" to the next generation. This is not true, however. Hitler's ashes were captured by the Russians and dispersed.

Werewolves

When Germany was on the verge of defeat in the closing days of World War II, a number of HJ were drafted into the so-called *Werwolven* (Werewolves). The Werewolves—secretly set up under the authority of Himmler's SS—were intended to be guerrilla units that would put up a last-ditch armed resistance to the Allies in all parts of Germany, but notably in the Alps. The *Werwolfen* would have been garrisoned at the *Alpenfestung* (Alpine Redoubt), the area on the Obersalzberg in the sacred hills of Nazi mythology, mountains charged with the legend of the Middle Ages emperor Barbarossa and sanctified by Hitler's residence. They were also expected to sally out from the Alpine bastion as trained commando units to create havoc among the Allied forces by sniping and ambushing, by sabotage and disruption of traffic, and by poisoning water and food supplies. The Werewolves regarded themselves as a resistance movement similar to the underground armies that had fought against the Germans in Poland, France, Italy, Russia and the Balkans. They were designed as a paramilitary formation, an auxiliary force to assist the German army; they expected to fight in uniform and, if captured, to claim the right of prisoners of war. They issued crude pamphlets threatening revenge on those who refused to support them. At the time of German surrender, the leader of the organization was *SS Obergruppenführer* Hans Prützmann. In early 1945, the threat was taken seriously by the Allied forces, as the SS and HJ's oath meant that they were willing and ready to sacrifice their lives for the Führer. Fanatic teenagers only knew one god—Adolf Hitler—and had been saturated from childhood with the aims and ideology of National Socialism. Most of them were so dedicated and convinced of ultimate victory that their mental attitude defied comprehension. Their fanaticism was so strong that it sometimes seemed to have penetrated the subconscious. They expected a heroic last stand, inspired by the myth of Hagen and the sinister last battle of the Nibelungen. Did not the battle song of the Hitler Jugend say that they would go marching on after everything was in ruins? ("*Wir werden weiter marschieren wenn alles in Scherben fällt!*")

HJ boy in the Volkssturm, Berlin, 1945. This Volkssturm HJ private wears the HJ dark-blue winter uniform with M1933 black ski-cap with HJ diamond cap badge, M1938 dark-blue trousers, and full insignia, including HJ and Volkssturm armbands on the left arm. On the right upper sleeve he wears two silver Panzervernichtungsabzeichen (tank destruction badge, instituted in March 1942) for his single-handed destruction of two Soviet tanks without the use of an anti-tank weapon. He is armed with the latest Sturmgewehr StG 44 (assault rifle model 1944) with ammunition magazine pouches fixed on the waist belt.

Civilian drafted into the Volkssturm *1945*

Heinkel He-162 Salamander

A secret propagandistic Werewolf broadcast was created by Goebbels which contributed to many misconceptions about the units. The propaganda was responsible for intoxication about the Werewolves' aims, achievements and real capacity. The Werewolves never materialized, however, never became an effective fighting force, as Hitler abandoned the idea of a final struggle against the Allies in the Bavarian Alps. Instead, the Führer decided to stay and die in Berlin. After his suicide on 30 April, his appointed successor—Admiral Karl Dönitz, the navy commander—ordered all members of the embryonic organization to cease operations. The order was obeyed, and the few *Werwolfen* stopped all resistance. A very small number of these few refused to surrender and tried to prolong the fighting, sacrificing themselves in a vain attempt to stem the Allied advance. They were rapidly captured and sentenced to restriction in their hometowns or to hard labor, including the exhumation of mass graves. A few hold-outs made isolated pockets of resistance and some of them were executed by the Allies. All the Werewolves achieved was a more suspicious and hostile Allied attitude toward the conquered German civilians.

Denazification and the Nuremberg Process

The war ended in May 1945 and members of the Hitler Youth went back to being regular civilians. It was a hard adjustment for many to go from being the elite of the German nation, high-ranking officers in the HJ, to normal schoolboys and students. After all they had been through, the idea of going back to school seemed for many ex-members preposterous. What could they possibly learn after the excitement and the horrors of war?

The members of the HJ and other Nazis were required to be denazified. After the fall of Hitler's regime, the process of *Entnazifizierung* (denazification) was intended to eradicate Nazism. It was an immensely complicated task for the Allies. All persons involved in Nazism were removed from public positions and by 1946 the process became more systematic. The Allied

Control Council had defined five categories of persons in relation to Hitler's regime:

1. *Hauptschuldige*: major offender who was sentenced to death or life imprisonment;
2. *Belastete*: activist, militarist, involved in war crimes and profiteering;
3. *Minderbelastete*: lesser offender, not known to have committed crimes;
4. *Mitlaufer*: fellow-traveler, one who joined the Nazis to demonstrate allegiance;
5. *Enlastete*: exonerated individual, innocent, or proven anti–Nazi.

Cadres of the HJ were, on the whole, defined as category 3, lesser offenders deserving leniency, who were to be placed on probation for two or three years. Common members generally fell under categories 4 and 5. All, however, were "denazified." Former HJ members were shown the evil of Hitler's regime. For example, they had to look at footage from the death camps, and many could not believe that the films were real. Many of them were so fanatic and indoctrinated that it took years for them to feel a sense of guilt for the Holocaust, the genocide of the Jews.

Denazification proceeded slowly and—with the establishment of the Cold War—in some cases those deserving punishment were able to escape. A number of former *Waffen SS* were allowed to enlist in the French Foreign Legion. Certain former Nazi policemen were engaged by both the West and the East in various intelligence services (e.g., Klaus Barbie, the "Butcher of Lyon"). Nazi scientists were engaged to develop new weapons and rocket programs, the most famous being Wernher von Braun (father of the V2 rocket) whose work was decisive in the 1969 NASA moon landing.

In 1947, the Allied occupation authorities proclaimed a general amnesty for all persons of both sexes born before 1 January 1919, provided they were not guilty of war crimes. The leaders of the Hitler Youth had to stand trial. After being relieved of his post as leader of the Youth in August 1940, Baldur von Schirach had been appointed *Gauleiter* (governor) of Austria. This German-speaking neighbor of Germany, with whom it had strong historical ties, had been forcibly annexed to Hitler's German Reich in 1938 under a thin cloak of legality. Renamed *Ostmark*, Austria was absorbed into the German economic and military system and placed until 1945 under the leadership of a Nazi appointed *Gauleiter*, first Arthur Seyss-Inquart, then Odilo Globocnik, and ultimately von Schirach. The unorthodox cultural policies of the new *Gauleiter* in Vienna had aroused Hitler's distrust. After von Schirach's visit to Hitler's home at Berghof in 1943, where von Schirach and his wife pleaded for a moderate treatment of eastern peoples and criticized the conditions of Jews, he lost all real political influence. Nevertheless von Schirach's administration of foreign workers, and the fact that he allowed the deportation of 185,000 Jews from Vienna to the extermination camps in Poland during his tenure as governor were major items in the indictment against him at his Nuremberg trial. The tribunal conceded that he did not originate the criminal extermination policy, but said that he had participated in the deportation. Von Schirach admitted that he had approved the "resettlement," but denied all knowledge of genocide. The court found him guilty of crimes against humanity, and sentenced him to twenty years' imprisonment. His wife Henriette appealed to the court for clemency on the grounds that "our children love America." Von Schirach was released in September 1966 and afterward lived a secluded life in southwest Germany. He wrote his memoirs, and a book titled *Ich Glaube an Hitler* (I Believed in Hitler) was published in Hamburg in 1967. Schirach's book should be read with considerable reservation, as the author attempts to take refuge in the role of an innocent young man, fatally seduced and fascinated by Hitler, who had misled German youth, but only

The final act: death or surrender

learned of the Nazi crimes when it was too late. Von Schirach died in Kröv on 8 August 1974.

Arthur Axmann, von Schirach's successor as leader of the Hitler Youth, was arrested in December 1945 when a Nazi underground network was uncovered which he had been organizing. A denazification court sentenced him in May 1949 to a prison sentence of three years as major offender, concluding that he had been a Nazi from inner conviction rather than base motives. After serving his sentence, Axmann subsequently worked as a sales representative in Gelsenkirchen and Berlin. On 19 August 1958, his case was reopened. A West Berlin court fined the former leader of the Hitler Jugend 35,000 marks, finding him guilty of indoctrinating German youth with Nazi values, but not guilty of having committed any crimes during Hitler's era. Axmann died in Berlin in 1996.

During the postwar years, former HJ boys and girls realized that they were especially tainted citizens of the most despised nation on the face of the earth. They developed harsh resentment toward their elders, especially educators who had robbed them of their youth, who had delivered them into the cruel power of the Nazis, who had nearly destroyed an entire generation of German children. It was not an easy task to be a grown-up, a father or a mother in the post–World War II years. Even today many German grandfathers and grandmothers are reluctant to speak about their youth during the Third Reich.

Appendix 1
Chronology

April 20, 1889—Adolf Hitler born in Austria.

November 9, 1918—Weimar Republic proclaimed in Germany.

November 11, 1918—World War I ended, Germany defeated.

June 28, 1919—Germany signs the Treaty of Versailles.

September 1919—Hitler joins the German Workers' Party.

April 1, 1920—Hitler renames the German Workers' Party the "National Socialist German Workers' Party" (Nazi Party—NSDAP).

March 1922—Hitler announces the first Nazi Party youth group.

November 8, 1923—Hitler's Beer-Hall Putsch ends in failure (Hitler is afterward sent to prison).

December 20, 1924—Hitler is released from prison and begins rebuilding the Nazi Party.

Late 1925—Hitler's book *Mein Kampf* is first published.

July 1926—The Hitler Youth is formally established, with Kurt Gruber as its leader.

August 19–20, 1927—Gruber leads 300 Hitler Youth members in a march at a Nuremberg rally, earning a tribute from Hitler.

April 1929—The Hitler Youth is declared the only official youth group of the Nazi Party.

July 1930—The *Bund deutscher Mädel*, the League of German Girls, is founded.

October 30, 1931—Baldur von Schirach is appointed Nazi youth leader.

April 13, 1932—The SA and the Hitler Youth are temporarily banned by the Weimar government.

January 30, 1933—Hitler is named chancellor of Germany.

February 27, 1933—The Reichstag building burns.

March 23, 1933—The Enabling Act grants Hitler dictatorial powers.

April 1, 1933—Nazis start boycott of Jewish shops.

May 10, 1933—Nazis and college students burn books.

June 1933—Baldur von Schirach named youth leader of the German Reich.

August 2, 1934—Hitler becomes *Führer*.

October 7, 1934—The Reich Land Service is introduced, sending city youths to work on farms.

September 15, 1935—The Nuremberg laws against Jews are proclaimed.

March 7, 1936—German troops reoccupy the demilitarized Rhineland.

December 1936—The Hitler Youth Law makes membership compulsory for youths aged 10 to 18.

March 13, 1938—Hitler annexes Austria.

November 9, 1938—*Kristalnacht* (Nazis attack Jews on the "Night of Broken Glass").

March 1939—Hitler annexes Czechoslovakia.

March 25, 1939—A new, tougher law concerning compulsory Hitler Youth membership conscripts all German boys aged 10 into the Hitler Youth.

September 1, 1939—Germany invades Poland, beginning World War II.

October 7, 1939—Nazis begin forcing Polish farmers off their land.

April 9, 1940—Germany invades Denmark and Norway.

May 10, 1940—Germany invades Belgium, the Netherlands, and Luxembourg.

June 14, 1940—Paris occupied by Nazis.

August 1940—Artur Axmann succeeds Schirach as Hitler Youth leader.

Fall 1940—The National Youth Directorate requires target practice and terrain maneuvers for boys 10 and older.

June 22, 1941—Germany invades the Soviet Union.

January 20, 1942—Wannsee Conference held during which Nazis formalize plans for the "Final Solution of the Jewish Problem."

March 13, 1942—Hitler orders new military training camps to provide three weeks of mandatory training for all boys aged 16 to 18.

January 28, 1943—Heimatflak anti-aircraft batteries are officially manned solely by Hitler Youth boys.

January 31, 1943—The German Sixth Army surrenders at Stalingrad.

May 1943—The last German strongholds in North Africa fall to the Allies.

June 24, 1943—The 12th SS Panzer Division *Hitlerjugend* was created.

June 6, 1944—D-Day; Allies land at Normandy in northern France. The Hitler Jugend tank division is sent to the Normandy front.

July 20, 1944—Assassination attempt on Hitler fails.

September 25, 1944—Hitler creates the *Volkssturm* (People's Storm) to defend Germany to the end.

February 1945—The Werewolf project begins training children in guerrilla warfare and sabotage.

April 20, 1945—On his 56th birthday, Hitler pins medals on Hitler Youth boys outside his bunker in Berlin.

April 30, 1945—Hitler commits suicide.

May 7, 1945—Germany surrenders unconditionally.

May 8, 1945—The 12th *Hitlerjugend* armored division surrenders to U.S. 7th Army.

October 1, 1946—At the Nuremberg Trials, von Schirach is sentenced to 20 years' imprisonment for crimes against humanity.

Appendix 2
Song of the Hitler Jugend

"Vorwärts! Vorwärts!"

Verse 1
Forward! Forward!
The clear marching bands sound
Forward! Forward!
The youth ignores danger.
Germany will shine on,
Even if we have to disappear.
Forward! Forward!
The youth ignores danger.
Even if the aim is high
The youth will reach it.

Chorus
Our flag waves before us.
We march to the future, man after man.
We march for Hitler through night and distress
With the flag of youth for liberty and bread.
Our flag is the new time.
It leads us to eternity.
Yes, the flag is beyond death!

Verse 2
Youth! Youth!
We are the soldiers of the future.
Youth! Youth!
We carry future prowess.
Führer, we belong to you.
We are comrades with you!

Vorwärts! Vorwärts!

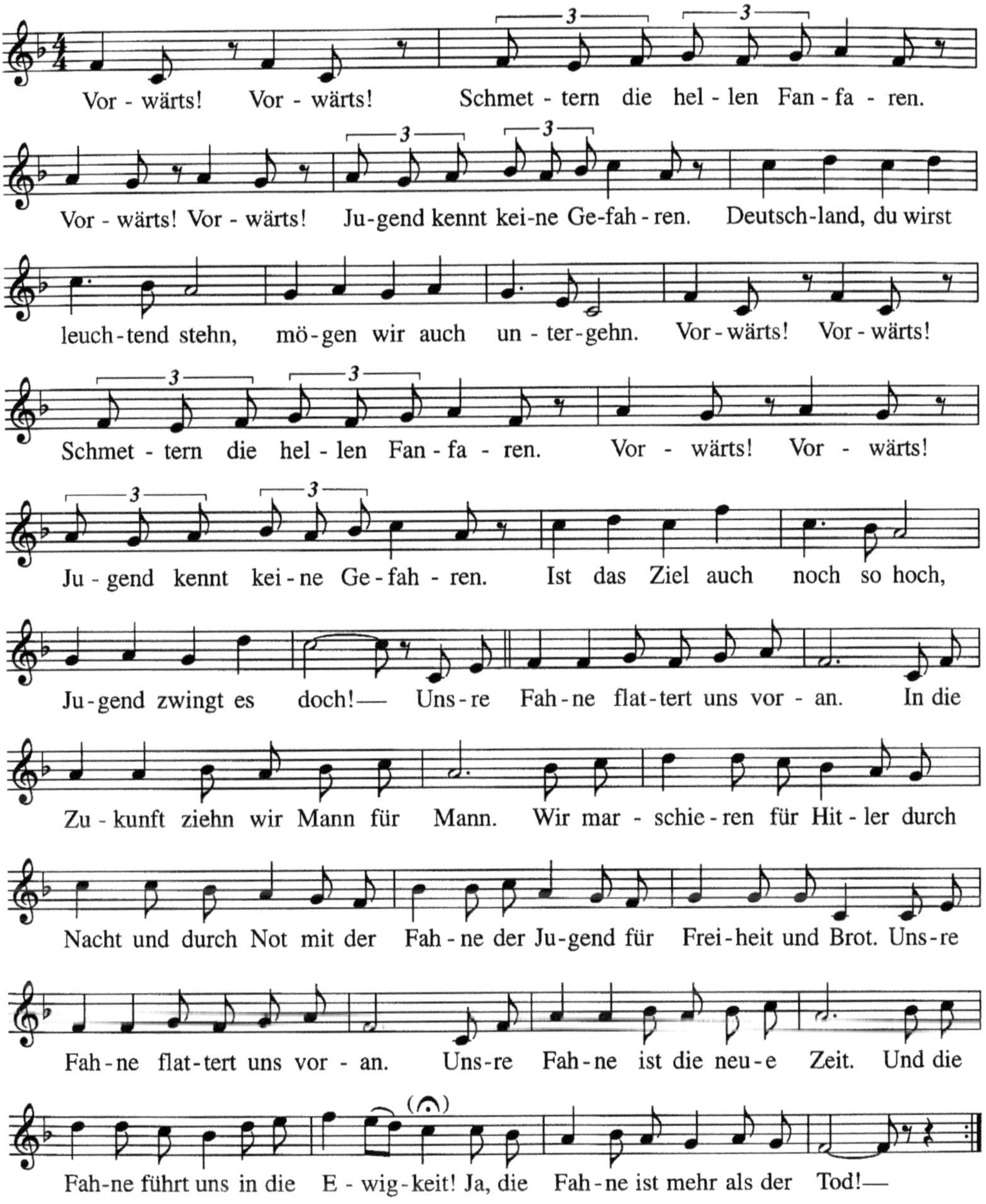
3
Vor - wärts! Vor - wärts! Schmet - tern die hel - len Fan - fa - ren.
Vor - wärts! Vor - wärts! Ju-gend kennt kei-ne Ge-fah - ren. Deutsch-land, du wirst
leuch-tend stehn, mö-gen wir auch un - ter-gehn. Vor-wärts! Vor-wärts!
Schmet - tern die hel - len Fan - fa - ren. Vor - wärts! Vor - wärts!
Ju - gend kennt kei - ne Ge - fah - ren. Ist das Ziel auch noch so hoch,
Ju-gend zwingt es doch!— Uns-re Fah-ne flat-tert uns vor - an. In die
Zu - kunft ziehn wir Mann für Mann. Wir mar - schie-ren für Hit - ler durch
Nacht und durch Not mit der Fah - ne der Ju-gend für Frei-heit und Brot. Uns-re
Fah-ne flat-tert uns vor - an. Uns-re Fah-ne ist die neu-e Zeit. Und die
Fah-ne führt uns in die E - wig-keit! Ja, die Fah-ne ist mehr als der Tod!—

Bibliography

Ayçoberry, P. *La Société Allemande sous le IIIe Reich.* Paris: Editions du Seuil, 1998.

Brandenburg, H. C. *Die Geschichte der Hilter Jugend.* Cologne: Verlag Wissenschaft und Politik, 1968.

Heck, A. *A Child of Hitler.* Frederick, CO: Renaissance House, 1985.

Kamer, H., and E. Bartsch. *Jugendlexikon National-Sozialismus.* Hamburg: Rowohlt Taschenbuch Verlag, 1982.

Klose, Werner. *Generation im Gleichschritt: Ein Dokumentarbericht.* Hamburg: Gerhard Stalling Verlag, 1964.

Koch, H. W. *The Hitler Youth.* New York: Stein and Day, 1975.

Mabire, J. *Les Jeunes Fauves du Führer.* Paris: Fayard, 1976.

Mann, Erika. *Zehn Millionen Kinder: Die Erziehung der Jugend im Dritten Reich.* Munich: Verlag H. Ellermann, 1986.

Peukert, D. J. K. *Inside Nazi Germany.* New Haven: Yale University Press, 1987.

Rempel, G. *Hitler's Children.* Chapel Hill: University of North Carolina Press, 1975.

Stoffel, G. *La Dictature du Fascisme Allemand.* Paris: Editions Internationales, 1936.

Index

Abetz, Otto 80
Abitur (graduation certificate) 93
Adler und Falken 11
Adolf-Hitler-Marsch 75
Adolf Hitler schools (AHS; Adolf-Hitler-Schulen) 96–97
Adolf-Hitler-Schulen (AHS; Adolf Hitler schools) 96–97
Afrika Korps 138, 140
Agricultural service 81
All Quiet on the Western Front (film) 26
Alpine Redoubt 155
Altendorf, Werner 33
Althing 77
Amt IV 121
Amt VII 138
Amt XI 98–99
Anti-intellectualism 89, 90
Anti-Semitism 5, 6, 10, 17, 21, 24, 28, 29, 87, 89, 91
Armbands 62
Armelbinde (armbands) 62
Armelstreifen (cuff-bands) 137
Armstrong, Louis 117
Arndt, E.M. 11
Artaman League (Bund der Artamenen) 16–17, 22, 23, 29, 81
Aryans 5, 10, 38, 39, 43, 45, 46, 47, 50, 51, 73, 78, 82, 91, 92
AT Riegel Mine 43 148
Ausbildungs- und Ersatzbataillon 152
Auschwitz (extermination camp) 17
Auslandsdeutsche (Germans in foreign lands) 59
Autarky 3
Autobahn 108

Axmann, Arthur 33, 108, 123–125, 130, 152, 154–155, 161

Baby Division 149
Bachant (Wandervogel fellow) 13
Ballilas 11
Banners 62
Barbie, Klaus 159
Barbusse, Henri 89
Bastogne 152
Battle of Coburg 21
Battle of Normandy 148–151
Battle of the Bulge 151–153
Bäumer, Gertrud 40
Bautruppen (construction troops) 113
"Believe! Obey! Fight!" 83
Bereichsleiter 10
Berger, Gottlob 131
Binoculars (Feldstecher) 145
Birth rate 45, 47
Bismarck Jugend 11
Blau Weiss (Blue-White) 13
Blitzkrieg 109
"Blood, Soil and the Sword" (SS slogan) 17
Blue-White (Blau Weiss) 13
Blum, Günther 33
Blut und Bodem (blood and soil) 17
Bolshevism 5
Book burning 89
Bormann, Martin 48, 74, 123, 153
Bouhler, Philip 92
Boxing 72, 133
Boy Scouts 11, 29, 70
Braun, Eva 44, 155
Braun, Wernher von 159
Bremer, Gerhart 131

Index

Bruderschaft (brotherhood or camaraderie) 133
Bücherverbrennung (public book burning)
Bund der Artamanen (Artaman League) 16–17, 29, 81
Bund deutscher Mädel (BdM; League of German Girls) 7, 32, 34, 37–39, 47, 57, 59, 62, 63, 67–68, 74, 80, 84, 111, 118, 124, 125, 154
Bursche (Wandervogel rank) 13

Camouflage 140–143
Catholic Church 30, 120
Celebrations 75–77
Chamberlain, H.S. 11
Chaplin, Charlie 74
"Children, church, kitchen" 38
Cold War 159
Combat League for the German Culture (Kampfbund für deutsche Kultur) 89
Committee for Schoolboys' Rambles (Wandervogel, Ausschuss für Schülerfahrten) 12–18
Communist Union of Youth (Komsomol) 11
Communist Youth Association (KJVD) 28
Compass (Kompass) 145
Concentration camps 4, 17, 82, 99, 121
Criminal-Biological Institute of the RSHA 120
Czechoslovakia 3

Dachau (concentration camp) 99
Daggers 69
Dähnhardt, Heinz 16
Darré, Walther 11, 17, 43
Darwin, Charles 11
Day of Homage to the Dead (Totengedenktag) 77
Death head guards 130
de Gaulle, Gen. Charles 149, 151
de Lagarde, Paul 11
Denazification (Entnazifizierung) 158
Deutsche Arbeiterpartei (DAP; German Worker's Party) 9
Deutsche Arbeitsfront (German Labor Front) 44, 48, 80, 97, 111–112
Der deutsche Erzieher (German educator) 90
Deutsche Falkenschaft 11
Deutsche Freischar 11
Deutsche Jungenschaft (DJ 1-11; German Youth Movement of November 1) 17–18
Deutsche Jungvolk Organisationsfahne (German Youth organization) 63
Deutsche Knabenschaft 34
Deutsche Kolberg 12
Das deutsche Mädel (publication for BdM girls) 78
Deutsche Pfadfinderbund 12
Deutschen Jugendnachrichten (News of the German Youth) 78
Deutscher Gruss (German salute) 70
Deutscher Volkssturm (popular army) 153–157
Deutsches Jungvolk in der Hitler Jugend (DJ; German Young People in the Hitler Youth) 22, 34, 59, 74, 84, 92, 96, 154

Deutschkunde 92
Dienstgraden (badges of rank) 137
Dienstrock (tunic) 138
Dietrich, Jozef "Sepp" 131, 135
Disciplinary Company of the HJ 120
Divini Redemptoris (letter) 31
Dolch (dagger) 69
Dönitz, Adm. Karl 158
Dorner, Adolf 92
Dorsey, Tommy 117
Drexler, Anton 9
Drinking bottle (Feldfasche) 144

Ebner, Dr. Gregor 47
Eckart, Dietrich 9
Edelweiss pirates 119–121
Ehrenzeichen der deutschen Mutter (Cross of Honor of the German Mother) 43, 44
Eichendorff, Joseph Freiherr von 13
Einheitsfeldmütze (field cap) 140
Einstein, Albert 89
Ellington, Duke 117
Emergency technical rescue 128–129
Entnazifizierung (denazification) 158
Erfurter Maschinefabrik Haenel und Suhl (Erma) 145, 146
Erma Maschinenpistole MPi 38 145
Eufrat (Wandervogel Parents and Friends Advisory Council) 13
Euthanasia 6
Evacuation of children 124

Fahrschulen (driving schools) 109
Fahrtenmesser (traveling knife) 69
Faith and Beauty 38
Fallschirmjäger (paratroopers) 105, 107
Fascism 10, 70, 80
Federal Organization of Women (Frauenwerk) 40
Die Feier der neuen Front (The Feast of the New Front) 24
Feldanzug (field/combat uniform) 138
Feldfasche (drinking bottle) 144
Feldherrnhalle (Hall of Heroes) 75
Feldmütze (forage cap) 140
Feldstecher (binoculars) 145
Female organizations 37–38
Feuerschutzpolizei (emergency rescue squads) 128
Feuerwehren (fire brigades) 128
Fichte, Johann Gottlieb 11
Field equipment 143–145
Fire brigades 127, 128
Fischer, Karl 12, 13
Flags 62–68
Flak artillery 114, 128
Flakhelfer (anti-aircraft gunners and searchlight personnel) 105
Flamethrowers 146
Flammenwerfer (portable flamethrower) 147

Flieger-Hitler-Jugend (Hitler Youth Flying Association) 104–105
Flieger-SA 104
Franco, Francisco 80
Frauenwerk (Federal Organization of Women) 40
Freikorps (Free Corps) 15–16, 21
Freischar (free groups) 16, 17, 29
Freischar junger Nation 11
Freischar Schill 11
Freud, Sigmund 89
Frick, Wilhelm 32
Front Youth (Frontjugend) 22
Frontjugend (Front Youth) 22
Führerprinzip 86
Führungs-Hauptamt (SSFHa; SS military headquarters) 98, 135, 138

Galsworthy, John 89
Gas mask (gasmaske) 144
Gasmaske (gas mask) 144
Gau Berlin 35
Gau Munich 37
Gauleiters (district leaders) 19
Gebirgsjäger (Storm-trooper mountain units) 73
Gefreiter 9
Generational conflicts 82
Georg Fock 102
German-American Bund 59
German diversity 115
German Girls League in the Hitler Youth (BdM; Bund deutscher Mädel in der Hitler Jugend) 7, 32, 34, 37–39, 47, 57, 59, 62, 63, 67–68, 74, 80, 84, 111, 118, 124, 125, 154
German Labor Front (DAF; Deutsche Arbeitsfront) 27, 44, 48, 80, 97, 111–112
German Labor Service (RAD; Reichsarbeitsdienst) 33, 77, 87, 97, 112–114, 120, 130, 131
German navy (Kriegsmarine) 104
German Protestant Church 30
German salute 70
German Socialist Youth Association (SAP) 28
German Song Week 78
German Worker's Party (DAP; Deutsche Arbeiterpartei) 9
German Young People in the Hitler Youth (DJ; Deutsches Jungvolk in der Hitler Jugend) 34, 59, 74, 84, 154
German Youth Movement of November 1 (DJ 1-11; Deutsche Jungenschaft) 17–18
German Youth Organization (Deutsche Jungvolk Organisationsfahne) 63
Gestapo 4, 116, 121, 124
Getarnte Drillichanzug M44 (camouflage suit) 143
Geusen 11, 29
Gide, André 89
Glaube und Schönheit (Faith and Beauty) 39
Gleichschaltung 27–29, 77, 115, 118
Gliederung der NSDAP (Nazi Party organization) 108

Globocnik, Odilo 159
Gobineau, Arthur 5
Goebbels, Josef 6, 26, 27, 44, 48, 73, 74, 84, 87, 89, 117, 153, 158
Goodman, Benny 117
Göring, Hermann 74, 104, 117
Görlitz, Julius 99
Graf, Willi 120
Granatwerfer GrW 34 146
Granatwerfer GrW 42 147
Granatwerfer 36 146
The Great Dictator (film) 74
Greater German Youth League (Grossdeutsche Jugendbund) 29
Grimm, Jakob 11
Grossdeutsche Jugendbewegung (GDJB; Youth Movement of Greater Germany) 21
Grossdeutsche Jugendbund (Greater German Youth League) 29
Gruber, Kurt 21–23, 34, 37, 79
Gruppe Austria 37
Gruppe Mitte 37
Gruppe Nord 35
Gruppe Nordwest 35
Gruppe Ost 35
Gruppe Ostland 35
Gruppe Silesia 37
Gruppe Süd 37
Gruppe Südwest 37
Gruppe West 35
Guderian, Heinz 109, 111
Günsche, Otto 155
Günther, Hans F.K. 11

Hand grenades 146
Harvest Thanksgiving Day 77
Hausser, Paul 130
Heer (German ground force) 113, 130
Hegel, G.W.F. 11
Heimabende (indoctrination meetings) 84
Heimat (homeland) 153
Heimatflak (homeland anti-aircraft artillery) 128
Heines, Edmund 22
Heissmeyer, August 95–96
Hemingway, Ernest 89
Heroes' Remembrance Day (National Day of Mourning) 76
Herrenvolk (master race) 92
Hess, Rudolf 74, 87, 117
Heusinger, Gen. Adolf 153
Heydrich, Reinhard 48
Hierl, Konstantin 112
Hiking 74, 75
Hilgenfeldt, Erich 48, 80
Himmler, Heinrich 6, 17, 43, 47, 48, 74, 82, 95, 96, 120–121, 128, 130, 152, 153, 155
Hindenburg, Paul von 20
Hindenburg Jugend 11
Hitler, Adolf 3–7, 9–11, 16, 18, 19–24, 27–34, 37,

42–46, 48–51, 69–70, 72, 73, 75–77, 82–91, 95, 96, 107, 108, 115–117, 119, 121, 123, 125, 130, 149, 150, 152, 153–155, 158–161
Hitler Jugend Ehrenabzeichen (Hitler Youth Badge of Honor) 68
Die Hitler Jugend: Idee und Gestalt (*The Hitler Youth: Idea and Form*; book) 79
Hitler Jugend Organisationsfahne (Hitler Youth Organization) 62
Hitler-Jugend-Zeitung (Hitler Youth newspaper) 78
Hitler Youth Driving Association 108
Hitler Youth Flying Association (Flieger-Hitler-Jugend) 104–105
Hitler Youth Organization (Hitler Jugend Organisationsfahne) 62
Hitler Youth Patrol Service (Hitlerjugend Streifendienst) 62
Hitlerjugend Streifendienst (Hitler Youth patrol service) 62, 128–129
Hitlerjugend Waffen SS 131
Hitlerjugend Zeitung (newspaper) 22
Hitlerjugendführer (Hitler Youth leader) 35
Hitlerjunge (Hitler Youth member) 34–35
Hitlerjunge Quex (film) 88, 89
Hoess, Rudolf 17
Hoffmann, Heinrich 24
Hoffmann, Henriette 24
Hoheitszeichen (Nazi official national emblem) 137
Holfelder, H. 22
Home Guard (Volkssturm) 41, 153–155
Homosexuality 14, 31, 45, 46
Horst Wessel 102
"Horst Wessel Song" (anthem) 70
Huber, Kurt 120
Huch, Ricarda 89
Hühnlein, Adolf 108–109
Hygiene 79–80

Ich Glaube an Hitler (*I Believed in Hitler*; book) 159
Insignia 59–62

Jahn, Erich 33
Jugend-Internationale 12
Jugendbund der NSDAP (League of the Youth of the National-Socialist Party) 21
Jugendbund Graf von Wartenburg 11
Jugendbünde 16
Jugenddienstpflicht (youth conscription) 123
Jugendherbergen (German Youth Hostels) 29, 75
Jugendschutzkammer (Youth Protection Chamber) 94
Jugendstraflager (punishment camp) 120
Jugendverbande 12
Junabu (Jungnationale Bund; League of Young Nationalists) 16
Jungdeutscher Orden (Jungdo) 11, 16
Jungdo (Jungdeutscher Orden) 16
Das Junge Deutschland (Young Germany, publication of the social service of the HJ specializing in labor) 78–79
Junge Dorfgemeinschaft (*Young Villagers*; publication for young peasants) 79
Die Junge Front (newspaper) 22, 78
Junge Welt (*Young World*; publication for junior girls) 78
Jungfront Verlag (publishing company) 79
Jungmädel im Bund deutscher Mädel in der Hitler Jugend (JM; League of Young Girls) 34, 63, 74
Jungmädelbund (JMB; League of Young Girls) 37
Jungmannen (Young Men of the Storm-troops) 99
Jungmannschaften (youth teams) 21, 34
Jungnationale Bund (Junabu; League of Young Nationalists) 16
Jungstahlhelm (Young Steel Helmet) 16, 28
Jungstrom Kolberg 12
Jungsturm Adolf Hitler 21
Jungvolk (junior branch of Hitler Youth) 22, 34, 59, 74, 84, 92, 96, 154
Jungwolf 11
Jürgensen, Arnold 133
Jüttner 98

Kampfbund für deutsche Kultur (Combat League for the German Culture) 89
Kampfgruppen (combat groups) 150
Kampfzeit (Time of Struggle) 19–20, 25–26, 91, 108
Karten (maps) 145
Kaufmann, Günther 79
KdF (Nazi free-time organization) 72, 112
Kenkmann, A. 116
Kenstler, August Georg 16
Kern 100
Kern Hitler Jugend (Hitler Youth proper) 34–35
Kerr, Alfred 89
"Kinder, Kirche, Küche" 38
Kinderlandverschickung (KLV; evacuation of children) 62, 124, 125
"Kindersegen" (blessed with children) 43
Kindertagesstätte (nursery schools) 43
Klintzsch, Lieutenant Johann Ulrich 21
Knappenschaft (Young Novitiates) 16
Knives 69–70, 144
Köbel, Eberhard "Tusk" 17–18
Kochgeschirr (mess kit) 144
Kompass (compass) 145
Komsomol (Communist Union of Youth) 11
Kraft durch Freude (KdF; Strength Through Joy) 72, 112
Krass, Hugo 151, 153
Krausse, Bernhard 133, 150
Kriegs-winterhilfswerk (KWHW; wartime winter relief organization) 80
Kriegseinsatz (mobilization) 124
Kriegsmarine (German navy) 104

Kristallnacht (Night of Broken Glass) 89
Kroll Opera House 76
Krutchinna, Horst 33
Kuhm, Fritz 59

Landdienst (agricultural service) 81
Landdienst der Hitler Jugend (agriculture service) 62
Landjahr der HJ 29
Langweiler, Heinrich 147
Lauterbacher, Hartmann 33
League for Aeronautic Sport (LSV; Luftsportverband) 104
League of German Girls (BdM; Bund deutscher Mädel) 7, 32, 34, 37–39, 47, 57, 59, 62, 63, 67–68, 74, 80, 84, 111, 118, 124, 125, 154
League of German Students (Nationalsozialistischen deutschen Studentenbunde) 89
League of the Youth of the National-Socialist Party (Jugendbund der NSDAP) 21
League of Young Girls (JM; Jungmädel im Bund deutscher Mädel in der Hitler Jugend) 34, 74
League of Young Girls (JMB; Jungmädelbund) 37
League of Young Nationalists (Jungnationale Bund; Junabu) 16
Leben rune (rune of life) 80
Lebensborn eingetragener Verein (Fountain of Life Society) 47, 50
Lebensraum (living space) 9, 84
Leibstandarte SS Adolf Hitler (LSSAH; Hitler's personal bodyguards) 131, 132, 136, 150
Lenin, Vladimir 5
Lenk, Gustav Adolf 21, 22, 23
Ley, Robert 48, 74, 87, 93, 96, 97, 111, 117
Lilienstern, Rühle von 11
Lilienthal, Otto 104
Lippisch, Alexander 105
London, Jack 89
Loose, Alfred 33
Lörzer, Bruno 104
Louis, Joe 73
Luftschutzpolizei (air-raid police units) 128
Luftsportverband (LSV; League for Aeronautic Sport) 104
Luftwaffe 40, 77, 104–105, 107, 114, 126
Luftwaffe-Helfern (air-force auxiliaries) 128
Lutze, Viktor 100

Machine guns 146
Machtergreifung (seizure of power) 76
Mahler, Gustav 78
Mahraun, Arthur 16
Make-up 45
"Malmédy Massacre" 152
Mann, Heinrich 89
Mann, Thomas 89
Mantel (overcoat) 138
Maps (Karten) 145
Marine-Hitler-Jugend (Navy Hitler Youth) 102

Marine-SA 102
Marsch auf die Feldherrnhalle (Munich Beer Hall) 11
Marschstiefel (leather jackboots) 140
Marx, Karl 5
Maschinen Karabiner 43 (MK 43, also called Maschinenpistole 43 or MP 43) 145, 146
Maschinengewehr MG 42 146, 147
Maschinenpistole MPi 28/II 145
Maschinenpistole MPi 34 145, 146
Maschinenpistole MPi 40 146, 147
Maschmann, Melitta 37
Mathematik im Dienst der national-politischen Erziehung (Mathematics at the Service of National Political Education) 92
Mauser Modell 1898 (Kar 98) 145
Medals 68–69
Mein Kampf (book) 84, 90
Mess kit (Kochgeschirr) 144
Messer (knife) 144
Meyen, Wolf 13
Meyer, Kurt 131, 136, 149–151
Milestone, Lewis 26
Military police (Waffen SS Feldgendarmerie) 136
Military training camps (Wehrertüchtigungslagern) 74
Mines 148
Mit brennender Sorge (*In Deep Concern*) 31
Model, Walther 152
Mohnke, Wilhelm 131, 150
Mortar 146
Mother Cross 43, 44
Mothering Day 76
Motor-Hitler-Jugend 108–111
Motor Sturm Abteilung (MSA) 108
Muller, Adam 11
Muller, Franz 45
Müller, Friedrich Max 5
Müller, Ludwig 30
Munich Beer Hall (Marsch auf die Feldherrnhalle) 9, 11, 16, 21, 77, 91
Music 77–78
Musikeinheiten (music units) 78
Mussolini, Benito 10, 11, 70, 80, 108
Mutprobe (tests of courage) 72
Mutterkreuz (Mother Cross) 43

Nabersberg, Karl 33
Nachrichten-Hitler-Jugend 111
Nachrichten-SA 111
Napola (Nationalpolitischen Erziehungsanstalten; national political institutes) 95–98
National Day of Mourning (Heroes' Remembrance Day) 76
National Labor Day 76
National material control office 51
National Socialism 3, 4, 16–18, 26, 28, 31, 33, 37, 50, 75, 76, 78, 83, 85, 119, 155

National-Socialist Automobile Corps (NSAK; Nationalsozialistischen Automobil Korps) 108
National-Socialist Driver Corps (NSKK; Nationalsozialistische Kraftfahrer-Korps) 108–111, 128
National Socialist German Students' League (NSDStB; Nationalsozialistischen Deutschen Studentenbund) 23–24, 89, 93
National Socialist German Worker Party (NSDAP; Nationalsozialistische Deutsche Arbeiterpartei) 9, 10, 11, 16, 19–24, 27, 31–34, 39–41, 44–45, 69, 70, 76, 96–99, 112, 124
National-Socialist League of Ex-Servicemen 16
National Socialist Women's Association (NSF; Nationalsozialistische-Frauenschaft) 38–43
National-Sozialistische Schülerbund (NSS; Nazi school league) 23–24
National-Sozialistische Schülerinnenbund (NSS; Nazi League for Schoolgirls) 37
National-Sozialistische Volkswohlfahrte (NSV; Nazi People's Welfare Organization) 80
National Youth Directorate 125
Nationale Jungsturm (newspaper) 21
Nationalpolitischen Erziehungsanstalten (national political institutes) 95–96
Nationalsozialistische Deutsche Arbeiterpartei (NSDAP; National Socialist German Worker Party) 9, 10, 11, 16, 19–24, 27, 31–34, 39–41, 44–45, 69, 70, 76, 96–99, 112, 124
Nationalsozialistische-Dozentenbund (NSDB; Nazi Lecturers League) 93
Nationalsozialistische Flieger-Korps (NSFK; Nazi Flyers Corps) 104
Nationalsozialistische-Frauenschaft (NSF; National Socialist Women's Association) 38, 39
Nationalsozialistische Jugend (newspaper) 21
Nationalsozialistische Kraftfahrer-Korps (NSKK; National-Socialist Driver Corps) 108–111, 128
Nationalsozialistische Lehrerbund (NSLB; Nazi teacher league) 90
Nationalsozialistische Volkswohlfahrt (NSV; Nazi People's Welfare Organization) 48–50, 80, 124
Nationalsozialistischen Automobil Korps (NSAK; National Socialist Automobile Corps) 108
Nationalsozialistischen Deutschen Studentenbund (NSDStB; National Socialist German Students' League) 23–24, 89, 93
Navy Hitler Youth (Marine-Hitler-Jugend) 102
Nazi Drivers' Corps 108, 109
Nazi Flyers Corps (NSFK; Nationalsozialistische Flieger-Korps) 104
Nazi League for Schoolgirls (NSS; National-Sozialistische Schülerinnenbund) 37
Nazi Lecturers League (NSDB; Nationalsozialistische-Dozentenbund) 93
Nazi Party program 9
Nazi People's Welfare Organization (NSV; Nationalsozialistische Volkswohlfahrt) 48–50, 80, 124
Nazi pilgrimages 75
Nazi school league (NSS; National-Sozialistische Schülerbund) 23–24
Nazi teacher league (NSLB; Nationalsozialistische Lehrerbund) 90
Nazi Women League (NS Frauenschaft) 154
Niemöller, Martin 30
Nietzsche, Friedrich 11
Night of Broken Glass (Kristallnacht) 89
Night of Long Knives 31
Norkus, Herbert 76, 88–89
NS Deutsche Oberschule Starnbergersee (National-Socialist German High School Starnbergersee) 99
NS Frauenschaft (Nazi Women League) 154
NSV Reich Adoption Service 50
Nuremberg laws 5
Nuremberg process 158
Nuremberg rallies 22, 75, 76

Oaths 85, 155
Oberbachant (Wandervogel senior fellow) 13
Oberkommando des Heeres (OKH; Germany's Army High Command) 153
Oberland (small Munich paramilitary group) 16
Ohlsen, Jürghen 88
Olböter, Erich 133
Olympic Games of 1936 73
Olympics 1936 (film) 40
Ordensburgen (finishing schools) 96–99
Ordnungspolizei 129
Ostpreussen Volkssturm 153

Panzer Artillerie Regiment 12 135
Panzer Aufklärungs Abteilung 12 135
Panzer Grenadier Regiment 25 Hitlerjugend 135
Panzer Grenadier Regiment 26 Hitlerjugend 135
Panzer Nachrichten Abteilung 12 136
Panzer Pionier Bataillon 12 135
Panzerbüchse 43 Panzerschreck 147, 148
Panzerdivision Hitlerjugend 151
Panzerfaust (portable anti-tank weapons) 41, 147, 148, 154
Panzergrenadier Division Hitlerjugend 131
Panzerschreckabteilungen (anti-tank battalions) 154
Panzervernichtungsabzeichen (tank destruction badge) 156
Panzerwurfmine (tank grenade) 146
Paratroopers 107
Patriotic Youth League of Greater Germany (Vaterländische Jugendverband Grossdeutschlands) 21
Patrol service 128
Peiper, Joachim 152
Penal Code of 1871 14

Pennants 62
People's Fighter (He-162) 155, 158
Pfarrer Notbund (Emergency League of Pastors) 30
Pfeife (whistle) 145
Der Pimpf (publication for junior DJ members) 78
Pirates 116, 119
Pistols 145
Pius XI, Pope 30, 31
The Poisonous Mushroom (anti–Semitic primer) 91
Porsche, Ferdinand 108
Prinz, Karl-Heinz 133
Probst, Christoph 120
Proficiency award 68
Propaganda Ministry 93
Propagandakompanie (PK; war reporters) 136
Protestant Church 30, 120
Proust, Marcel 89
Prützmann, Hans 155

Race and Settlement Main Office (RuSHA; Rasse- und Siedlungshauptamt) 47, 48
Rähm, Ernst 31, 74
Rallies 75–77
"Rally for Honor and Freedom" 77
"Rally for Unity and Strength" 77
"Rally in Honor of Work" 77
"Rally of Freedom" 77
"Rally of Greater Germany" 77
"Rally of Victory" 77
Rasse-und Siedlungshauptamt (RuSHA; SS Race and Settlement Main Office) 47, 48
Ratti, Achille *see* Pius XI, Pope
Rauschning, Hermann 6
Regalia 50–59
Reich Labor Service for Young Women (RAD/wJ; Reichsarbeitdienst der weibliche Jugend) 39, 112
Reich Party Day (Reichsparteitag) 11
Reich Teachers' League (RLB; Reichslehrerbund) 90
Reichsarbeitsdienst (RAD; German Labor Service) 33, 77, 87, 97, 112–114, 120, 130, 131
Reichsarbeitsdienst der weibliche Jugend (RAD/wJ; Reich Labor Service for Young Women) 39, 112
Reichsarbeitsdienst Manner (RAD/M) 112
Reichsfunkschule (school for the training of HJ broadcast personnel) 79
Reichsjugendamt (Reich Youth Office) 33
Reichsjugendführer (National Youth Leader) 23, 35
Reichslehrerbund (RLB; Reich Teachers' League) 90
Reichsmotorschule (driving school) 109
Reichsparteitag (Reich Party Day) 11, 22, 75
Reichsseesportschulen (schools for sea sport) 102
Reichstag 27

Reichszeugmeisterei (RZM; central ordnance office of the NSDAP) 50–51, 69, 138
Reiter-Hitler-Jugend (Hitler Youth cavalry) 111
Reiter-SA (equestrian corps of the storm-troops) 111
Reitsch, Anna 40
Remarque, Erich Maria 26
Rentein, Adrian von 23
Repression of dissidents 120, 121
Reserve troops (SS-VT) 130
Resistance 115, 121
Riefenstahl, Leni 39
Ritter, Robert 120
Röhm, Ernst 24
Rommel, Erwin 100, 135, 149, 150
Roquette, Otto 13
Rosenberg, Alfred 11
Rossbach, Gerhard 16, 22
Rousseau, Jean-Jacques 18
Rüdiner, Jutta 37
Rundstedt, Gerd von 135
Rundstedt, Marshall von 149, 151
Runes 22, 92, 137
Rust, Wilhelm Bernhard 32, 90, 93, 95, 96

Salmuth, Gen. Hans von 135
Salutes 70
Samurai 17
Sanitäts-SA (medical corps of the stormtroops) 26
Schairer, Eberhard 45
Schanzzeug (entrenching tool) 144
Scharnhorst Jugend 11, 28
Schenzinger, Karl Alois 88
Schiessauszeichnung (HJ shooting medal) 68, 99–100
Schilljugend (Austrian youth nationalist movement) 16, 22
Schirach, Baldur von 23–33, 46, 79, 87, 88, 93, 96, 123, 128, 159, 161
Schirach, Henriette von 31, 159
Schirmmütze (service cap) 138
Schmeisser, Hugo 146
Schmeling, Max 72, 73
Schmorell, Alexander 120
Scholl, Hans 120–121
Scholl, Sophie 120–121
Scholtz-Klink, Gertrud 40, 43, 117
Schoniger, Erich 45
Schools 90–99
Schulterklappen (shoulder straps) 62
Schutzbrillen (sunglasses) 145
Schutzluft (Civil Defense) 127
Schwarz, Franz Xaver 96
Schweppenburg, Gen. Geyr von 135, 149
Schwertworte (sword words) 92
Seghers, Anna 89
Sexuality 17, 45, 46
Seyss-Inquart, Arthur 159

Shooting awards 99
Shoulder straps 62
Shovel (Schanzzeug) 144
Social-Democrat Socialist Youth (SAJ) 28
Social Office of the Reich Youth Leadership 123
Sohnrey, Heinrich 13
Sondereinheiten (special units) 100
Spielmannzug (marching band) 78
Squadristi 108
Stahlhelm (steel helmet) 16, 138
State labor service (RAD; Reichsarbeitsdienst) 33, 77, 87, 97, 112–114, 120, 130, 131
Steinbrück, Hans 116
Steinhoff, Hans 88
Stielhandgranate (stick grenade) 146
Stöcker, Adolf 11
Stoppuhr (stopwatch) 145
Stopwatch (Stoppuhr) 145
Storm troopers (SA; Sturm Abteilung) 5, 9, 16, 21, 26, 31, 32, 46, 51, 69, 89, 94, 99–100, 104, 108
Strasser, Gregor 19
Streicher, Gauleiter Julius 22, 74
Streifendienst (patrol/police auxiliary service) 62, 128–129
Strength Though Joy 112
Student, Kurt 107
Study Group for German History Books and Educational Material 92
Sturm Abteilung (SA; storm troopers) 5, 9, 16, 20, 21, 26, 31, 32, 46, 51, 69, 89, 94, 99–100, 104, 108
Der Stürmer (newspaper) 22, 74
Sturmgewehr (StG; also MPi 44) 44 (assault weapon) 145
Sturmjugend (*Storm Youth*) 78
Submachine guns 145, 146
Sunglasses (Schutzbrillen) 145
Swing Jugend (Swing youth) 117–118

Tannenbergbund 12
Tarnkappe (also called Zeltbahn; camouflage cape) 144
Technical Emergency Service (TeNo; Technische Nothilfe) 128–129
Technische Nothilfe (TeNo; Technical Emergency Service) 128–129
Teddy boys 121
Tellermine 35 148
Tellermine 42 148
Tierkampf 98
Tobacco 45
Totalitarianism 3
Totengedenktag (Day of Homage to the Dead) 77
Totenkopf (death's head badge) 137
Totenkopfverbände (death's head concentration camp guards) 130
Treaty of Versailles 9, 18, 104

Treitschke, Heinrich von 11
Trevor-Roper, Hugh 155
Triumph of the Will (film) 40
Tropenanzug (tropical service uniform) 138
Trotha, Adolf von 29, 104
Trust No Fox (anti–Semitic primer) 91

Udet, Ernst 104
Uniforms 50–59
Unteroffizieren (NCOs) 137
Usadel, Georg 33

V-1 flying bomb 150
Vaterländische Jugendverband Grossdeutschlands (Patriotic Youth League of Greater Germany) 21
Verfügungstruppen (SS VT; reserve or task troops) 130
Versorgungs Einheit 12 136
Victory of Faith (film) 40
Völkischer Beobachter (*The Popular Observer*, newspaper) 9, 21, 88
Volksdeutsche 130
Volksgemeinschaft 72
Volksjäger (people's fighter) 155
Volkssturm (Home Guard) 41, 153–155
Volkswagen 108

Waffen SS 98–99, 102, 111, 129–134, 136–146, 148–149, 152, 159
Waffen SS Feldgendarmerie (military police) 136
Waffen SS Tarnjacke (camouflage tunic) 140, 143
Waffenfarbe (color of service) 111
Wagner, Richard 11, 78
Waldmüller, Hans 133, 150
Wandervogel, Ausschuss für Schülerfahrten (Committee for Schoolboys' Rambles) 12–18, 28–30, 75, 118
War reporters (PK; Propagandakompanie) 136
Wartime winter relief organization (KWHW; Kriegs-winterhilfswerk) 80
Weapons 145–148
Weber, Friedrich 16
Wehrertüchtigungslagern (military training camps) 74
Wehrmacht (national armed forces) 33, 76, 88, 96, 99, 109, 113, 114, 130, 150, 151
Wehrmannschaften (defense teams) 100
Wehrsport (contact sport) 133
Weimar Republic 11, 19, 32, 42, 70, 77, 91
"Weltmacht oder Niedergang" (World Domination or Downfall) 154
Werewolves (Werwolven) 155–158
Werwolven (Werewolves) 155–158
Wessel, Horst 91
Westwall (fortification line) 113
Whistle (Pfeife) 145
White Rose 121

Wilhelmine period 12
Wille und Macht (*Will and Power*; publication for HJ leadership) 78
Winter Help (WHW; Winterhilfswerk) 80
Winterhilfswerk (WHW; Winter Help) 80
Wirtschafts und Verwaltungshauptamt (Main Office for Economy and Administration) 138
Witt, Fritz 131, 133, 135, 136, 149, 150
Wolff, Karl 47
World War I 3, 9, 14, 15, 26, 50, 70, 74, 90, 104, 147, 154
World War II 6, 41, 47, 73, 76, 77, 83, 87, 98, 107, 111, 113, 114, 116, 123, 130, 145, 146, 155, 161
Wünsche, Max 131, 150, 151

Young Novitiates (Knappenschaft) 16
Young Steel Helmet (Jungstahlhelm) 16
Youth Movement of Greater Germany (GDJB; Grossdeutsche Jugendbewegung) 21
Yule (winter solstice) 77

Zander, Elsbeth 40
Zazous 117
Zeltbahn (also called Tarnkappe; camouflage cape) 144
Zola, Emile 89
Zoot-suiters 117
Zuckmayer, Carl 89
Zweig, Stefan 89

www.ingramcontent.com/pod-product-compliance
Ingram Content Group UK Ltd.
Pitfield, Milton Keynes, MK11 3LW, UK
UKHW050523150426
52171PUK00026B/1767